ACCOUNTING
for DANTE

THE WILLIAM AND KATHERINE DEVERS
SERIES IN DANTE STUDIES

Theodore J. Cachey, Jr., and Christian Moevs, editors
Simone Marchesi, associate editor
Ilaria Marchesi, assistant editor

ACCOUNTING

for DANTE

Urban Readers and Writers in Late Medieval Italy

JUSTIN STEINBERG

University of Notre Dame Press · *Notre Dame, Indiana*

Manufactured in the United States of America

The publisher gratefully acknowledges the support of the Aldo and Jeanne Scaglione
Publication Award for a Manuscript in Italian Literary Studies (Modern Language
Association of America) and of the Division of Humanities of the University of
Chicago in the publication of this volume.

Reproductions in any form of images obtained with permission from the Ministero
per i Beni e le Attività Culturali of the Archivio di Stato, Bologna, the Archivio di Stato,
Florence, the Biblioteca Nazionale Centrale, Florence, and the Biblioteca Medicea
Laurenziana, Florence, are forbidden.

Library of Congress Cataloging-in-Publication Data
Steinberg, Justin.
Accounting for Dante : urban readers and writers in late medieval Italy / Justin Steinberg.
    p.   cm. — (The William and Katherine Devers series in Dante studies)
Includes bibliographical references and index.
ISBN-13: 978-0-268-04122-9 (pbk. : alk. paper)
ISBN-10: 0-268-04122-9 (pbk. : alk. paper)
    1. Dante Alighieri, 1265–1321—Influence.   2. Italy—Intellectual life—1268–1559
3. Italian literature—To 1400—History and criticism.   I. Title.
PQ4390.S774   2007
851'.1—dc22

                                                                    2006032466

∞The paper in this book meets the guidelines for permanence and durability of the Committee
on Production Guidelines for Book Longevity of the Council on Library Resources.

For my parents

Contents

About the William and Katherine Devers Series in Dante Studies

The William and Katherine Devers Program in Dante Studies at the University of Notre Dame supports rare book acquisitions in the university's John A. Zahm Dante collections, funds an annual visiting professorship in Dante studies, and supports electronic and print publication of scholarly research in the field. In collaboration with the Medieval Institute at the university, the Devers program has initiated a series dedicated to the publication of the most significant current scholarship in the field of Dante Studies.

In keeping with the spirit that inspired the creation of the Devers program, the series takes Dante as a focal point that draws together the many disciplines and lines of inquiry that constitute a cultural tradition without fixed boundaries. Accordingly, the series hopes to illuminate Dante's position at the center of contemporary critical debates in the humanities by reflecting both the highest quality of scholarly achievement and the greatest diversity of critical perspectives.

The series publishes works on Dante from a wide variety of disciplinary viewpoints and in diverse scholarly genres, including critical studies, commentaries, editions, translations, and conference proceedings of exceptional importance. The series is supervised by an international advisory board composed of distinguished Dante scholars and is published regularly by the University of Notre Dame Press. The Dolphin and Anchor device that appears on publications of the Devers series was used by the great humanist, grammarian, editor, and typographer Aldus Manutius (1449–1515), in whose 1502 edition of Dante (second issue) and all subsequent editions it appeared. The device illustrates the ancient proverb *Festina lente,* "Hurry up slowly."

Theodore J. Cachey, Jr., and Christian Moevs, *editors*
Simone Marchesi, *associate editor*
Ilaria Marchesi, *assistant editor*

Advisory Board

Illustrations

Acknowledgments

First and foremost, I wish to thank Ronald Martinez, who generously commented on this book at every stage of its development. At the University of Minnesota, Rita Copeland and David Wallace similarly provided me with insight, direction, and encouragement. The conversations I had with Armando Petrucci in the early stages of the present work were pivotal for its conceptualization.

I would like to single out Albert Ascoli, Zygmunt Barański, and Theodore Cachey for their help and guidance while the manuscript was completed and then revised. In addition, for their comments and criticism, I am grateful to Roberto Antonelli, Steven Botterill, Gary Cestaro, Ralph Hanna, Robert Hollander, Lino Leonardi, Christian Moevs, Marco Ruffini, Cesare Segre, Stefanie Solum, and Wayne Storey. I would also like to thank the staffs at the Italian archives and libraries in which I worked, especially Giorgio Marcon of the Archivio di Stato in Bologna. Finally, the editorial staff and the readers at the University of Notre Dame Press have done much to improve the book in its final stages: special thanks go to Ilaria and Simone Marchesi, fierce editors and real friends.

An earlier version of chapter 4 appeared in *Scrittura e civiltà* 24 (2000): 251–269. Chapter 5 is a substantial revision of an article that first appeared in *Italian Studies* 58 (2003): 5–30. Initial research for this book was supported by a Fulbright-Hays grant, and it was finished with the generous support of the Franke Institute for the Humanities.

Unless otherwise noted, all English translations from Italian and Latin texts are my own.

Introduction

Is there any medieval poet more concerned than Dante with the public circulation and reception of his works? From the beginning of the *Vita Nova*—Dante's first attempt at self-anthology—he foregrounds the relationship with his readers and the related problem of the interpretation of his texts. According to the prose narrative, the first sonnet of the *libello*, "A ciascun'alma presa e gentil core," was sent to the famous poets ("famosi trovatori" [*VN* 1.20]) of his time, but no one understood the true meaning ("verace iuditio" [*VN* 2.2]) of this dream-poem as a foreshadowing of Beatrice's death.[1] This tension between publication and interpretation continues throughout the *Vita Nova* and runs through some of the key episodes of the narrative, including the reframing of the epochal *canzone* "Donne ch'avete intelletto d'amore," which Dante specifies had already been circulated in public, "divulgata tra le genti." Indeed, the insistent reinterpretation and reframing of previously circulated works—regardless of the extent of this circulation—is one of the hallmarks of Dante's poetic curriculum. The *donna gentile* of the *Vita Nova* is transformed into Lady Philosophy in the *Convivio,* and the self-citations of "Amor che ne la mente mi ragiona" and "Donne ch'avete" in the *Purgatorio* prepare the way for the revisionary account of Dante's poetic career in the encounter with Beatrice in Earthly Paradise.

Critics typically treat these episodes of self-reflexive commentary for what they reveal about Dante's psychological, moral, and poetic development. Viewed as palinodes, they signal the existential shifts in Dante's career as he progressed from Florentine love poet to exiled philosopher to prophetic *scriba Dei*.[2] Rarely, if ever, does anyone consider how historical circumstances—namely, the early reception of Dante's work and its historical readers—may have motivated this process of revision and reinterpretation. But if the self-referentiality of Dante's poetry suggests the author's internal and personal development, it also speaks to the external conditions of literary production, dissemination, and reception. Whether "theologus-poeta" or "profeta,"[3] Dante always remained a vernacular author working within specific historical circumstances, and his revisions illustrate a concern for readership. Authorial strategies such as self-commentary and self-anthologizing are necessarily in dialogue with previous episodes of publication and interpretation. Yet despite the critical attention paid to dialogic aspects of Dante's work, such as the implied audience of the *Vita Nova* or the addresses to the reader in the *Commedia,* we have yet to consider fully who those readers were that Dante was addressing.[4]

Notable exceptions to the general neglect of Dante's historical readership are the influential studies of his relationship with contemporary and near-contemporary poets. Dante engaged directly with his contemporaries through poetic debates, or *tenzoni,* and indirectly through literary allusion, linking his texts verbally and thematically with those of his friends and rivals. At least since the fundamental contributions of Gianfranco Contini, Dante's use of intertextuality has been at the forefront of modern criticism.[5] More recently, the related question of Dante's role as literary historiographer has come under scrutiny. Scholars have examined how Dante not only engages with an already defined poetic community, but also actively constructs, through a careful process of inclusion and exclusion, a new vernacular literary canon.[6] In this light, works such as the *Vita Nova,* the *De vulgari eloquentia,* and the *Commedia* (especially in the frequent encounters with the Italian love poets in the *Purgatorio*) can be viewed as literary anthologies embodying a highly subjective literary tradition. As is increasingly recognized, our own reliance on Dante's biased historiographical judgments clearly needs to be re-evaluated, especially with respect to highly influential—if "municipal"—poets such as Monte Andrea, Chiaro Davanzati, and the much-maligned Guittone d'Arezzo.

Despite these often groundbreaking contributions, the social and political rarely enter into discussions of Dante and his contemporaries. Scholars typically speak of the intertextual and historiographical elements of Dante's work in stylistic or psychological terms. They analyze the Guinizzellian or Cavalcantian aspects of his lyric poems or reveal, especially in his early work, the traces of Guittone's ineluctable influence. These formal and thematic influences, in turn, are used to explain Dante's censuring and obscurantist literary history. In this view, Dante's oedipal anxiety with respect to rivals such as Guittone and even former friends such as Guido Cavalcanti lies behind his very personal rewriting of the literary canon. As part of a self-authorizing strategy, Dante elides the innovations of competing vernacular poets while promoting the originality of his own role as philosopher-poet and theologian-poet. While Dante's conscious efforts at poetic self-fashioning are by now undeniable, the representation of the medieval Italian literary field as a struggle among strong poets does not fully account for what is at stake in these poetic debates and contending literary histories. When the social field is left out of literary criticism, we are left with accounts of competing egos and interpersonal rivalry.[7] But competition among egos is hardly unique to Dante and his time and place. In the end, such intertextual analyses cannot bring us much closer to understanding Dante as a historically specific reader and author interacting with a historically specific community of readers and authors.

The current reliance on modern editions for almost all texts no doubt contributes to the formalist and psychologizing tendencies of studies of the early Italian lyric. At least since the publication of Contini's magisterial *Poeti del Duecento,* scholars, especially outside of Italy, have approached early Italian poetry through standardized printed editions. These editions are invaluable for both establishing reliable texts and disseminating comprehensible commentaries on these often-elusive works. At the same time, however, removed as they are from the historical, social, and political contexts of medieval book production, they inevitably distance modern readers from the literary and historiographical practices encountered by Dante and his circle. The advantage of printed texts, as Walter Ong has suggested,[8] lies in their capacity to be endlessly recreated in evolving contexts. Yet this potentially endless reproduction comes at a cost: the loss of the original textual event, the socialized meaning locked in a specific historical and geographical moment. When we consider the printed medium in which the early Italian lyric has been disseminated, the prevalence of formalist and stylistic approaches is not surprising. Removed from its moment in time, the lyric text is transformed on the typographical page into an artifact of an idealized and self-contained aesthetic space—a "verbal icon," to borrow the terminology of the New Critics.

On the other hand, when studied through the lens of manuscript culture, the early Italian lyric emerges as a vital participant in socially and politically charged discourse. From an anthropological perspective, manuscripts of the early lyric still share various structural similarities with oral performance.[9] Each manuscript is a temporally specific textual event, produced in a specific locale for a specific audience. The social freight of this textual event is not limited to the text itself, but extends to codicological "codes" such as handwriting, illumination, page layout, parchment, rubrication, and marginalia.[10] The medium here is also the message. By studying the material forms in which these early poems circulated, we can begin to understand how meaning is manifest in their contextualized uses, in what they do as well as what they say. In addition, when examining the various compilations of these thirteenth-century poems, or *canzonieri,* it becomes clear that we need to discuss not Dante and the singular history of the Italian lyric, but rather plural histories of the lyric, since each early anthology represents its own politicized vision of the Italian poetic canon. Dante's own interventions as literary historiographer and anthologizer, whether in *De vulgari* or *Purgatorio,* respond directly to the contending anthologies of his time, to the competing visions of literary history evident in the extant manuscripts.

This book is about competing histories. One of its primary aims is to trace a history of *duecento* lyric culture that takes into account the localized and socially stratified centers of textual production active in late medieval Italy. The first chapter examines the mini-anthologies of lyrics created by the notaries of Bologna from the end of the thirteenth-century to the beginning of the fourteenth: the so-called *rime* from the Memoriali bolognesi. These vernacular *rime* were copied into the margins and in between Latin contracts in the official registers, or *memoriali,* of the Bolognese government. At a time of intense political upheaval and democratic advance for the new government known as the *popolo,* the notaries copied into the public record books the poetry of (among others) Giacomo da Lentini, Bonagiunta Orbicciani, and Guido Guinizzelli, as well as the earliest extant transcriptions of Dante's lyrics and the earliest fragments of the *Commedia.* In other words, they created a canon of early lyric poetry strikingly similar to the version of literary history Dante articulated in the *De vulgari* and *Purgatorio.* In fact, notably absent from the Memoriali are the poems of the Aretine poet Guittone and the Guittonians—this in spite of Guittone's frequent dealings with Bologna through the local chapter of the Knights of the Glorious Virgin Mary, or

"*Frati guadenti*" ("Jovial Friars"), an originally derogatory nickname derived from the wealth and relative ease enjoyed by the lay order to which he belonged.

The notaries' decisions to include or exclude certain poets from their transcriptions in the Memoriali bolognesi cannot be explained by poetic envy or anxiety of influence. The philosophically sophisticated vernacular poetry of Guinizzelli and Dante spoke to the cultural independence and newly achieved intellectual and political status of the upwardly mobile and newly educated notaries of Bologna. And the distaste for Guittone, the newly converted friar-poet, was as political as it was personal. After all, the vernacular poetry and prose of Fra Guittone promoted the values and legitimacy of the Jovial Friars, a politically strong coterie of local aristocrats that directly opposed the social gains made by the notaries and the *popolo.* Guittone was even a personal friend and ally of the local founder of the Jovial Friars, Loderingo degli Andalò, a powerful member of the Bolognese oligarchy whom Dante infamously punished as a hypocrite in *Inferno* 23. Re-examined within a socially fraught local context, the much-studied poetic debates between Dante/Guinizzelli and Guittone emerge as representative of concrete and competing visions of society. The doctrinal disagreements in these poets' work regarding the uses and abuses of love poetry or the proper role of philosophical and even theological learning went much beyond interpersonal rivalry. These were ideological battles that mattered, that had social and political consequences.

Attention to manuscript culture not only brings new meaning to well-known poetic debates, it also reveals the historical importance of poets and poetic discussions that have been neglected by critics. The case of the Florentine banker-poet Monte Andrea in the lyric anthology Vatican anthology Latino 3793 stands out for the contrast between the prominence of the poet in the manuscript—both the *canzone* and sonnet sections conclude with several quires of his compositions—and the current lack of scholarly interest in him. Containing over a thousand poems, the Vatican anthology is responsible for preserving more than half of the early Italian lyric corpus.[11] Visual and material aspects, moreover, distinguish it from other thirteenth-century *canzonieri,* especially the use of a *mercantesca* script for transcriptions and its rudimentary page layouts. In fact, as the analysis in chapter 4 will show, the anthology resembles a merchant's account book and can be identified as a product of the Florentine mercantile elite. Not surprisingly, the powerful bankers and merchants behind the assembly of the codex present one of their own, the Florentine banker Monte, as the legitimate heir of the already rich tradition of Italian lyric poetry; in the manuscript, all roads lead to Monte, who, with his odes to wealth and to the material basis of Fortune, embodies the ethos of the new mercantile ruling class.

Dante, on the other hand, seems to pass over Monte Andrea in silence and so, following his example, has most of the critical tradition. It is not difficult to imagine possible reasons for this rejection of Monte, including his municipality and *guittonismo.* Yet although Dante does not deign to mention Monte by name, the latter's popularity and influence are evident in a series of important, if submerged, intertextual references to his work in *Inferno.* The presence in the *Commedia* of difficult rhyme words (*rimas caras*) drawn from Monte's corpus is often explained as mere stylistic borrowing.[12] When his place in the Vatican anthology is taken into account, however, these stylistic echoes emerge as part of a sustained critique on Dante's part of the Florentine mercantile class, with Monte, as their privileged poet and ideologue, serving as the perfect target. Dante counters the material vision of Fortune put forth by Monte (and promoted by the merchant compilers of the Vatican anthology) with his own providential perspective on earthly events, first suggested in *Inferno* 7. As in the case of the politicized anti-*guittonismo* that will be discussed in chapter 1, the relationship explained in chapter 5 between Dante and Monte's texts is political and ideological as well as aesthetic and interpersonal.

Reading early Italian poetry in light of the historicized readership encoded in the Memoriali bolognesi and in the Vatican anthology makes visible elements of lyric culture that we, as moderns, can no longer "see." In fact, one of the most important recent developments in medieval studies is a return to the visible evidence of the manuscript as the locus of cultural meaning. Across a variety of fields and disciplines, a renewed emphasis on the social text and the material expression of literary works has produced important studies on the cultural meaning of anthologies and compilations, the relationship between text and image, and the shifting historical importance of the author and author's book. Yet these analyses, many influenced by the New Philology,[13] tend to privilege a single codicological "event" and typically do not investigate or seek to establish a textual tradition. Citing the Western prejudice for absence over presence that lies behind the traditional philological emphasis on textual reconstruction, scholars following the precepts of the New Philology prefer the evidence of a historicized extant manuscript to what they see as the anachronistic privileging of a nonexistent, original author's text.[14]

In these studies, the implicit critique of philological *emendatio* — the attempt to improve the text of a given manuscript with alternative readings culled from other manuscripts (or, when necessary, with an informed conjecture) — underestimates, in my opinion, the ultimate dependence of historical criticism on filling in the gaps, both textual and contextual. While in the past philologists may have too zealously focused their endeavors on recovering the unknowable intentions of the author, recent analyses of specific manuscripts are no less occupied in a process of reconstruction. The difference is that now they are concerned with the makers of a book instead of the author of a text. In fact, even the supposed "presence" of the singular manuscript is suspect, since the correct interpretation of its textual and codicological codes depends on a variety of suppositions regarding the intentions of editor, compiler, scribe, illuminator, etc. At the same time, by cutting off a manuscript from a family of texts, this neo-Bédierism risks placing the codex in a historical parenthesis, trapping its meaning between the covers of the book, as an earlier generation trapped interpretation within the limits of the text.[15] The practical consequences of this approach, perhaps not surprisingly, are that many innovative studies on medieval manuscripts remain essentially formalist/structuralist in nature.[16] Even when examining the material intersections of text and image or closely analyzing an individual *compilatio,* these approaches often neglect the complex historical circumstances and vicissitudes of a literary work. When treated as an exclusive, even fetishized receptor of meaning, the historical manuscript can actually pose an impediment to historicist criticism.

The textual event embodied by the manuscript is not an island of meaning unto itself. The full historical significance of a given text and codex emerges only when we consider how they differ from what came before and followed. While close analysis of the handwriting, illumination, and editorial principles of a single manuscript may shed light on its social role within a synchronic framework, its diachronic history is too often elided. For what they reveal about historical change, the neo-Lachmannian methods pioneered by Italian philologists, at least since Contini's groundbreaking contributions, remain crucial for understanding the genealogy of a given work and the history of its reception in time. For our purposes, one advantage this *Nuova filologia* has over the New Philology is the former's overriding concern with placing each manuscript in a relationship with other manuscripts,[17] locating each historicized text among other historicized texts. The genealogy of texts and codices that emerges from any hypothesized stemma, however tentative, can nevertheless, if read historically and not only hierarchically, illustrate the important trajectory of a work from composition to reception, author to public.

Some of the most innovative work in this tradition concerns authorial variants and multiple redactions of a text, both of which foreground the actual labor of writing and the intimate connection between composition and reception.[18] Yet even these cases tell only half the story, since they continue to examine the historical movement from authorial text to material reception, rather than the reverse movement. Almost no study of manuscript culture explores the possibility that medieval authors were directly influenced by how their work was or could be received, transcribed, and circulated, that texts and codices mutually affected each other. In the case of Dante, this neglect is conspicuous, since, as already mentioned, he explicitly thematizes the question of the public dissemination of his work, especially of his lyrics. This is most evident in the *Vita Nova,* where the public is incorporated into the actual narrative,[19] but it is equally central to key encounters in the *Purgatorio,* such as with Casella and Bonagiunta. In these scenes of contact between the poet and his readers (and auditors) Dante revisits and re-performs, in a sense, the reception of his work—only this time, it is under his direct authorial control.

The absence of scholarly discussion of the ways in which Dante might have been affected by the circulation of his work is especially striking since we have extant written evidence of that circulation. Dante's lyric texts circulated during his lifetime, and yet critics tend to use these contemporary transcriptions only for what they contribute to the postlapsarian world of reception studies. Authorial composition remains, in this way, insulated from the vagaries of contemporary reading and misreading. *Accounting for Dante* is an attempt to understand how Dante anticipated and responded to his public, especially the urban public of readers and writers represented in the Memoriali bolognesi and the Vatican anthology. In short, how are Dante's self-anthologies informed by the ways he had already been anthologized?

With the *Vita Nova,* Dante begins a process of collecting and re-collecting his own poems that continues throughout his career. And just as Dante's literary historiography assumes new levels of meaning when viewed against the backdrop of contemporary histories of the lyric, his self-anthologizing cannot be separated from the ways his poems were actually anthologized in contemporary books and documents. Indeed, even a preliminary study into Dante's earliest reception reveals a striking contrast between how he imagines the materiality of his texts and the historical reality of extant transcriptions. Whether Dante is describing the rubricated, divided, and glossed "book of memory" in the *Vita Nova* or the university-standard *libro da banco* (desk book) implicit in *Paradiso* 10, his codicological metaphors inevitably evoke the material resources and reading practices that characterized High Scholasticism and university culture. Yet the transcriptions in the Memoriali bolognesi and the Vatican anthology 3793 were made by urban readers and writers, notaries and merchants, in cursive *cancelleresca* and *mercantesca* scripts. These scripts and these transcriptions are more characteristic of the urban and professional world of documents than of scholastic book culture. Even after his death, most early manuscripts of the *Commedia* were transcribed in hybrid notarial scripts in books resembling archival registers more than in university textbooks or juridical manuals.

This contrast between Dante's conception of his texts' materiality and the actual materiality of his texts suggests not only a gap between imagination and reality, but also the elusive relationship between texts and contexts. The frequent codicological metaphors in Dante's corpus—elegantly discussed by Ernst Robert Curtius and Charles S. Singleton—are informed by and even in contention with contemporary book production and reproduction.[20] As historical circumstances provided Dante with ever-less institutional authority and effective control over the circulation of his work—in sharp contrast with the obsessive control over texts asserted by his near contemporary Petrarch—he increasingly incorporated illumination, rubrication, gloss, script, and even readers and writers into the body of the work itself. In *Inferno,* for example, Paolo and Francesca represent a model of how to read, or rather how not to read; the self-citations and frequent allusions to other vernacular poets in *Purgatorio* turn the mountain into a literary anthology, a living *compilatio;* and the incisive memorial images that mark each heaven in *Paradiso* facilitate the *divisio* of the text, just as illuminations organize the sections of a manuscript book. Indeed, Dante's masterpiece is masterful in part because it encompasses so many aspects of the reading experience. Confronted with such voracious textualizing, it is even more important to resist the temptation of equating Dante's narrative of history with History itself, taking part for whole, and to recognize instead the external circumstances that at once lay outside of and influence his work. Even the model of the universe (and by association the *Commedia*) as God's book, bound by Love in one "volume" (*Par.* 33), provides a significant contrast to the scattered and hermeneutically unstable *quaderni* in which notaries and merchants first copied Dante's texts in late medieval Italy.

Textuality and materiality are contiguous phenomena for Dante because he recognized, perhaps more than any other medieval author, the spatial element of literature. Dante's works form sophisticated territories—incorporating cosmology, numerology, geography, contemporary architecture, and, of course, the space of the book. From the spheres of *Paradiso* to the private rooms of the *Vita Nova,* from the numerological structure behind the arrangement of verse, canto, and *cantica* to the precise location of Earthly Paradise, space and place are crucial for understanding Dante's texts. Above all, the medieval conception of memory as an actual place, a place often represented as a book, further blurs the line between text and context, or rather, text and codex.[21] And for Dante, the book of memory is a psychic container as real as the material spaces of contemporary books. Indeed, the complicated formal structures, rationalized topography, and heightened visuality Dante employs in his work can be seen as a means of maintaining spatial-textual integrity within the "place" of the memory of individual readers, a sort of memorial transmission that rivals and might even replace the unstable material circulation that he would have witnessed in the early dissemination of his lyrics. If the vernacular poet cannot control the new methods of book production and reproduction, perhaps he can influence the books of memory of his urban readers.

Ultimately Dante's spatializing poetics reveal that he understood—as many critics have not—that just as textual events are time-specific, they are always inevitably place specific as well. Yet, despite the increasing influence of Carlo Dionisotti's literary geography on Italian studies,[22] early Italian poetry and especially the early lyric are still typically read in a vacuum. And mapping out various Siculo-Tuscan, or even Florentine and Pisan, schools of poetry is only the first step in understanding the social "place" of these vernacular texts. This is especially true in the epistolary genre of the *tenzone*,[23] the most functional of poetic genres, yet one that is often interpreted solely in conceptual or thematic terms. The *tenzoni* between Guittone and Guinizzelli about love poetry are politicized, for example, when located within a specific city (Bologna), among specific social groups (the Jovial Friars and the emergent *popolo* government), and even on a specific page space (the margins of the Memoriali bolognesi). That Dante revisits this geographically and socially concrete debate from the perspective of the afterlife, especially in his encounters with poets in *Purgatorio* 24 and 26, only underlines the importance of recuperating the historical places where these poems first circulated and these debates first occurred before being relocated within the *Commedia*'s transcendent vision and otherworldly topography.

In fact, the social and political specifics of contemporary poetry are frequently submerged by Dante's universalizing poetics, and over time they become increasingly difficult to recover. Only traces are left in the sixth and seventh terraces of Purgatory of the politicized, contentious world of thirteenth-century Bologna, and there are few hints in Dante's digression on Fortune in *Inferno* 7 that he was influenced by the cultural poetics of Florence's mercantile elite. In fact, without the contemporary evidence found in the Memoriali bolognesi and the Vatican anthology, much of the social and historical context for this poetry would all but fade away, and with them some of the richness and complexity of Dante's project. In order to check this leveling of time, and Dante's complicity with it, the detail—whether philological, intertextual, or paleographic—is always the starting point in *Accounting for Dante*. Rather than simply providing a neutral and positivist datum, the "technical" detail can at times compel us to rethink our notions about a text and/or its context. Technical evidence can complicate or potentially challenge received narratives and is ultimately crucial because it sticks out,[24] because it cannot be seamlessly assimilated by what we consider to be the habits, norms, and practices of a given period.

Moreover, in a society that often privileges tradition and reproduction over innovation and production, the details do literally make the difference. Revealing the temporal and spatial specificity of texts, they restore the heterogeneous, divided, and dynamic qualities of medieval urban experience. The three major thirteenth-century lyric anthologies—the Laurentian, Palatine, and Vatican—could all, for example, be described as pre-stilnovist in nature, with each presenting a relatively homogenous early vernacular canon heavily influenced by Guittone and the Guittonians. However, recent studies, particularly those by Roberto Antonelli and Lino Leonardi, of the textual, paleographic, and codicological "clues" of these manuscripts have demonstrated that they are,[25] in fact, unique textual events, containing distinct historiographical perspectives and produced by diverse, even contending, social groups.[26]

An important precept of modern textual criticism is that copyists tend to simplify and level a text in the process of transmission, replacing what is confusing or unfamiliar with what is more common to their own historical and social backgrounds. In an attempt to counter this phenomenon of banalization, when presented with readings of equal probability, the philologist often opts for the more difficult reading, the *lectio difficilior*. The reception of literary works, more broadly speaking, often follows a similar process of banalization. For example, as we shall see, some of the contemporary poets who first read Dante translated, in their responses, what they found foreign and illegible in his innovative poetry back into the conceptual framework with which they were most familiar. But the preference for the *lectio difficilior* in textual editing has not taken root, for the most part, in literary and literary-historical analyses. When confronted with an interpretive gap in the understanding of a work, the more economical (*facilior*) explanation is favored, the one more in line with established ideas about medieval culture, the *textus receptus*. Still, at times it can be useful to allow the more difficult reading to stand, to resist incorporating its irreducible specificity into the known categories of an epoch, culture, or class. Indeed, in the following chapters, a conceptual misreading, a textual "error," or a nonstandard method of transcription will often serve as an entryway for understanding what really mattered for contemporary readers and writers in their experience of a highly conventional and ritualized Italian poetic tradition. By illustrating the cracks in a supposedly shared worldview, these "difficult" details reveal that behind the production and consumption of countless, almost indistinguishable love poems, lay real divisions between not only stilnovists and Guittonians, but also magnates and *popolani,* merchant-bankers and notaries. I will propose, furthermore, that these divisions were not only reflected in the circulation of Italian poetry but re-affirmed, redrawn, and contested.

There are, however, certain inherent risks involved in this sort of "close reading" of medieval culture, such as reading profundity into surface, meaning into accident. The part is valuable only if it can be integrated into a whole, the details into historical and theoretical paradigms. Moreover, the available evidence in such an inquiry is often fragmentary. Gaps exist, and the risks of producing a misleading *emendatio* are serious. Still, these are the risks of any historical inquiry, which is always, to an extent, archeological in nature. Working with what time has wrought, the literary historian can attempt only to collect the fragments into a cohesive, if contingent whole. For this reason, *Accounting for Dante* remains a "working hypothesis."[27]

The following chapters examine the complicated intersections of materiality and textuality. I begin with the material evidence provided by the Memoriali bolognesi of the politicized poetic debates that Dante included in his *Commedia*. I conclude by speculating on what he left out: the social and material reality that supported the poetics of the Florentine banker Monte Andrea.

In chapter 1, as already noted, I examine the *rime* of the Memoriali for their political and historiographical importance, challenging the traditional view that the poems served a purely legalistic purpose by filling in blank spaces in the registers to avoid future tampering. Instead, I argue that the newly empowered notaries, writing quite literally in the margins of official Latin culture (with visual layouts recalling the *mise-en-page* of their registers and instruments), reflect the anti-magnate sentiment of the period in their exclusion of Guittone and the Guittonians and their inclusion of Dante, Guinizzelli, and the Sicilian-school poets. This antagonism toward the converted Fra Guittone and his aristocratic order of Jovial Friars sheds light on the ideological contrasts and political stakes informing Dante's historiography of the early Italian lyric.

Chapter 2 examines how Dante was influenced by the reception of his own early texts, in particular the way the framing of "Donne ch'avete intelletto d'amore" in the *Vita Nova* responds to the *canzone* "Ben aggia l'amoroso et dolce chore." "Ben aggia" was itself a response to "Donne ch'avete," written in the voice of the ladies of Dante's intended audience, sharing the same rhymes, and transcribed directly after his *canzone* in Vatican anthology 3793. In particular, I argue that, the vexed treatment of the female voice, which is at the center of the *Vita Nova,* was Dante's attempt to contain the misreadings of his poetry that he would have encountered in his own reading of "Ben aggia" and anticipated in future readers. As evidenced in the Vatican anthology, the practice of writing in the female voice, often in *tenzoni* between two male poets, formed part of an important social ritual for the Tuscan ruling elite. In contrast, throughout the *Vita Nova,* Dante frames his dialogues with female readers and interlocutors as private speech acts. In doing so, he underlines the authenticity and interiority of his vernacular poetry, contextualized within a private feminine community and located indoors, in private rooms, as opposed to the masculine public constructed through poems written *in voce di donna* and represented in Vaticano 3793.

Although scholars generally agree that Dante's early exposure to the Italian lyric must have been through a manuscript similar to Vatican anthology 3793, no one has analyzed in detail the importance of the Vatican anthology for the *De vulgari eloquentia.* In chapter 3, I propose that the simultaneous historical, geographical, and linguistic narrative in Dante's text is fully intelligible only if understood as a reaction to the politically grounded anthologizing exemplified by Vaticano 3793. The Vatican anthology reproduces in microcosm the shifting political power of the Italian peninsula and foregrounds the new cultural and political prominence of Florence's mercantile oligarchy through a sophisticated history of early Italian lyric poetry. The anthology begins with the poets of Frederick II's court and continues through the poets of the emergent Emilia and the Tuscan communes (Pisa, Lucca, Siena, Arezzo) before finally culminating with the socially prominent Florentine poets Chiaro Davanzati and Monte Andrea. However, except for "Donne ch'avete," Dante's poetry is ignored by the compiler of the Vatican anthology and, in fact, undocumented in the thirteenth-century manuscript tradition. In his rewriting of literary history in the *De vulgari,* Dante instead appoints himself and his circle (Cavalcanti, Lapo Gianni, and Cino da Pistoia) as the legitimate heirs of the Sicilian-school canon while criticizing the Guittone-centric tradition reproduced in contemporary *canzonieri.*

When Dante critiques, as part of his revisionist history, Guittone's plebeian poetics, his target is not purely linguistic. Guittone and the Guittonians are associated with the dialogic poetic genres that characterize the Vatican anthology—poetic genres that represent and impersonate the voices of women or the middling classes. Their poetry of impersonation foregrounds the gross inauthenticity and rhetorical cynicism of the Italian love lyric, where the social function of the poem is more important than its content and truth-value. The ritual of writing in the female voice and the social cohesion enacted by the *tenzone* genre outweigh any "authentic" lyric voice. Municipal poets are thus not just linguistically inferior, they are also confined to a restricted social and semiotic "place"—limited by a performative model of poetry to the political vicissitudes of the Italian city-state. Against this concept of compromised municipality, Dante offers the perspective of exile, the permanence of the written word, and the abstract and microcosmic space of the *canzone* form.

In chapter 4, I turn to the specific physical and codicological aspects of the Vatican anthology only touched upon in previous chapters. I analyze the handwriting, binding, parchment, page layout, and *modi scribendi* of the Vatican anthology alongside contemporary documentary culture, in particular the notarial registers and merchant accounting books found in Florentine archives and libraries. The physical similarity between the Vatican anthology and contemporary accounting books reveals the unique fusion of mercantile and lyric culture behind the making of the Vatican anthology and demonstrates the impossibility of separating the social from the literary in our understanding of the history of early vernacular poetry. An illustrative case is the abbreviation *Mo* for the Florentine poet Monte Andrea—centered in the page and surrounded by brackets. We find a visually identical practice in account books in which *Mo* stands for *Monta,* or the sum of an individual account.

The Vatican anthology also shares with contemporary account books a new relationship to blank space. In addition to the transcriptions of the primary copyist of the anthology, subsequent possessors of the Vatican anthology continued adding to and expanding it, transforming the compilation into an open work in progress and underlining the manuscript's status as a physical object. Influenced by innovations in accounting and contemporary bookkeeping, these later copyists treat the Vatican anthology as a bound blank book, a series of homogenous blank pages, as opposed to the long-standing medieval model of a book divided into a hierarchy of quires, sheets, and pages. In a dramatic shift in the history of the book (and anticipating the emergence of the journal and diary), the homogenous blankness of the bound book is perceived as pre-existing the composition of a text. The potential epistemological and existential ramifications of this shift are numerous and, for the most part, unexamined, including its influence on modern "bounded" identity, the integrity of which is enabled by the perception of individual consciousness as a discrete, book-like objective space. For our purposes, the private, noncirculating status of the Vatican anthology and its tangible presence as a physical space evokes other important literary phenomena of the period, such as the emergence of the autograph manuscript and the author's book. In one sense, the private and open-ended nature of the Vatican anthology anticipates Petrarch and the obsessive elaborations of his autographs. Yet it also serves as a background that contrasts with Dante's textualization of contemporary book production and his attempts at absorbing, through the frequent use of codicological metaphors in his writings, the material aspects of lyric transmission from which he was barred because of historical circumstances. The concept of the book of memory is both enabled by and a response to the private blank book.

The final chapter, as also mentioned above, explores Dante's implicit dialogue in *Inferno* with Monte Andrea, the thirteenth-century Florentine banker and poet whose poems conclude the Vatican anthology. Given his profession, the series of odes he composed in praise of material wealth, and even his name, as we see in chapter 4, Monte represents perfectly the mercantile class that compiled Vatican anthology 3793. In crucial passages of *Inferno,* Dante alludes to Monte in the context of a larger critique of the Florentine mercantile class and its production and transmission of poetry, both exemplified by the Vatican anthology. In addition, Monte's poetry—representing a materialistic vision of society and Fortune—is evoked at points in *Inferno* at which Dante illustrates his own opposing view, one of providential Fortune and sacred history. Yet the echoes of Monte in the *Inferno* are subtle, perhaps even deliberately submerged. The banker-poet's brutally realistic interpretation of contemporary events remains a challenge to a transcendent vision of history in which a political exile is transformed into a visionary and a prophet. Through the lens of Dante's treatment of Monte Andrea and his poetry, we see Dante unavoidably engaged with the social and material realities of contemporary lyric transmission and production at the same time as he attempts to write himself out of that historical actuality. These contradictions lead to a final reflection on the contrasts between Dante's historiography and his own historicity, between the textualization of literary history in Dante's works and the inclusion and exclusion of his own texts in contemporary manuscripts and documents.

In an epilogue, I ask what is in a name. What changes when we identify Dante's treatment of Fortune specifically with the Florentine banker-poet Monte Andrea? More importantly, what is the role of Dante's name, announced in *Purgatorio* 30.55? In particular, the ambiguity as to whether we should read "Dante" primarily as a common noun—for "the one who gives"—or as a proper name referring to a historically identifiable individual serves as an ultimate reflection on what is within and without Dante's texts. Finally, that Dante's signature is spoken in the female voice brings us back full circle to the poetics of impersonation of Vatican anthology 3793 and the fraudulent rhetoric of Guittone and his followers.

chapter one

Dante's First Editors

The Memoriali bolognesi and the Politics
of Vernacular Transcription

The Memoriali bolognesi are the official registers of the Bolognese communal government, in which all social contracts and financial transactions were
required to be recorded and notarized. From the end of the thirteenth century
to the first quarter of the fourteenth, notaries appointed by the city government to record contracts in the Memoriali also inserted vernacular poems
in the end pages, lower margins, and in the spaces between Latin contracts.[1]
The *rime* were discovered relatively late and first published only in 1876 by the
poet and professor Giosuè Carducci.[2] Over the ensuing years, Carducci and
his followers continued publishing selections from the Memoriali, spurred by
a postromanticist enthusiasm for what they perceived as representations of
a popular oral tradition in late medieval Bologna.

The Memoriali bolognesi registers received more systematic scholarly
attention between 1900 and 1921 in preparation for an exhibition held in Bologna marking the six-hundredth anniversary of the death of Dante Alighieri.[3] A great deal of energy was spent searching for archival evidence in
the Memoriali of Dante's sojourn in Bologna—mentioned in Giovanni Boccaccio's *Vita* of the poet. Although modern scholars agree that Dante did
indeed live for a period in Bologna, no documentary support was found for
his stay.

Yet the Memoriali do provide evidence of Dante's presence in another sense. Collected in the notarial registers are the oldest surviving transcriptions of his texts.[4] First, in 1287, when Dante was only twenty-two years old and at least five years away from the composition of the *Vita Nova,* the notary Enrichetto delle Quercie transcribed in Memoriale 69 "Non me poriano zamai far emenda" (fig. 1), a sonnet that refers to the Garisenda, the truncated, leaning tower still found in Piazza Ravegnana in the center of Bologna. In 1293, Pietro Allegranza copied in his register (Mem. 82) several fragments of Dante's epoch-making "Donne ch'avete intelletto d'amore." The *ballata* "Donne, i' non so di ch'i' mi prieghi Amore" was copied into a register in 1310 (Mem. 120), and the opening verses from Dante's *rima petrosa* "Così nel mio parlar voglio esser aspro" are found in a *memoriale* from 1320 (Mem. 132).

Finally, and perhaps most dramatically, in a register from 1321 (Mem. 143), the same year as the poet's death, hurriedly scrawled as prose at the bottom of a series of contracts (fig. 2), is a fragment from the *Inferno*—the second oldest manuscript evidence we have for the transmission of Dante's masterpiece.[5] The terzina—lines 97–99 of canto 19, which describes the punishment of the simoniacs—includes one of the poet's most vehement attacks in the *Commedia* against the worldliness and political meddling of church figures. It is directed against Pope Nicholas III, who is buried head first in an infernal parody of the baptismal font: "Or te sta, che tu se' ben ponito; / et guarda bem la maltolta moneta / ch'eser te feçe contra Charlo ardito" (Now you stay there, for you are justly punished, and take a good look at your ill-gotten coin that made you bold against Charles). The anticlerical sentiment underlying the transcription of these verses is further evident in the reading "Or te sta"—even more forceful and immediate than the "Però ti sta" (Therefore stay there) of the *textus receptus.*[6] In addition, the notary seems unsure of the decasyllabic line, crossing out and then rewriting "Or" before continuing the rest of the fragment; the attack on the corrupt pope was thus likely copied from memory.

The entries of Dante's poetry in the Memoriali bolognesi are even more important when we consider that, with the sole exception of "Donne ch'avete" in Vaticano 3793 (discussed in the next chapter), the great Tuscan lyric anthologies ignore or even exclude Dante from their compilations.[7] The state archives of Bologna contain the only extant records of Dante's poetry copied during his lifetime, albeit limited to the noncirculating world of municipal documents. In metaliterary passages such as the opening to the *Vita Nova* or

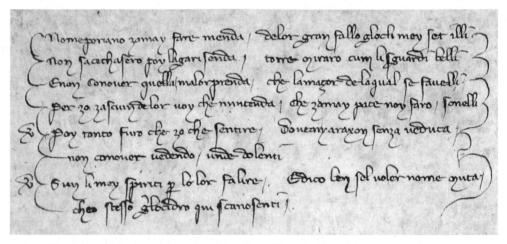

Fig. 1. Dante's first appearance in writing (1287). Transcription of the sonnet "Non me poriano zamai far emenda" by the notary Enrichetto delle Quercie. Bologna, Archivio di Stato, Memoriale 69, fol. 203v. Reproduced by permission of the Ministero per i Beni e le Attività Culturali, Archivio di Stato di Bologna.

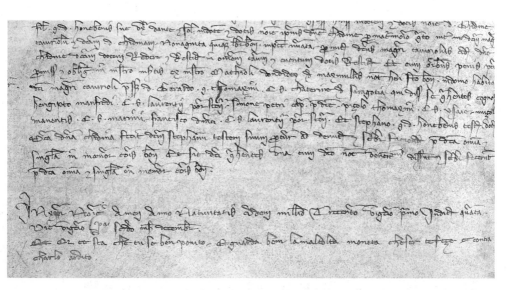

Fig. 2. *Inferno* 19.97–99 copied in the lower margin of a page of contracts from 1321 (below invocation and date). Bologna, Archivio di Stato, Memoriale 143, fol. 281v. Reproduced by permission of the Ministero per i Beni e le Attività Culturali, Archivio di Stato di Bologna.

Paradiso 10, Dante tended to imagine his texts as inhabiting the prestigious space of the *libro da banco,* or desk book—the type of annotated manuscript book consulted in juridical and scholastic environs. Yet the early reception of his work is characterized predominantly by the archival and memorializing functions of writing.

Despite their role in preserving the earliest records of Dante's poetry, the notaries of the Memoriali bolognesi, Dante's first editors, have been largely neglected by literary critics and historians. The texts themselves are occasionally studied from a philological perspective or in order to date Dante's works, but the possible motives behind the notaries' selections have remained, for the most part, unexamined.[8] Modern critics generally concur in finding a purely legal, functional role for the *rime:* they were used to fill in the blank spaces of registers in order to prevent tampering and forgery.[9] The notaries thus copied the vernacular poems mechanically, without any intervention of their own. They were, in the end, "semplicemente dei notai."[10]

But what did it mean to be "simply a notary" in late medieval Bologna— during a period in which the power of the notaries in governmental positions was so overwhelming that Giorgio Tamba has described the city as "una repubblica dei notai" (a republic of notaries)?[11] And does a legal and functional application of vernacular fragments in the Memoriali bolognesi necessarily exclude historical and literary explanations? In fact, even a preliminary survey of the registers reveals evidence contradicting the argument that the *rime* serve solely to fill in blank spaces. Various *memoriali* containing *rime* are interspersed with not only blank spaces, but even entire blank pages. While many notaries clearly use the incipits and fragments of vernacular poems to fill up the bottom margins of their registers, others demonstrate a distinctly literary consciousness and metrical awareness in their transcriptions. For example, in his famous transcription of Dante's "No me poriano zamai far emenda"(fig. 1), Enrichetto delle Quercie copies the poem alone on a blank page, separated from the surrounding contracts, in a calligraphic, upright hand that is careful to clearly separate words, verses, distichs, and even quatrains and tercets (indicated with the initial *V* for *versus* or *volta*).[12]

The notaries of the Memoriali bolognesi, it turns out, copied vernacular poetry into their official registers in a variety of ways for a variety of reasons, ranging from the predominantly legal to the predominantly literary.[13] Furthermore, the ways in which poems were copied changed over time. The earliest *rime* were transcribed on the first and last pages of registers. These vernacular

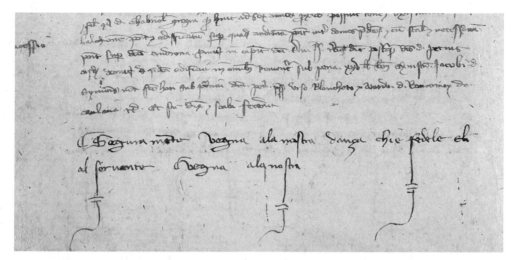

Fig. 3. The dance song "Seguramente" copied in the lower margin by Nicola *Johanini Manelli,* with characteristic elongated descenders of *S*'s and *F*'s filling up blank space. Bologna, Archivio di Stato, Memoriale 67, fol. 21v. Reproduced by permission of the Ministero per i Beni e le Attività Culturali, Archivio di Stato di Bologna.

"traces" are mixed in with other preparatory writings found in the end pages of the *memoriali,* including rough drafts, notes, handwriting practice, and pen testing.[14] In the next phase, the *rime* move from the unnumbered end pages into the body of registers, either sharing page space with official Latin contracts or inhabiting the margins. In the registers of Nicola *Johanini Manelli,* Memoriali 67 and 78 (1287 and 1290), poetic fragments and incipits often complete a page of contracts, filling up the bottom margins (figs. 3 and 5). The transcriptions of Biagio *Auliverii* (Mem. 63, 1286) and Nicola *Phylippi* (Mem. 64, 1286), written as indented prose paragraphs, are interspersed among the Latin contracts themselves, from which they are almost indistinguishable (fig. 4). Another method emerged in the early fourteenth century, when poems began to be clearly separated from contracts and written as carefully distinguished verses beneath or above the inscription or subscription of a register (figs. 6, 7, and 9). Framed by blank space and distinctly literary in layout, these later transcriptions will be discussed in the final section of this chapter.

This brief sketch of the development of various modes of transcribing vernacular poetry in the Memoriali bolognesi can only begin to account for the surprising heterogeneity and continuous innovation behind the copying of the *rime.* Even within a single time frame, notaries experimented with a

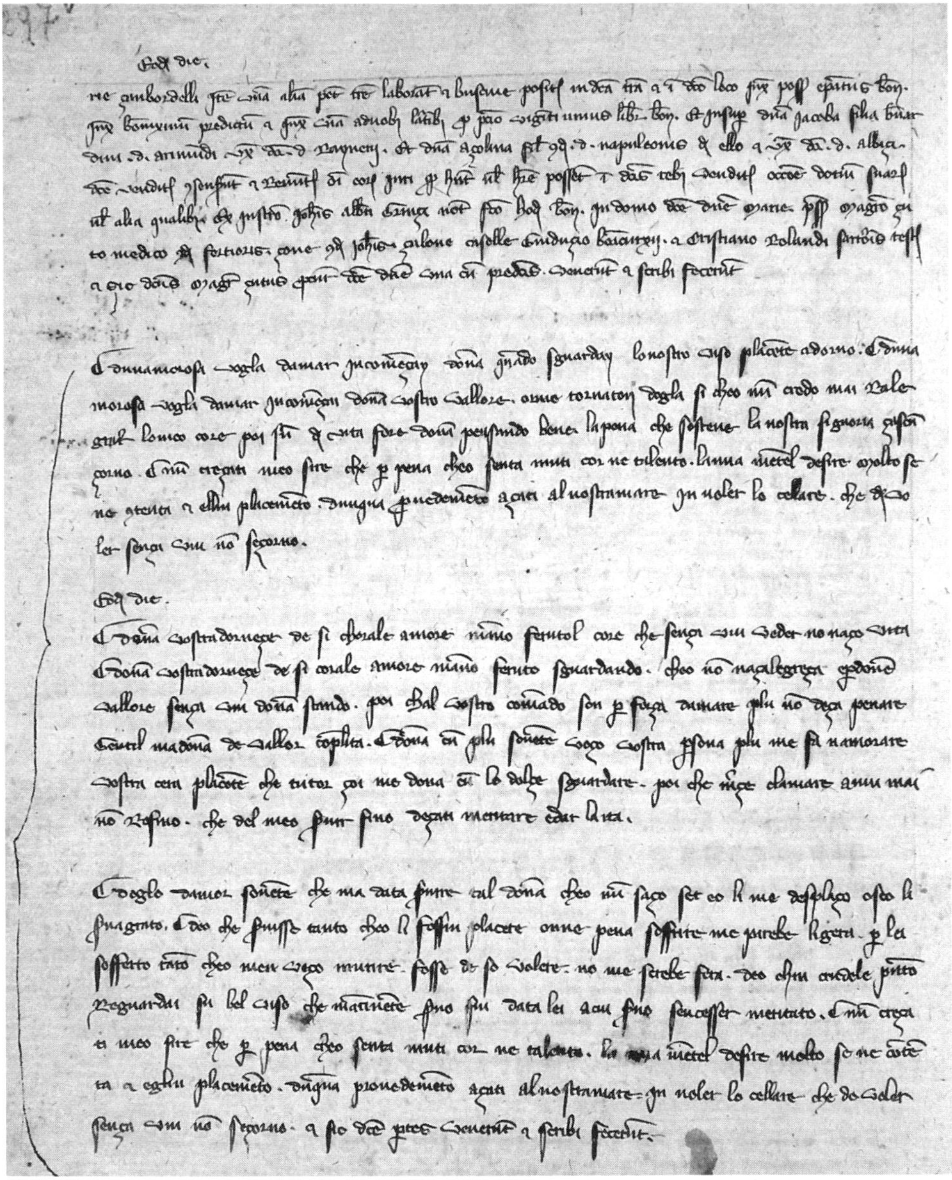

Fig. 4. "D'un'amorosa voglia," "Donna, vostr'adorneze," "Doglio d'amor sovente," and another fragment of "D'un'amorosa voglia" written out as contracts by Biagio *Auliverii*. The poems are transcribed in prose paragraphs, dated, and concluded with Latin formulas. Bologna, Archivio di Stato, Memoriale 63, fol. 297v. Reproduced by permission of the Ministero per i Beni e le Attività Culturali, Archivio di Stato di Bologna.

variety of techniques for recording vernacular poetry, and no single trend was ever exclusive. Most of the notaries, however, at least until the fourteenth century, were influenced by documentary and archival models of writing in their treatment of literary texts. In the poetic transcriptions of Nicola *Johanini Manelli,* for example, he elongated the stems of the descenders of the *S*'s and *F*'s in the bottom line of the text several inches below the writing line, creating vertical pen flourishes that fill up the space remaining between the bottom of the text and the bottom of the page (figs. 3 and 5). In contemporary notarial registers, similar pen flourishes were added after the completion of Latin contracts and were typically used to fill in the space left blank in the lower margins. In addition, in the left-hand margin next to his *rime,* Nicola identified their metrical genre (*ballata, sonecto, cantinele*) in the same fashion as he labeled his notarized contracts (*testamentum, venditio,* etc.). Biagio *Auliverii* and Nicola *Phylippi* took the nexus of notarial and literary culture even further, finishing transcriptions with notarial formulas such as "et sic dicti contrahentes presente dicto notario dixerunt et scribi fecerunt" (and the aforementioned contracting parties, in the presence of the aforementioned notary, declared and had it recorded).[15] Biagio even dated his poems in the same manner as his contracts (fig. 4).

In these registers, it is at first difficult to distinguish vernacular poetry from Latin prose, and no doubt the late discovery of the *rime* is due in part to their being "disguised" as contracts. When copying vernacular poems, notaries such as Nicola *Johanini Manelli,* Biagio *Auliverii,* and Nicola *Phylippi* reproduced the visual layouts and bookkeeping methods of their protocols, incorporating literary anthologizing into their professional duties as legal writers. In many ways, these apparently rudimentary layouts are in fact more original and telling than the more literary transcriptions, those carefully separated from Latin contracts and written out as verse. With the former, the notary-copyists created an innovative material container for the emergent vernacular literature, a new transcribing language organic to their professional background. (Chapter 4 will discuss a similar phenomenon with the merchant-copyists of Vaticano 3793.) That many of the *rime* also served a legal and practical purpose only increases the significance of their transcription and their value as literary-historical artifacts. Rather than simply representing a primitive stage in the transmission of vernacular literature, this documentary style of transcription demonstrates that authority over the preservation of Dante's poetry, and that of his contemporaries, was still fluid and contested among different categories of writers with their different conceptions of writing.

Given the functional nature of many of the *rime,* it is generally assumed that they were copied passively and mechanically, without regard for literary concerns. But various notaries of the Memoriali bolognesi were discriminating cultivators of vernacular poetry. These copyists acted at least in part as incipient editors of poetry, as a review of some of the evidence that underlies our basic assumptions about the Memoriali will show. In the necessarily brief philological excursus that follows, I will focus on a single poem, "D'un'amorosa voglia." This *ballata* is especially useful for understanding the phenomenon of the *rime* because it was copied four times, twice each by Biagio *Auliverii* and Nicola *Phylippi.* Moreover, the poem served as a crucial test case in Santorre Debenedetti's groundbreaking demonstration that the *rime* were copied from written manuscripts and not transmitted orally and by memory.[16] Confuting the romanticist portrayal of the *rime* as written traces of a popular and regional tradition, Debenedetti's essay remains a turning point in the history of the criticism on the Memoriali bolognesi, and it continues to influence our perceptions about the early transmission of Italian literature.

There are five extant redactions of "D'un'amorosa voglia": a complete version in the register of Biagio *Auliverii,* Memoriale 63, fol. 297v (A); verses 15–24 on the same page of the same register (B); a complete version in the register of Nicola *Phylippi,* Memoriale 64, fol. 113r (C); verses 1–20 on fol. 157r of the same register (D); and a complete version in Banco Rari 217 of the Biblioteca Nazionale Centrale of Florence, attributed to both Riccucio de Florença and Albertucio da la Viola (P). Eliminating B and D as containing only formal variants, Debenedetti identified four textually significant readings in his comparison of A and C. By correlating these variants with the readings found in P, he was able to produce the following table:

15	*crezati* A	*dotati* C	*pensati* P
18	*La mia mente* A	*El meo core* CP	
19	*contenta* A	*talenta* CP	
23	*volerlo* AP	*saverlo* C	

As the table indicates, the readings "El meo core" (18) and "talenta" (19) in C and "volerlo" (23) in A find corresponding readings in P.[17] By ascribing these scribal variants to two distinct branches of a manuscript tradition, Debenedetti proved that the *rime* were copied from written evidence and not the result of a haphazard oral tradition.

Debenedetti's findings are now universally accepted, so it is worth pointing out a possible oversight in his examination of "D'un'amorosa voglia" that, to my knowledge, has gone unnoticed. Namely, he claims that Nicola *Phylippi*'s second transcription (verses 1–20) of "D'un'amorosa voglia," D, contains only insignificant formal variants.[18] In fact, in D Nicola replaces the reading "atalenta" in verse 19 of his previous transcription (C)—a reading that is in agreement with the *lectio* in P—with "acontenta," a reading found only in the transcription of his fellow notary Biagio *Auliverii*. While in D Nicola still prefers the Occitanism "dotati" in verse 15 to the *lectiones faciliores* "crezati" and "pensati" in A, B, and P, he appears to correct the error "talenta" (suggested perhaps by the rhyme word *talento* in verse 17) with the reading preferred by Biagio in A and B. The possibility that Nicola communicated and perhaps even collaborated with Biagio for his transcription of "D'un'-amorosa voglia" is heightened when we consider that the two notaries worked together on a daily basis during their semester in the Office of the Memoriali (January–July, 1286) and copied two of the same poems in their registers: "D'un'amorosa voglia" and "Donna, vostr'adorneze." But even within this proposed collaboration, the two versions of "Donna, vostr'adorneze" copied by Biagio (Mem. 63, fol. 297v) and Nicola (Mem. 64, fols. 100v–101r) provide further evidence of two distinct approaches to recording vernacular poetry. Biagio's transcription, described as "ottima" by Debenedetti,[19] appears once again to be faithful to a single exemplar. Nicola, on the other hand, introduces a number of diverse readings and includes an extra stanza of the *ballata* not found in Biagio's version.[20]

Biagio and Nicola *Phylippi* are not the only notaries in the Memoriali to demonstrate a certain textual awareness, especially in this early, fertile period of poetic transcription. Nicola *Johanini Manelli* interrupts his transcription of the sonnet "Vixo che d'one flore se' formato" (Mem. 67, fol. 121v) after realizing that he skipped from line 1 to 4 (having committed the common scribal error known as a *saut du même au même*). In a particularly elegant expression of the fusion of notarial and literary culture, he crosses out the flawed transcription with the same undulating line used by contemporary notaries to void contracts (fig. 5). Nicola then provides a complete and correct version of the poem on another page of the same register (fol. 34v). Sandro Orlando

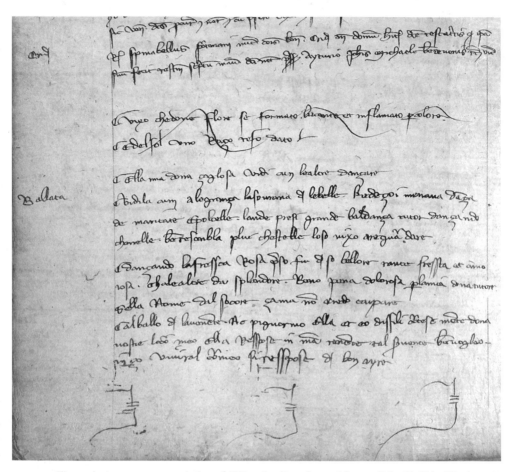

Fig. 5. An inaccurate transcription of "Vixo che d'one flore se' formate" "voided" by Nicola *Johanini Manelli*. "Ella mia dona zogliosa" is identified in the margin as a "Ballata." Bologna, Archivio di Stato, Memoriale 67, fol. 121v. Reproduced by permission of the Ministero per i Beni e le Attività Culturali, Archivio di Stato di Bologna.

has already pointed out, moreover, that in the same register the variant readings in Nicola's transcriptions of Guinizzelli's sonnet "Omo ch'è saggio non corre leggero" (Mem. 67, fols. 28r and 117r)—in particular "quand'ha" and "penseri" in line 3—are drawn from different branches of the manuscript tradition, demonstrating that he likely culled readings from two different versions of the text. Finally, in his own transcriptions of the Guinizzellian sonnet (Mem. 74, 1288, fols. 281v and 386v), Bonaccursio *de Rombolinis* switches between the readings "po[i] ch'à" and the now preferred "quand'ha" with the same sort of inclusiveness toward variant readings we have seen in Nicola *Phylippi*'s versions of "D'un'amorosa voglia."[21]

Although Debenedetti's magisterial essay convincingly argues that the *rime* are drawn from written sources (with important exceptions, such as the transcription from *Inferno* 19), his description of the passive, automatic role of the notaries in transcribing vernacular verse is more open to question. The evidence provided by the variants in the poems found in Memoriali 63 and 64 suggests a more active involvement on the part of the notaries, including examples of scribal *contaminatio*. Above all, the *rime* examined so far indicate a noticeable degree of interest on the part of the notaries in how and what they transcribed. Nor should this sort of active participation be entirely unexpected from members of a professional category known for their contributions to the new vernacular literature. Yet the perception of the *rime* found in the Memoriali bolognesi as a largely unconscious and thematically insignificant phenomenon has resulted in an underestimation of their historical significance. The question thus remains: Why did notaries begin to copy vernacular poems in the Memoriali bolognesi at a specific moment, and what were the motives behind the selection of certain authors and texts?

The Rise of the Notarial Guild and the *popolo* Government

The Memoriali Bolognesi were instituted in 1265 at a time of political upheaval and dissension within the city-state of Bologna. Between 1260 and 1280, in part in reaction to the constant warring between the noble families of Guelph and Ghibelline allegiance, the recently formed *popolo* government wrested power from the older aristocratic *podestà* government. Consensual if not truly democratic, the *popolo* government was constituted of representatives drawn from the ranks of urban professionals, mid-level merchants, and skilled laborers, who elected them through the guilds and guild militias, organized by neighborhood.[22] In opposition to the self-destructive violence of the magnates, the *popolo* promoted themselves as peacekeepers, as the sole protectors of a *status et pacificus et tranquillus*. In the name of legality and civil order, they were able to gain power and enact ordinances against the ruling classes, the anti-magnate laws. These were designed to combat the factional strife and lawlessness among the nobility—embodied in their private courts and militias and in their adherence to the irrational justice of revenge, the ever-present *vendetta*.[23]

With their juridical training and legal experience, the powerful and ubiquitous notaries of Bologna were naturally at the forefront of this legal revolution of the *popolo*. Without counting apprentices and employees, over one thousand authorized notaries were working in Bologna in 1283, a city with a population of perhaps less than fifty thousand.[24] They helped administer and perform legal duties for the guilds that made up the new representative *popolo* government. Significantly, notaries had held important positions in the older *podestà* regime, enabling them to facilitate the transition to the new guild-based political system.[25] So, while they sympathized with the tradesmen, the notaries understood the bureaucratic administration of the nobles.

But the true power of the notaries was more cultural than explicitly political or economic. They held a practical monopoly on written legal verity in Bologna and enjoyed an almost unconditional public trust. In the thirteenth and fourteenth centuries, in Bologna as in other cities of central and northern Italy, the increasing professionalization of the notariate dramatically enhanced the notaries' power as public stewards of truth, lending an authoritative stamp to their every act of writing, a true *fides publica*. In previous centuries, the private contract, or *charta*, although drawn up with the help of a notary, required the signatures of contracting parties and witnesses at the bottom of the text (*subscriptiones*) in order for it to be considered truthful and legal. By the thirteenth century, the *charta* was replaced by another private contract, the *instrumentum publicum*. The *instrumentum* lacked subscriptions and was acknowledged as a legally binding document based solely on the authority of the notary who copied it.[26] Salathiel Bononiensis, in the introduction to his *Ars notaria*, underlines the newly acquired prestige of the notaries' *fides publica* when he defines the notary as that public person who, invested with the public trust, publishes the citizens' transactions.[27] The prestige that this *fides* allotted the notaries and their documents cannot be overemphasized for a society that increasingly relied on written documents to ensure social and economic bonds, yet lacked the technology to prevent the numerous forgeries of the period. Social order depended on the trustworthiness of the autonomous notarial guild.

The growing power of the *popolo* government and the notarial guild was challenged in 1265 by a new experimental *podestà* government controlled jointly by the magnates Loderingo degli Andalò and Catalano dei Catalani. Loderingo and Catalano are now infamous as the two Jovial Friars (*Frati gaudenti*) punished as hypocrites in canto 23 of *Inferno.* Most commentators on this canto explain the condemnation of the Jovial Friars by Dante and his contemporaries in terms of the knightly order's conspicuous worldliness and corruption. However, it is important not to lose sight of the originally class-based nature of the antagonism toward the friars.[28] After all, the Knights of the Glorious Virgin Mary, as the predominantly lay order was properly known, was composed almost entirely of noble knights and members of the older ruling classes, "cavalieri a speroni dorati."[29] According to the chronicler Salimbene da Parma, even the pejorative *"Frati gaudenti"* had its origins in class conflict, since it derived from the hostility of the humbler classes, the *rustici,* who objected to the greed and privileges of the friar-knights.[30] Protected by the church, the friars were exempted from burdensome taxes and could claim that for their members ecclesiastical jurisdiction took precedence over the laws of the city government.[31] At the same time, unlike other religious orders, they did not have to renounce property, business dealings, or family ties. It was through the Jovial Friar order, moreover, and the government of Loderingo and Catalano that the ruling families of Bologna were able to regroup and regain some of the power and privileges they had lost under the legislation of the popular movement. Loderingo himself was not only the founder of the Jovial Friars, but also one of the leaders of the Ghibelline party and a member of the wealthy and influential Andalò family, one of the noble families that had the most to lose under the anti-magnate laws.[32]

During their brief rule in Bologna, Loderingo and Catalano placed the guild militias under the direct control of the *podestà* and of the Knights of the Glorious Virgin Mary.[33] They also instituted severe penalties for acts of violence against magnates—basically turning on its head the anti-magnate legislation of the previous decades.[34] The greatest threat, however, to the emergent *popolo* government was the appropriation on the part of the Jovial Friars of the *popolo*'s rhetoric of peace and civil order, of their claim to being the sole maintainers of a *status et pacificus et tranquillus.* Through their religious order, the Ghibelline Loderingo and the Guelph Catalano transformed themselves from instigators of civil war to supposed protectors of the peace.[35] In doing so, the co-governors were able to co-opt the demands of the *popolo,* especially their calls for transparent justice, as a means of maintaining power. In particular, one of the friar-knights' first acts in public office in 1265 was a series of statutes aimed nominally at restoring order to the city. The forty-sixth chapter of the ordinances required all contracts involving more than twenty lire of bolognini to be recorded in the central registers of the *podestà* government by one of the four notaries appointed by the commune.[36] In other words, Loderingo and Catalano instituted the Memoriali bolognesi.

Like other governmental attempts at regulating the notariate,[37] the Memoriali bolognesi represented a more or less direct attack on the independence of the notarial guild by appropriating their legal authority and *fides publica*. According to the statute of 1265, any public act copied by a notary was recognized as valid only if it corresponded to a second contract copied in the Memoriali. Otherwise it was considered "cassum et nullius valoris,"[38] and any party attempting to use these "worthless" contracts for legal purposes would be fined. The ordinances justified this appropriation of authority by assaulting the truthfulness of the notaries' writings; the Memoriali were necessary to remedy the numerous cases of forgeries and fraud increasingly found in legal instruments, so that "falsitatibus que circa instrumenta fiebant omnimode obvietur" (one could remedy in any way the falsehoods that were committed in contracts).[39] A preamble from one of the first *memoriali* echoes the rhetoric used by the central city government to undermine the prestige of legal verity enjoyed by notaries with their private registers:

Quia Bononia quae mater est veritatis et iuris inhundantibus falsitatibus hominum et malitia succrescente videbatur a rectitudinis limite deviare et in laberinthum corruere falsitatis inventus est per prudentes viros usus laudabilis scripturarum remedium et memorialium officium nuncupatum. . . . Ego Amator quondam D. Petri de Butrio . . . memorialium officium deputatus seguendo formam et mandatum per viros venerabiles et colendos Fratres Loterengum et Catelanum ordinis gloriose Virginis Marie pro excludendis fraudibus et falsitatibus.[40]

[Since Bologna, the mother of truth and laws, was flooded with the falsehoods of men and ever-increasing malice, so that she appeared to deviate from the right path and to precipitate into the labyrinth of falsehood, judicious men have found as a solution a praise-worthy use of writing called the Office of the Memoriali. I, Amator of the late D. Petri de Butrio . . . have been put in charge of the Office of the Memoriali, to follow the form and mandate set forth by those venerable and honorable men, Friar Loderingo and Friar Catalano of the Order of the Glorious Virgin Mary, in order to flush out acts of fraud and falsehoods.]

In an ideological reversal, thanks to the "remedium" of the Memoriali, the aristocratic joint governors of Bologna, the venerable Loderingo and Catalano, were now the sole arbiters of stable, legal authority in Bologna. Even the notaries' private archives of carefully organized preparatory drafts and protocols were superceded by the centralized preservation of the Memoriali. Each original *memoriale* was guarded in the city's archives, the Camera Actorum, and two additional copies were entrusted to the Dominican and Franciscan orders.

The reign of the Jovial Friars, however, did not last, and their attempts at diminishing the prestige and status of the notariate ultimately fell short. In the last decades of the thirteenth century, the *popolo* movement continued to make gains under the charismatic leadership of the illustrious notary and professor of *ars notaria,* Rolandino Passageri. Under his guidance, the *popolo* became the principal governing organism of the city-state and the notaries held the ruling positions.[41] The successes of the *popolo* have their most explicit expression in the *Ordinamenti sacrati e sacratissimi* in 1282–1284. These ordinances excluded the magnates from the government, revoked their fiscal privileges, and, above all, placed them under strict juridical control—anticipating by more than a decade similar events and legislation in Florence.

Changes in the governing structure of the Bolognese commune also brought changes to the structure of the Memoriali,[42] which went from being a means of social control over the increasingly powerful notarial guild to an administrative instrument for that same social group. Most noticeably, the registers from the period 1279 to 1289 are reduced in size and made of paper instead of parchment.[43] Unlike the stately registers of previous years, the paper registers of this period resemble the humble daily protocols that the Memoriali were supposed to supplant. In fact, within this period (Mem. 40–60, 1279–1285), notaries actually used the unnumbered first or last pages of their registers as if they were protocols, filling them with notes and even first drafts of contracts.[44]

It is exactly in this period of political crisis and physical transformation of the structure of the Memoriali bolognesi that we find another innovative phenomenon: the insertion of vernacular verse in the margins and in between

Latin contracts. Almost half of all the *rime* present in the Memoriali are copied in this decade (1280–1290) of intense political ferment and concentrated poetic transcription. The significance of the mixing of official Latin contracts and vernacular verse is even more striking when we consider the poetic genres preferred by the early copyists.[45] Popular *ballate* appear with particular frequency in the registers from 1280 to 1290, as do poems constructed as dialogues in which at least one of the speakers is female. For example, in his register (Mem. 47, 1292), Antonio *Guidonis de Argele* collected a series of bawdy drinking songs and poems in the comic-realist tradition treating such uncourtly subject matters as sex, gluttony, and bodily functions. The vividness and concreteness of theme and diction in these ballads, reminiscent of goliardic poetry in their carnivalesque celebration of everyday subject matter, make it almost impossible not to consider the implications of the revolutionary date of their transcription: 1282. It seems unlikely that a recently matriculated notary working during the first years of the guild-based government would be unaffected by the victorious tones of the class-biased *Ordinamenti sacrati*—the emblem of legislative power for this "repubblica dei notai." In some sense, by copying down Italian poems in his official register, Antonio *Guidonis de Argele* was participating, consciously or not, in a broader contemporary rhetorical enthusiasm for the rights of *popolani,* in a political movement claiming to ensure that the "lupi rapaces et agni mansueti ambulent pari gradu" (meek lambs are on equal footing with rapacious wolves).[46] The revolution in social hierarchy taking place within the governmental walls of the *palazzo comunale* appears to have been accompanied by a playful inversion of linguistic and generic hierarchy within the politicized pages of the Memoriali. At the very least, the selection of poems and the documentary style of their transcription speak to the cultural autonomy of the notaries, an autonomy that finds expression at the very moment a long-sought political autonomy was achieved.

Nicola *Johanini Manelli*: Editor of Guinizzelli

The registers of Nicola *Johanini Manelli* (Mem. 67, 1287, and Mem. 78, 1290) demonstrate a particular disregard for the traditional hierarchy of literary styles, combining the sophisticated stilnovist poems of Guido Guinizzelli with popular vernacular ballads and dances. The notary-copyist, whose technical innovations in poetic transcription were discussed above, recorded for the first time Guinizzelli's "Omo ch'è saggio non corre leggero," part of the important *tenzone* with Bonagiunta Orbicciani in which the latter accuses Guinizzelli of contaminating the traditional love lyric with the university learning ("senno" [13]) of Bologna. Not surprisingly, the Bolognese's defense of this learning in "Omo ch'è saggio" was destined to be a great favorite in the Memoriali bolognesi, appearing in six different registers. Nicola was the only notary, however, who also recorded Guinizzelli's influential sonnet "Io voglio del ver la mia donna laudare" and, further indicating his interest in the poet, he transcribed each sonnet twice in his registers.

At the same time, alongside the sophisticated poetic manifestos "Io voglio del ver" and "Omo ch'è saggio," Nicola seamlessly inserts into his registers compositions drawn from oral and performative culture, namely the dance songs "Seguramente" and "Ella mia dona zogliosa." In particular, "Seguramente" is copied before "Omo ch'è saggio" in Memoriale 67 (fols. 21v [fig. 3], 28r) and after "Io voglio del ver" in Memoriale 78 (fols. 131r, 165r). And while the learned compositions of Guinizzelli were almost certainly transcribed from written evidence and manuscripts, the dance "Seguramente" was apparently copied down from memory, evidence of an important oral tradition in Bologna. Compared to the almost identical redactions of Guinizzelli's texts, the two versions of "Seguramente" are notably divergent. In the second version of the *danza,* in Memoriale 78, Nicola reduces the verse "fedel d'amor servente" to "lial servente," inserts the verse "et à gli cor e sperança" between the third and fourth verses, and then adds five extra lines at the end of the poem. Underlining their oral and popular origins, Nicola labels the dances with the curious title "cantinele," written in small script in the left-hand margin where one would normally expect to find a description of the Latin contract.[47] Other metrical genres are identified by Nicola as "ballata" and "sonictum" accordingly, indicating he possessed a degree of literary sophistication and that at some level he must have been aware of the significance of juxtaposing the philosophical poetry of the Bolognese judge with the bawdy limerick "Turlù, Turlù, Turlù."

The contrasts between high and low genres in Nicola's register are even more significant when we consider that Guittone most likely utilized the profane *danza* "Seguramente" in composing his sacred ballad, or *laude,* "Vegna—vegna—chi vole giocundare."[48] In particular, the *ripresa* of the Guittonian ballad, "Vegna—vegna—chi vole giocundare / e a la danza se tegna" (Come,

come, whoever wants to amuse themselves, and take part in the dance) [1–2][49] recalls the Bolognese dance that begins with:

> Seguramente
> vegna a la nostra danza
> chi è fedel d'Amore
> e hagli cor e speranza
> vegna a la nostra danza.

[Certainly, come to our dance, whoever is a loyal follower of Love and has his heart and hope in him, come to our dance.]

Both compositions are defined by the repeated invitation "Vegna . . . a la danza," directed either at "chi vole giocundare" or at " chi è fedel d'Amore."[50]

Guittone almost certainly encountered the popular ballad during one of his extended stays in Bologna. The Aretine poet, a converted member of the Jovial Friars, had frequent dealings (religious, commercial, and personal) with the Bolognese chapter of the Knights of the Glorious Virgin Mary. He even addressed letters and verses to Loderingo degli Andalò, the founding member of the order and instigator of the Memoriali bolognesi, to whom he left several properties in Ronzano outside of Bologna.[51] Guittone's transformation of the profane dance "Seguramente" into his sacred *laude* would thus seem another confirmation of his frequent and substantial contacts with Bologna. Indeed, considering Guittone's close ties with the city, we might expect to find numerous transcriptions of his poetry in the Memoriali bolognesi. Yet while contemporary poetic anthologies are, to different degrees, Guittonian in spirit, he is completely absent from the Memoriali, as are, for the most part, his followers. Instead, the notaries transcribed the poetry of Giacomo da Lentini, Bonagiunta, Guinizzelli, Cavalcanti, Lapo Gianni, Cino, and Dante—a canon of early lyric poetry much more in line with Dante's own historiography of the lyric.

How are we to explain the exclusion of one of the most popular and important poets of the thirteenth century—an exclusion that predates even Dante's censuring influences? At least in part, the selections in the Memoriali were contingent on the availability of vernacular poetry at this time, on what the notaries found in the manuscripts they used as exemplars. Yet the composition of primary sources cannot explain fully why the standing of Dante and of Guittone in the Memoriali is the exact opposite of what is found in the contemporary manuscript tradition. Nor does it explain why even Guittonian poets living in Bologna are absent from the Memoriali. For example, although the Florentine exile Monte Andrea appears in several Latin contracts within the Memoriali, his vernacular production, including *tenzoni* with Emilian poets, is neglected by the notary-copyists. Except for the late entry of the sonnet "Quella crudel staxon ch'al çudegare" in 1320, even Onesto da Bologna fails to enter the corpus of the politicized Memoriali. The exclusion of Onesto is especially significant since, in exchanges with Cino, he critiques the philosophical poetry of the stilnovists, denigrating Dante, in particular, as that poet who "sogna e fa spirti dolenti" (dreams and creates languishing spirits).[52] While the *rime* from the Memoriali embody, in many ways, the fertile intellectual exchanges between Tuscany and Emilia in this period, Guittone's school—or, more accurately, faction—appears extraneous to this urban, university-educated milieu.

Given the political explanation I have proposed for the transcriptions in the Memoriali, the notaries may have had an even more specific reason for excluding Guittone from their ranks.[53] In the context of the social conflicts discussed above, Guittone's familiarity with the ex-governor of Bologna and founder of the Memoriali, Loderingo degli Andalò, and his involvement with the Knights of the Glorious Virgin Mary, could only have contributed to the hostility of the notaries toward the vernacular production of the friar-poet.[54] For Guittone was more than simply a member of the Jovial Friars, he was also their primary epistolographer and ideologue. And he placed his conversion to the tenets of the order at the center of the diegetic narrative of his lyrics—reproduced visually and codicologically in the manuscript tradition in which love poetry and religious and moral verse are divided into two sections under the rubrics "Guittone D'Arezzo" and "Frate Guittone."[55] In his new institutional position, moreover, Fra Guittone frequently targeted the rhetoric and ideology of secular poetry, especially its disregard for the proper hierarchy of sacred and profane. In order better to understand Guittone's polemic and its social implications, and how these would have been received by Nicola *Johanini Manelli* and his peers, the following section will examine an implicit debate between Guittone and Guinizzelli about love poetry and heterodoxy, *laude* and *fraude*.

Guittone, Guinizzelli, and the Question of *laude* and *fraude*

The canonical place for beginning a discussion about the relationship of Guinizzelli to Guittone is the sonnet the former addressed to the latter, "O caro padre meo, de vostra laude":

> [O] caro padre meo, de vostra laude
> non bisogna ch'alcun omo se 'mbarchi,
> ché 'n vostra mente intrar vizio non aude,
> che for de sé vostro saver non l'archi.
>   A ciascun rëo sì la porta claude,
> che, sembr', ha più via che Venezi' ha Marchi;
> entr'a' Gaudenti ben vostr'alma gaude,
> ch'al me' parer li gaudii han sovralarchi.
>   Prendete la canzon, la qual io porgo
> al saver vostro, che l'aguinchi e cimi,
> ch'a voi ciò solo com'a mastr'accorgo,
>   ch'ell'è congiunta certo a debel' vimi:
> però mirate di lei ciascun borgo
> per vostra correzion lo vizio limi.

[O my dear father, it is not necessary that any man undertake to praise you, since in your mind vice does not dare to enter without your wisdom keeping it at bay with arrows. It closes the gates to all evils, which seem to outnumber the Marks in Venice. Your spirit well enjoys itself among the Jovial Friars, who, to my mind, have overflowing joys. Take this *canzone,* which I offer to your wisdom, to cut and trim it, for I entrust it to you as the sole master, for it is certainly joined by weak bonds. Therefore examine all of its forts, excise the vice through your correction.][56]

Traditionally, "O caro padre meo" has been read as a face-value tribute from the young Bolognese poet to the more established Aretine.[57] In this view, a still pre-stilnovist Guinizzelli wrote the sonnet to accompany one of his earlier *canzoni,* most likely "Lo fin pregi' avanzato," when he sent it to be corrected by his poetic father figure.[58] The chronological position of "O caro padre meo" within Guinizzelli's corpus is especially significant because of the role the poem plays in *Purgatorio* 26, in which Dante encounters Guinizzelli's character. As has long been recognized, the canto contains various allusions to both "O caro padre meo" and "Omo ch'è saggio." According to the influential study by E. H. Wilkins, Guinizzelli is thus both "praised and corrected" in the canto—praised for inaugurating a new philosophical style of poetry (which he defends in "Omo ch'è saggio") and corrected for his youthful adherence to Guittone, exemplified in "O caro padre meo."[59]

Recent scholarship on "O caro padre meo" has begun to question our received notions about the sonnet. Several critics have argued that the poem that most likely accompanied "O caro padre meo" was the epochal stilnovist *canzone* "Al cor gentil rempaira sempre amore" rather than the earlier composition "Lo fin pregi' avanzato."[60] Others have raised doubts about the sincerity of Guinizzelli's praise, suggesting that the poem might be polemical or at least ironic.[61] In my reading of the sonnet, Guinizzelli is poking fun at both the institution of the Jovial Friars and the poetic style of Guittone. For example, the incipit of "O caro padre meo" mimics the language Fra Guittone uses in addressing his new devotional public, from the sonnets "O carissimi miei, qual è cagione" and "O frati miei, voi che disiderate" to the *canzoni* "O cari frati miei, con malamente" and, perhaps most importantly, "Padre dei padri miei e mio messere," addressed to none other than Fra Loderingo degli Andalò. More obviously critical are lines 7–8, "entr'a' Gaudenti ben vostr'alma gaude, / ch'al me' parer li gaudii han sovralarchi," which target the privileges of the Jovial Friar order and their various *gaudii,* as well as the word play on forms of *gaudere* in Guittone's poetry. In his postconversion compositions, Fra Guittone replaces the *adnominatio* of *gioia*—the *senhal* of his love poetry—with repetition of lexical forms of sacred *gaudio.*[62] Indeed, if we count the occurrences of forms of *gaudio* in "Vegna—vegna—chi vole giocundare," ("gaudio" [23], "gaudo" [23], "gaudendo" [24], "gaudio" [27], gauda[27], "gaudio" [30]), they are, as Guinizzelli says, truly "sovralarchi" (8), overabundant. In a similar fashion, in describing Guittone's "saver" (4) in successfully fending off all evil ("A ciascun rëo sì la porta claude" [5]), Guinizzelli is also playing on the friar-poet's frequent use of the term *reo,* both as a noun and an adjective. Indeed, in Guittone's tirade against Love in "O tu, de nome Amor, guerra de fatto," we find the term used repeatedly: "condizion rea" (15); "via reo se' più ch'omo" (46); "reo mal" (68); "ch'omo laudi el reo" (82); "principio n'è reo" (35); "'l mezzo è reo" (39); and, finally, "la fine è pur rea: pur che, destrutto / principio e mezzo, reo te solo coso" (the end is still evil, so that even without considering the beginning and the middle, I declare you [love/war] pure evil)[44–45]. By linking Guittone's lofty moralizing with his overbearing style, Guinizzelli is hinting in these two instances that the friar-poet's division of experience into religious joys and worldly evils, *gaudii* and *rei,* might be overly facile.

Poetics and ethics are in fact inseparable in any discussion of "O caro padre meo" because it was Guittone himself who, in his literary conversion, first called attention to the problem of good and bad poetry. In palinodic poems such as "Ora parrà s'eo saverò cantare," "Ahi, quant'ho che vergogni e che doglia aggio," and "O tu, de nome Amor, guerra de fatto," Guittone condemns secular poetry, courtly love, and the praise he wasted on his lady and pledges henceforth to dedicate his writing to Christ and the Virgin in the form of religious *laudi*.[63] For the purposes of our discussion about the reception of the early Italian lyric in the Memoriali, it is crucial to note that Guinizzelli emerges (as we will soon see) as one of the fiercest critics of Guittone's parsing of the uses and abuses of poetry. Already in "O caro padre meo," Guinizzelli takes aim at Guittone's fusion of bourgeois morality and poetics, although the level of irony in the sonnet becomes evident only when compared to other texts. In the quatrains, the poet-friar is portrayed as a soldier valiantly defending the castle of his mind and soul, "mente" and "alma" (7). He uses bows and arrows against the incessant assault of vice and slams the door in the face of evil. Just as he is safely protected from the outside world within his confraternity of the Jovial Friars, so is his consciousness sealed off against evil thoughts and desires ("'n vostra mente intrar vizio non aude"[3]). The spatial metaphors in these verses create sharp contrasts between interior and exterior, between sin and vice on the outside ("for de sé"[4]) and the impenetrability of Guittone's moral fortress (*'n vostra mente intrar vizio non aude*" echoed a few lines later with "*entr' a' Gaudenti*"[7]).

As a devoted Christian soldier and member of the Knights of the Glorious Virgin Mary—who were entrusted with rooting out possible threats to the church—Fra Guittone is then invited in the tercets of "O caro padre meo" to turn his attention to Guinizzelli's *canzone.* Just as in the first part of the sonnet Guittone successfully defends the fortress of his mind from vice, in the second section he is asked to purge the metaphorical towns or forts of the *canzone* space: "però mirate di lei ciascun borgo / per vostra correzion lo vizio limi" (13–14). Guinizzelli is thus provocatively asking Guittone to ensure that his *canzone* is orthodox, offering it up for "correzion." Addressing the friar-poet as both moral and poetic "mastr[o] (11),[64] he entreats him literally to censor his *canzone*—to cut away ("l'aguinchi e cimi" [10]) the corrupt or even sinful portions. Nor was Guinizzelli alone in addressing Guittone as a sort of amateur inquisitor. Influenced no doubt by the converted poet's attacks on heresy in poems such as "Ahi, como è ben disorrato nescente," "Sì come no a corpo è malattia," and "O tu, om de Bologna, sguarda e sente," the Cathar Matteo Paterino sought doctrinal advice from Fra Guittone in the *canzone,* "Fonte di sapïenza nominato."[65]

But in the case of Guinizzelli, what are the possible heterodox elements in need of correction, since they are clearly not the principles of Catharism? Of his extant *canzoni,* only "Al cor gentil" provides the sort of doctrinal analysis that Guittone would object to. In fact, in the last stanza of the poem, Guinizzelli envisions God accusing him of the heresy of idolatrous, profane love:

> Donna, Deo mi dirà: "Che presomisti?"
> siando l'alma mia a lui davanti.
> "Lo ciel passasti e 'nfin a Me venisti
> e desti in vano amor Me per semblanti:
> ch'a Me conven le laude
> e a la reina del regname degno,
> per cui cessa onne fraude".
> Dir Li porò: "Tenne d'angel sembianza
> che fosse del Tuo regno
> non me fu fallo, s'in lei posi amanza." [66]
>
> (51–60)

[Lady, God will say, when my soul is before him, "How dared you? You went past the heavens and came unto Me, and you gave profane love my semblance. Praise is appropriate to Me and to the queen of the worthy realm, through whom all fraud ceases." I will tell him: "She had the likeness of an angel from your realm, it was not my fault if I placed my love in her."]

After the impersonal scientific exposition on love in previous strophes, in this concluding stanza Guinizzelli suddenly addresses his lady directly and describes for her an imagined dialogue with God after his death. Not surprisingly, given what He has heard in "Al cor gentil," God is not at all happy with the poet in this exchange. He rebukes the poet for his metaphorical impropriety, for comparing his *donna* to the heavens and even to God Himself (" 'Lo ciel passasti e 'nfin a Me venisti / e desti in vano amore Me per semblanti' " [53–54]), and for subsequently neglecting the praise properly due to Him and the Virgin ("ch'a Me conven le laude / e a la reina del regname degno" [55–56]). Yet Guinizzelli does not back down. He daringly defends his conflation of sacred and profane love by turning the accusation of tropic language back onto God Himself, who was, after all, the first to blur the distinction between the earthly and the divine when he gave his lady an angelic "sembianza" (58).[67]

In this brief exchange about the proper uses of poetry and poetic language, the perspective of the all-seeing Father recalls quite strikingly that of the poetic father of "O caro padre meo."[68] As mentioned above, Guittone's palinodic poetry turns on the rejection of courtly love and secular poetry in favor of religious *laudi,* especially for the Glorious Virgin of his order, "la reina del regname degno" (56). The word play in this circumlocution for the Virgin seems to echo, in fact, one of Guittone's spiritual *laudi,* discussed above, "Vegna—vegna—chi vole giocundare," especially the lines, "regna—regna—in me sì, che regnare / mi faccia com' giusto regna" (reign, reign in me so that you make me reign like a just man reigns) [31–32]. The rhyme words *degno–regno* (56, 59) also recall *degna–regna* (26, 32) of the laud—where -*egna* functions as the recurring *x* rhyme in the reprise of the *ballata.* The question in "Al cor gentil" of true and false praise, moreover, turns on two other rhyme words, *laude* and *fraude,* which almost certainly link the *canzone* to "O caro padre meo, de vostra laude."[69] Indeed, in the thirteenth-century manuscripts of Italian poetry, the sole examples of the rhyme -*aude* are from "Al cor gentil," "O caro padre meo," and "Figlio mio dilettoso, in faccia laude"— Guittone's obscure response to "O caro padre meo."[70]

Although God's reprimands in "Al cor gentil" are probably meant to evoke the form and content of Guittone's postconversion poetry in general terms, one potential intertext does stand out. In "O tu, de nome Amor, guerra de fatto" (O you, with the name of Love, in reality, war) Guittone embarks on a moral battle, recalling the military imagery of "O caro padre meo," against the heresy, "resia" (10), of love and love poets, "guerrer ditti amanti" (warriors called lovers) [13].[71] Above all, the lovers and poets in question are accused of idolatry. They mistake erotic love for God and worship the lady instead of Him: "ch'el mesconosce Dio e crede e chiama / sol dio la donna ch'ama" (God goes unrecognized by him and instead he believes and calls God only the lady he loves) [50–51]. Even worse, they perpetuate and even encourage this dangerous heresy by singing Love's praises in erotic lauds:

> Peggio che guerra, Amor, omo te lauda,
> tal perché fort' hailo 'ngegnato tanto
> ch'ello te crede dio potente e santo
> e tal però ch'altrui ingegna e frauda.
>
> (16–19)

[Love, worst than war, men praise you. One because you have so tricked him that he believes that you are a powerful and sacred god and another so that he can trick and deceive others.]

Error breeds error, and Guittone sees his role as breaking down this false ideology of courtly love, exposing it and the poetry it produces as a "frauda."[72]

The rhyme words *lauda* and *frauda* (16, 19) in the passage above and the question of the idolatrous love of the lady bring us back to "O caro padre meo" and the last stanza of "Al cor gentil." We can now see how Guinizzelli daringly identifies himself with the indefinite "tal" (17, 19), the anonymous target of "O tu, de nome Amor, guerra de fatto," accepting and even elaborating upon Guittone's accusations of misplaced *lauda* and heretical *frauda*. In the manner of the heretical love poets of "O tu, de nome Amor," he has mistaken erotic love, "vano amor" (54), for God Himself and worshiped at the altar of his lady, confusing a sign, a "sembianza" (58), with the divinity it signifies. According to this critique, the poet of "Al cor gentil" has truly "misrecognized" God and instead "crede e chiama / sol dio la donna ch'ama" (50). In this way, Guinizzelli incorporates Guittone's attack on the idolatry of love and love poetry into his own idolatrous poem, enacting a virtual *tenzone* between the two poets set in the afterlife.

Guinizzelli had good reason, moreover, for projecting himself as Guittone's ideological opponent regarding the question of poetic praise. As various readers have pointed out, Guittone's "S'eo tale fosse ch'io potesse stare" is a thinly veiled criticism of Guinizzelli's stilnovist sonnets "Io voglio del ver la mia donna laudare" and "Vedut'ho la lucente stella diana."[73] In particular,

Guittone objects to how Guinizzelli compares his lady to objects in nature, such as a flower, a precious stone, or a star:

> che, quando vuol la sua donna laudare,
> le dice ched è bella come fiore,
> e ch'è di gem[m]a over di stella pare,
> e che 'n viso di grana ave colore.
>
> (5–8)

[who, when he wants to praise his lady, says that she is beautiful like a flower, and that she seems like a gem or a star, and in her face is the color of carmine.]

In Guittone's view, by employing similes drawn from the natural world, Guinizzelli has violated a natural hierarchy, since the lady is higher in the scale of creation than what she is being compared to and only slightly lower than man himself, "d'alquanto l'om mag[g]ior si cosa" (man is called somewhat greater) [14].

It now seems likely, as Vincent Moleta first suggested,[74] that Guinizzelli's discussion of nature and poetic praise in "Al cor gentil" functions in part as a response to the implicit critique of "S'eo tale fosse." Not only does an unreformed Guinizzelli compare his lady once again to a star, "donna a giusa di stella lo 'nnamora" (the lady, in the manner of a star, makes him fall in love) [20], but he raises the stakes by associating her effects with the virtues of the heavens and even the beatific vision of God. In other words, for the Guittone of "S'eo tale fosse" he aims too low in his comparisons, while for the Guittone of "O tu, de nome Amor" he reaches too high. More importantly, the justification for his elaborate praise of the lady is based on a complicated vision of nature that weds a Neoplatonic conception of participation to an Aristotelian ontology of potency and act. As a result, in the universe of "Al cor gentil," God and angel, lover and beloved, star and virtuous stone are all brought together by the actualizing force of Love. As Guinizzelli explains to God in the last stanza, the created universe is fundamentally structured around the principles of similitude and simile and is thus already in a sense "poetic." When Guinizzelli announces at the beginning of the *canzone*, "né fe' amor anti che gentil core / né gentil core anti ch'amore, natura" (nature did not make love before the noble heart nor the noble heart before love)

[3—4], the inversion and chiasmus in these lines serve as a sort of poetic and scientific manifesto for a vision of existence, based on the teachings of natural philosophy, that is deeply relational. Despite using similar language, Guittone had instead insisted in "S'eo tale fosse" on the absolute status of the lady: "Ché Natura [né] far pote né osa, / fat[t]ura alcuna né mag[g]ior né pare" (that Nature neither can nor dares make any creature equal or greater) [12—13]. As part of an unchanging natural hierarchy, her allotted place remains both unapproachable and incomparable.

The love poet of "S'eo tale fosse" shares an insistence on natural hierarchy with the converted friar of "O tu, de nome Amor." For both Guittone and Fra Guittone, there exists a natural vertical ordering to the universe, expressed in the inviolable divisions between heaven and earth, sacred and profane, the Virgin and the beloved, man and woman, animate and inanimate. In the historical period in question, it is not difficult to imagine how such unassailable categories might serve to legitimize by analogy other "natural" hierarchies, such as those between ruler and ruled or even noble and notary. In this context, the mirroring semblances of Guinizzelli's vision of nature take on renewed significance and cannot but challenge the easy moralizing of the friar-knight represented in "O caro padre meo" or his stand-in, the God of "Al cor gentil." For Guinizzelli does not only compare the lover to a stone and an angel and the beloved to a star and God; he also equates a noble by birth with mud: "dis' omo alter: 'Gentil per sclatta torno' / lui semblo al fango, al sol gentil valore"(the haughty man says: "I am noble through my lineage." I compare him to mud, noble worth to the sun) [33—34]. When we consider the social mobility promised by the new learning of the universities, it is not surprising that Guinizzelli's defense in "Al cor gentil" of philosophical love poetry and the transcendent *donna-angelo* is tied to a critique of those who claim an inherited right to rule by lineage, "per sclatta." As recognized in the indignation of the proud noble and the offended God of "Al cor gentil," challenges to cultural hierarchy threaten social ones as well. For in a cosmology of simile and metaphor, an angelic lady may be ontologically superior to a man, a self-conscious love poem less fraudulent than a hypocritical *laude,* and a university-educated judge or notary more noble than an aristocrat.[75]

Having shed light on the sociopolitical framework underlying the literary debate between Guittone and Guinizzelli, we are in a better position to judge the full import of the vernacular poems found in the Memoriali bolognesi. The cultural struggles between the Jovial Friars and the popular government must have made Guittone's vocal defense of his order and his attack on love poetry particularly noxious to the notaries of the Memoriali. In particular, while Loderingo and Catalano attacked the "fraudibus and falsitatibus" (fraud and falsity) found in the protocols of the notaries, Guittone characterized their literary activity as fraudulent. In this light, the transcriptions by the notaries can be read as an expression of autonomy against both the professional control formerly imposed upon them with the institution of the Memoriali and the cultural repression carried out by Guittone and the Jovial Friar order. Not only do they exclude Guittone and the Guittonians, but they also prefer to copy the sort of erotic and profane poetry that Guittone condemned as heretical.[76] This is especially evident in the registers of Nicola *Johanini Manelli,* whose editorial choices—"Io voglio del ver" and not "S'eo tale fosse," "Seguramente" and not "Vegna—vegna—chi vole giocundare"—suggest a polemical response to Guittone's strict hierarchy of praise.

The possibility that Nicola and other notaries followed the dispute about poetry between Guinizzelli and Guittone is supported by their interest in a similar poetic debate between Guinizzelli and Bonagiunta. Of all the poems by Guinizzelli the notaries could have chosen to copy, the popularity of "Omo ch'è saggio non corre leggero" is striking. For one, the sonnet is not easily comprehended by itself, since, as a response to Bonagiunta's "Voi ch'avete mutata la maniera," its full significance emerges only when considered as part of a larger discussion involving several different texts.[77] In "Voi ch'avete," Guinizzelli is accused of having contaminated love poetry, "li plagenti ditti de l'amore" (the pleasant sayings of love) [2], with the philosophy and philosophical jargon of the schools, namely the Aristotelian ontology of potency and act, *forma* and *essere* (3). As critics have recognized, both the concepts and language of Bonagiunta's sonnet target the innovations of "Al cor gentil." In Guinizzelli's response, he justifies his disregard for the proper hierarchies separating difficult philosophy from pleasant poetry by citing a more fundamental intellectual hierarchy. According to Guinizzelli, differing degrees of intelligence, "despari senni e intendimenti" (13), will view a question differently, and only a fool claims to be the sole repository of truth: "Foll'è chi crede sol veder lo vero" (A foolish man believes that he alone sees the truth) [5]. Within Guinizzelli's intellectual scale of being, Bonagiunta, like the "omo alter" in "Al cor gentil" (33), has assumed a position he does not merit; he regards himself too highly ("non se dev'omo tener troppo altero" [7]).

For "Omo ch'è saggio" to be held in such high regard by the Bolognese notaries, they must have, in varying degrees, understood and been concerned with the terms of the debate. It is not difficult, moreover, to determine which side they were on, since Guinizzelli's response to Bonagiunta was copied eight times in the Memoriali. Indeed, their various transcriptions of "Omo ch'è saggio" can be seen as an affirmation of the right of vernacular poetry—and the readers and writers who cultivated it—to embrace an increasingly comprehensive subject matter. Regardless of the objections of Bonagiunta and Guittone, the reach of the early Italian lyric was expanding in this period to include philosophy, cosmology, and even theology. And the boundaries between high Latin culture and popular Italian literature were continuously eroding. At least in part, the breakdown of traditional literary categories was the result of a concurrent shift in political hierarchies and the establishment of a new "natural" order based on learning and individual merit (as hinted at in "Al cor gentil" and "Omo ch'è saggio"). In the Memoriali, these new hierarchies were reproduced by the notaries through their editorial choices. A new class of university-educated professionals perceived courtly and comic, philosophical and literary, written and oral poetry as all belonging to a common cultural heritage. In their compilations, the notaries of the Memoriali demonstrate an inclusiveness that corresponds to Guinizzelli's defenses of poetic variety against the narrower vision of Guittone and Bonagiunta.

Of course, it is impossible to know for certain the extent to which these urban readers discerned the sophisticated intertexts characterizing contemporary poetic debates. Even Nicola *Johanini Manelli* may not have been completely aware of the implications of his editorial choices. Still, whatever their level of understanding of the formal and conceptual issues in dispute, the notaries demonstrate, through their transcriptions in the Memoriali, that taking sides in literary debates was an important element of their collective identity. Before the circulation of a popular *tenzone*, potential social alliances may have been latent and shared literary opinions unrecognized. But once a notary copied into his registers one kind of poem and not another—Guinizzelli instead of Bonagiunta, Dante instead of Guittone, Cino instead of Onesto— he actualized a specific ideological perspective and participated in collective self-representation. Thus the act of writing was itself meaningful, even if the texts copied were then archived, never to circulate.

The sociopolitical aspects of the *rime* from the Memoriali bolognesi also shed light on how Dante Alighieri might have experienced the literary debates of his day. Dante's engagement with the early Italian lyric will be treated in more detail in subsequent chapters. However, the nature of his relation to contemporary poetry, revealed in the context of the Memoriali, is worth touching upon, since it is often neglected in the scholarly debate. In particular, the frequent criticism of Guittone in Dante's works is traditionally explained in terms of interpersonal or even oedipal rivalry. Yet, as in the poetry of Guinizzelli or the Memoriali bolognesi, Dante's anti-*guittonismo* has a social and institutional basis, and it targets the politics of the Jovial Friar order in particular.

One of the most famous examples of Dante's anti-*guittonismo* appears in lines spoken by Guinizzelli himself in *Purgatorio* 26. This passage shows that Dante read the debate between Guinizzelli and Guittone as one between contrasting social groups, not just individuals:

> A voce più ch'al ver drizzan li volti,
> e così ferman sua oppinïone
> prima ch'arte o ragion per lor s'ascolti
>   Così fer molti antichi di Guittone,
> di grido in grido pur lui dando pregio,
> fin che l'ha vinto il ver con più persone.
>   Or se tu hai sì ampio privilegio
> che licito ti sia l'andare al chiostro
> nel quale è Cristo abate del collegio,
>   falli per me un dir di un paternostro.
>   (121–130)

[They turn their faces more to reputation than to the truth, and thus they fix their opinion before listening to art or reason. Thus of old many did with Guittone, still praising him in cry after cry, until the truth overcame him in the judgments of more people. Now if you have such ample privilege that you are permitted to go to the cloister where Christ is abbot of the college, say a Paternoster to Him for me.]

In this discussion about the fickleness of public opinion, Guinizzelli underlines how, with time, artistic truth wins out over fashion, and so the reputation of Guittone has fallen. Lines 121–126 of this passage are often cited as an example of Dante's biased and self-serving historiography, part of an authorizing strategy aimed at promoting himself as official *cantor rectitudinis.* Yet the oft-neglected verses that follow Guinizzelli's critique (127–130), in which he asks Dante to recite a Paternoster for him in heaven, add an ideological element to the attack on Guittone's poetry, framing it as a contrast between true and false "brothers." In these lines, Guinizzelli describes Dante as entering a cloister where Christ is the abbot and everyone lives under a collective rule, a "collegio." If heaven is a monastic community, the assembly of poets atop Mount Purgatory resembles, in many ways, a lay order of *laudesi.* As if they were members of a confraternity, the love poets encountered in cantos 23–26 defer patriarchal hierarchies, address fellow members as "frate," sing praises to the lady—such as "Donne ch'avete"—and cite each other's poetry as if it were common property, part of an anonymous profane *laudario.*

At the same time as Dante is transformed into a virtual friar, Fra Guittone, author of religious *laudi,* is associated, though the rhyme words *privilegio* and *collegio* (127, 129), with the hypocrites of *Inferno* 23. In this canto, Dante encounters Catalano and Loderingo themselves, who are still obsessed with the private individual privilege that characterized their order:

> "Costui par vivo a l'atto de la gola;
> e s'e' sono morti, per qual privilegio
> vanno scoperti de la grave stola?"
> Poi disser me: "O Tosco, ch'al collegio
> de l'ipocriti tristi se' venuto,
> dir chi tu se' non avere in dispregio."
>
> (88–93)

["That one seems alive, by the motion of his throat; but if they are dead, by what privilege are they exempt from the weighty stole?" Then they spoke to me: "O Tuscan who have come to the college of the sad hypocrites, do not disdain to say who you are."]

Loderingo and Catalano, who in life accused others of legal fraud, are now themselves punished in the circles of fraud as hypocrites.[78] In a similar fashion, Guittone, who had accused the love poets of literary *fraude,* now finds himself associated with the hypocrites and corrected by the truth, "il ver" (*Purg.* 26.126), of his wayward poetic "son." By alluding to the episode of Loderingo and Catalano from *Inferno* 23, Guinizzelli links Guittone's undeserved literary fame with his role in promoting the fraudulent Jovial Friar order, now re-baptized as a "collegio" of wretched hypocrites. That the ethical context of Guinizzelli's critique is conveyed through an intertextual reference suggests that Dante also read "O caro padre meo" as a subtle, allusive jibe at Guittone's moralizing poetry rather than a tribute to it. The allusions to "O caro padre meo" in *Purgatorio* 26 would thus constitute a rearticulation in the afterlife of Guinizzelli's critique of Guittone's poetry and not, as previously thought, a repudiation of his early *guittonismo*.

Scholars have certainly been correct in calling into question the existence of well-defined schools of poetry at this time. The anachronistic use of *dolce stilnovo* from *Purgatorio* 24.57 to indicate Dante and his circle also needs to be applied with caution since it is difficult to determine to whom exactly Bonagiunta is referring in this specific passage. Yet Dante speaks consistently in the plural when he considers the state of poetry in these cantos and seems to be aware of the collective and even institutional function of vernacular poetry at this time. He refers to "vostre penne" [58] and "nostre" [60] in *Purgatorio* 24, and in *Purgatorio* 26 the truth about Guittone is finally arrived at by "più persone" (126). His discussion of Guittone, moreover, almost always targets the poet's devotional public as well as the poet himself. In *De vulgari eloquentia* he rails against the "ignorantie sectatores" (2.6.8), the ignorant followers of the Aretine poet, and in *Purgatorio* 26 he disparages the "molti antichi" (124) who formerly sang his praises. In fact, as we have seen, the famous debates and *tenzoni* involved more than just the authors and their interpersonal rivalry. Even if a community of readers and writers did not exist before a dispute, one was soon constructed around it. From this perspective, instead of referring to a set canon, we should perhaps speak of a potential "community" of stilnovists, which would include not only Guinizzelli, Cavalcanti, Dante, and Cino, but also their followers, their *sectatores,* such as Nicola *Johanini Manelli,* and others among Dante's first editors.

Ugolino delle Quercie, the *scuola ciniana,* and the Final Poems of the Memoriali bolognesi

The return of the Memoriali registers in 1290 to a larger format and to parchment instead of paper marks the end of a period of concerted experimentation in vernacular transcription that was begun during the first decades of the *popolo* government. Instead of thick paper registers resembling private protocols, the Memoriali bolognesi after 1290 consist of large, carefully ordered parchment registers, divided into quires with all the external and internal characteristics of official public record books. At the same time, vernacular fragments—normally the incipit to a poem—are much less frequent and tend to take up only a line or two at the bottom of the page. Indeed, from 1294–1301, in Memoriali 86–101, no *rime* are recorded. The common Paternosters and Ave Marias once lining the lower margins of registers also disappear in this period. Most likely some sort of ordinance, whether official or unofficial, was behind the elimination of poetry from the Memoriali in these years.

The Latin and Italian *marginalia* return in the second phase of the *rime,* 1301–1325 (Mem. 102–153), but less frequently and less cohesively. The occasional nature of the vernacular transcriptions in these years makes it difficult to discuss larger movements or collaborations. Most appearances of vernacular poetry can at best be traced back to the singular personality and background of an individual notary. Nevertheless, several characteristics do stand out, and, in concluding this chapter, I will briefly touch upon the later transcriptions in the Memoriali because they contrast sharply with, and thus help further define, the poetic, scribal, and political discourses we have seen revealed in the *rime* of the 1280s.

A new, hybrid mode of transcribing vernacular verse is evident in several of the later fourteenth-century registers, incorporating elements common to both contemporary documents and books. The poems transcribed in the registers of Gregorio *condam Aldrevandini Prevedelli,* Ugolino delle Quercie, and Antonio *Johannis Speciallis*—carefully set off visually and spatially from the rest of the Latin contracts—are in many ways at odds with the experimental fusion of literary anthologizing and notarial graphic practices found in the earlier registers of Biagio *Auliverii,* Nicola *Phylippi,* and Nicola *Johanini Manelli.* Most of the characteristics of this new style of transcribing poetry are anticipated in Enrichetto delle Quercie's historical transcription of Dante's "No me poriano zamai far emenda" (Mem. 69, 1287), discussed briefly at the beginning of this chapter (fig. 1). Enrichetto copied the sonnet on the first page of his register, before the contracts, and he clearly separated it from them. The transcription itself is written in an elegant, spacious, and upright *cancelleresca,* with restrained flourishes finishing the ascending and descending stems. The verses are written two per line, with a space and slash mark additionally separating each pair. Each *pes* and *volta* is indicated with a curved paragraph symbol on right and left margins, and the *voltae* are marked with a *V*.[79]

The second wave of *rime* in the Memoriali begins in the tradition of Enrichetto delle Quercie. The notary who copied the sonnet "Chusì di gl'ocli soi foss'ella mancha" (Mem. 102, 1301) placed it under the notarial inscription on the first page of his register (fig. 6), clearly separated from Latin contracts in the same manner as Enrichetto. The transcription of "Chusì di gl'ocli soi," moreover, shares all the visual characteristics and divisions of "No me poriano": two verses per line, pauses indicated by spaces and slashes, *voltae* symbols, and capital letters marking metrical divisions. In addition, the careful handwriting used in the sonnet demonstrates a slight chiaroscuro, thus further distinguishing it from the rounded cursive script evident in the Latin contracts. Indeed, "Chusì di gl'ocli soi" appears to be written by a different hand from that of the contracts, perhaps at a later date by one of the notaries in charge of the Memoriali archive. Nothing could be further from the transcriptions of the early Memoriali bolognesi, in which notaries combined their literary interests with their legal duties, copying Italian poems in the same way and at the same time as Latin contracts.

These new developments in vernacular transcription were codified and enforced by the notary par excellence of the fourteenth-century Memoriali bolognesi, Ugolino delle Quercie. Ugolino was the son of the same Enrichetto delle Quercie and the nephew of another notary of the Memoriali, Guido delle Quercie. Already matriculated in the Society of Notaries in 1309, Ugolino worked as a notary from 1312 until 1343, active almost every year and transcribing forty registers in the course of his career.[80] In the three registers containing *rime*—Memoriale 126 (1313), Memoriale 132 (1316), and Memoriale 151 (1324)—Ugolino carefully separated his one transcription per register from the rest of the Latin contracts (fig. 7). He copied the poem in an isolated space below the notarial subscription in an orderly *cancelleresca,* clearly marking metrical divisions and separating words and verses. In addition to composing his own registers, Ugolino, as a career notary, worked side by side with the other notary-scribes and oversaw their work, as evidenced by the appearance of a small "ugolinus" in the margins of his colleagues' registers. This institutional supervisory activity led Giovanni Livi to suggest that Ugolino was responsible for the disappearance of vernacular *rime* from the Memoriali beginning in 1325.[81]

Ugolino's influence is most clearly demonstrated in the differences between the two registers of Antonio *Johannis Speciallis,* Memoriale 123 (1311) and Memoriale 153 (1325), the latter being the last register to contain vernacular poetry. Unlike Enrichetto and Ugolino, Antonio at first incorporated his poetic transcriptions into the main body of his first register (Mem. 123), "masking" them as Latin contracts (fig. 8). They are written as prose in a fluid documentary hand and identified by the left-hand marginal notation "cantio," recalling the experiments in poetic transcription of earlier notaries working in the 1280s. In Memoriale 153, on the other hand, he copied a single composition, the *ballata* "Amor la cui vertù per gratia sento" by Girardo da Castelfiorentino (fig. 9). Placed under the notarial subscription, the poetic text was purposely separated from the Latin contracts, with verses and words carefully divided. The handwriting is calligraphic, and the elongated capital letters *A* and *L* and the round *s* of "sento" further set off the literary transcription from the rest of the register. Antonio not only transcribed "Amor la cui vertù" according to the *modus scribendi* of Ugolino delle Quercie; this was a poem that Ugolino had already copied in his own register in 1313 (Mem. 126, fig. 7). The very last vernacular entry into the Memoriali bolognesi thus bears the mark of Ugolino, albeit indirectly.

The same notaries who took up new methods of transcribing poems in the fourteenth-century registers also demonstrate a different approach to their selections of poems. Above all, by copying only one poem per register, they avoided the contamination of high with low styles found in the earlier registers. In fact, these notaries neglect almost entirely the comic and popular aspects of contemporary poetry and instead prefer the compositions of a small circle of late stilnovist poets, in particular Cino da Pistoia, Girardo da Castelfiorentino, and Guido Novello da Polenta. Cino's "Amor la doglia mia non ha conforto" was transcribed in 1311 (Mem. 123) by Antonio *Johannis Speciallis,* who, as we have seen, also copied, along with Ugolino, Girardo da Castelfiorentino's "Amor la cui vertù per gratia sento." Two ballads by Guido Novello—Dante's host and patron during the composition of *Paradiso* and the nephew of Francesca da Rimini—were also transcribed in these years: "Sendo da voi, madonna mia, lontana" in 1310 (Mem. 120) and "Novella zoia 'l core" in 1315 (Mem. 130). Scholars have pointed out the stylistic and thematic influences of Cino's poetry on Guido Novello and Girardo da Castelfiorentino; indeed, the similar language and shared phrasing in the poetry of

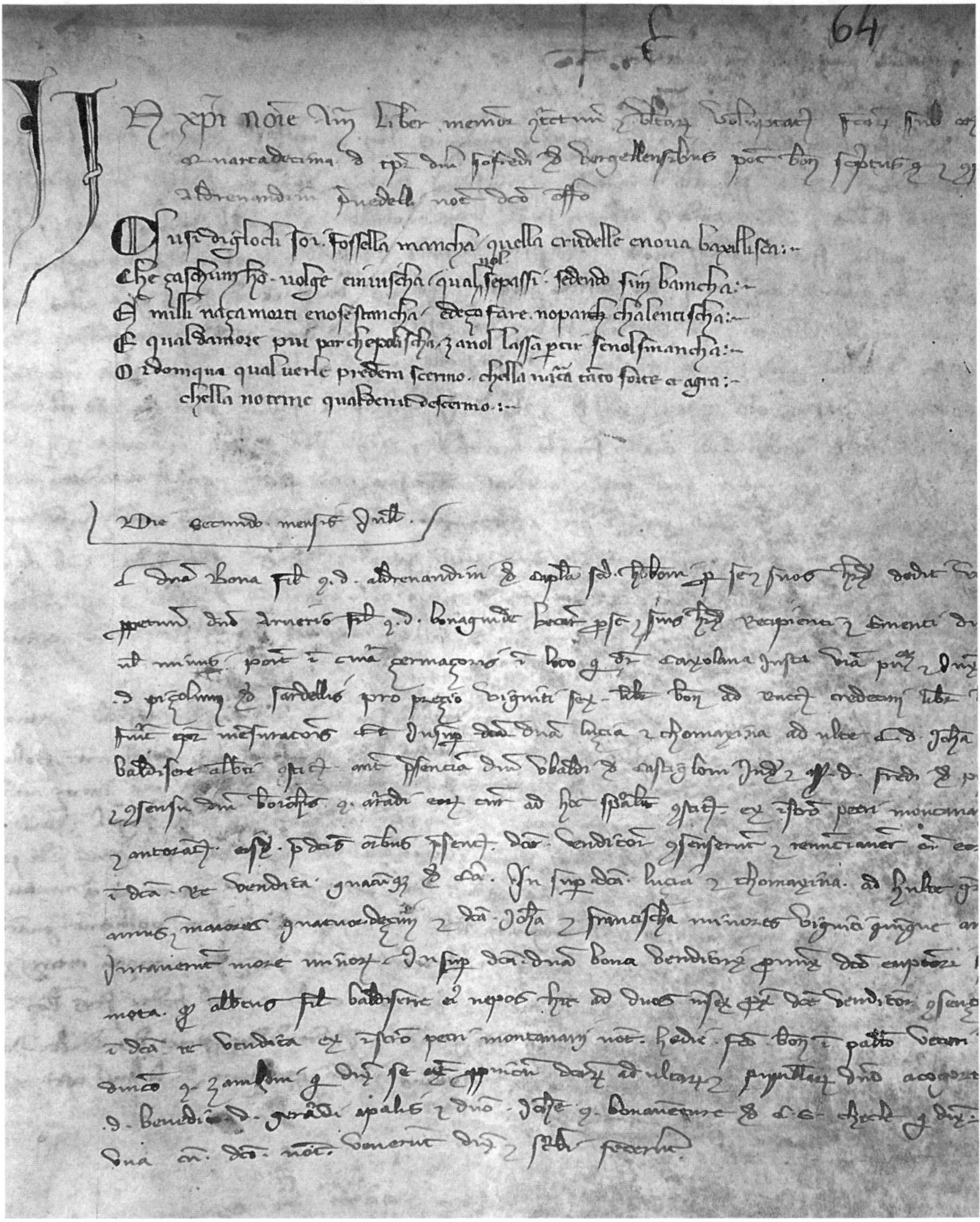

Fig. 6. Transcription of "Chusì di gl'ocli soi foss'ella mancha" below notarial inscription, separated from and in different hand than Latin contract. Bologna, Archivio di Stato, Memoriale 102, fol. 64r. Reproduced by permission of the Ministero per i Beni e le Attività Culturali, Archivio di Stato di Bologna.

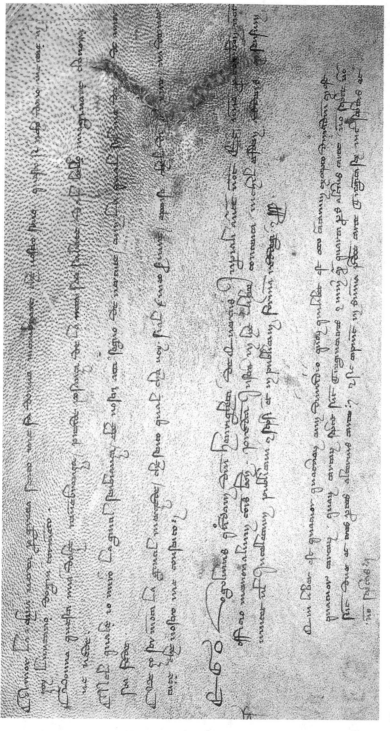

Fig. 7. Transcription of Girardo da Castelfiorentino's "Amor la cui vertù per gratia sento," separated from contracts and copied above notarial subscription by Ugolino delle Quercie. Bologna, Archivio di Stato, Memoriale 126, fol. 528r. Reproduced by permission of the Ministero per i Beni e le Attività Culturali, Archivio di Stato di Bologna.

Fig. 8. Cino da Pistoia's "Amor, la doglia mia non ha conforto" (identified as a "cantio" in left margin) and the unattributed "Se me departo non è di mia vogla," transcribed as and among contracts by Antonio *Johannis Speciallis*. Bologna, Archivio di Stato, Memoriale 123, fol. 381r. Reproduced by permission of the Ministero per i Beni e le Attività Culturali, Archivio di Stato di Bologna.

this *scuola ciniana* can even lead to uncertain attributions. "Amor la doglia mia non ha conforto," for example, is ascribed to Guido Novello in the fourteenth-century Escorial *canzoniere* and can be included only cautiously in Cino's corpus.[82] In addition to their similar style and content, the poems of Cino and Girardo may have been copied into the Memoriali for personal and professional reasons as well; as we will see below, the future judges Cino and Girardo also played an important role in the legal community in Bologna at this time.

From a social and political perspective, the notaries who identified with Cino, Girardo, and other representatives of a *tardo stilnovismo* had little in common with those who had first transcribed the fragments of Guinizzelli and Dante in the 1280s. Ugolino himself was not an ordinary, rank-and-file member of the notarial guild. His famous father, Enrichetto, was proconsul of the Society of Notaries, the highest position in the guild, and an active and respected member of the *popolo* government.[83] Ugolino also served on various government councils, and his tenure with the Office of the Memoriali coincided with the virtual *signoria* government of the merchant-banker Romeo Pepoli and the official *signoria* of Cardinal del Poggetto.[84] In fact, in his supervisory position with the Office of the Memoriali, Ugolino participated in a process typical of emergent *signorie* in which individuals were elected to temporary positions that increasingly were rendered permanent. In a related development, many of the Memoriali notaries of this period were continuously reelected, and the office was gradually rendered inaccessible to the recent matriculates, whose predecessors had filled the pages of the earlier Memoriali.

The closing off of the notariate, however, began even earlier with the required fee for the entrance exam into the guild. If an aspiring notary was not a family member of an already matriculated notary, he was required to pay a fee in order to take the notarial entrance exam. This fee grew from ten to fifteen lire in 1302, to twenty-five lire in 1309, and even to an extraordinary fifty lire in 1316.[85] The augmentation for non–family members of the already steep cost of the entrance exam precluded social movement within the notariate and created a caste of state functionaries. The notaries in charge of the Memoriali during this period were often family members and reappointed notaries from earlier years. These well-instituted, governing notaries differ greatly from their predecessors in the first years of the *popolo* government, who in large part were drawn from the artisanal classes.[86] Not surprisingly, as representatives of a new urban elite, they showed little interest in the comic poems and profane dances found in the earlier Memoriali, with their associations with popular vernacular culture. In their style of transcription as well, influenced as much by books as by documents, they attempted to set apart—both literally and figuratively—their own Italian literary cultivation from the everyday practices of rank-and-file notaries.

At the same time, developments within the Memoriali bolognesi— regarding which poems were selected and how they were copied—were more than simply a reflection of changing historical conditions. In fact, the changes in the *rime* examined so far represent only one facet of a heterogeneous corpus of vernacular poetry found in the fourteenth-century registers. As late as 1320, for example, Santo *Ugolini Santi* transcribed in his register (Mem. 140) both Guinizzelli's "Omo ch'è saggio non corre leggero" and the metrically irregular "Novella danssa," compiling a mini-anthology that recalls the registers of Nicola *Johanini Manelli*. Poetic transcriptions also continued to be written out as prose, incorporated into the body of the registers with the same *mise-en-page* of the contracts, as in the first register of Antonio *Johannis Speciallis*. Thus, innovations found in the fourteenth-century registers were neither automatic nor socially determined in a mechanistic fashion, but were instead actively brought about by a select group of notaries overseen by one of their most privileged members. Promoting a hybrid transcription method and illustrious vernacular literature, Ugolino and his colleagues re-established the lines of demarcation between literary and documentary writings and courtly and comic styles. Even in their transcriptions in the Memoriali, a new class of professional elites were distinguishing themselves from the *popolani* of earlier registers and rejecting their "common" interest in Italian poetry.

The repeat occurrences of a small group of later stilnovist poets in the fourteenth-century Memoriali may have specific political implications in addition to the social ones just discussed. In fact, the registers of the fourteenth century provide evidence of a discrete community of Tuscan judges (especially Cino, Girardo, and Francesco da Barberino) whose collective identity was solidified by reading Dante and writing vernacular poetry. Once these law students and professors are recognized as a poetic community, it also becomes easier to identify their common juridical practices and professional appointments. Too often, the intersection of legal and literary activity in notaries and judges of this period is evoked merely to explain the rhetorical background of their poetry. Yet the relations between the legal and literary worlds are much more subtle and symbiotic than can be expressed in a simple formula of cause and effect. If studying the legal training of notaries and judges can help us better to understand their poetry, perhaps examining the importance of their poetic activity can in turn shed light on their legal responsibilities. What effect, if any, might a specific vision of Italian poetry have had on the subsequent legal approaches of these former law students in Bologna?

Evidence of the popularity of a *scuola ciniana* in the Memoriali suggests that Bologna played an important role in fostering a legal-literary community centered around the Tuscan poet and judge. Cino was educated in law in Bologna before 1302 and, after a period of exile and political disillusionment, returned there and received his doctorate in 1314.[87] Girardo da Castelfiorentino also studied law in Bologna at least from 1300 to 1305,[88] and he and Cino appear together as students of law in a document dated 1302.[89] Scholars have pointed out that the elder Cino—who already knew and exchanged poems with Girardo's father, Terino da Castelfiorentino—likely functioned as a *tutor-repetitor* for Girardo.[90] After serving as a judge in various Tuscan cities, Girardo also returned to Bologna in 1312 as judge of the Water Commission (Ufficio delle Acque). These are the same years that the poetry of Cino and his circle appear in the Memoriali, making it seem likely that the Bolognese notaries responsible for these transcriptions had direct personal and professional contact with the Tuscan judges they anthologized.[91]

Several poet-judges anthologized in the fourteenth-century Memoriali also went on to play an important role in the burgeoning Florentine Inquisition. As an eminent legal professor and scholar, Cino da Pistoia served in 1319 on an important advisory council for the Franciscan inquisitor in Florence, Frate Pace da Castelfiorentino. In the next year, Cino stayed on as one of the judges in charge of deciding cases brought before the inquisitional court.[92] Following in his poetic and juridical master's footsteps, Girardo da Castelfiorentino also served as jurist-consulate for his countryman Frate Pace in 1320 and 1322.[93] Girardo must have been considered a particularly adept inquisitional judge, for he continued his consultation with Frate Pace's successor, Frate Michele d'Arezzo (1322–1325).[94] But Girardo's most dramatic decision occurred in 1327, while he was working for Frate Accursio Bonfantini. Along with his fellow judges, he condemned Cecco d'Ascoli—the Bolognese former professor, astrologer, and critic of Dante—to be burned at the stake. The sentence was carried out immediately; having been handed over to the secular authorities, Cecco was burned, along with his works, on September 16, 1327.[95]

One of the most surprising and, especially in light of the present discussion, provocative elements of Cecco's unfortunate end is the role that Dante and Bologna played in the story. We have already seen the popularity of Judge Girardo's poetry among an elite circle in Bologna, where he apprenticed under Dante's friend and interlocutor, Cino da Pistoia. Of course, Cecco was a former professor of medicine at the university in Bologna as well as a harsh critic of Dante in his vernacular treatise, *L'Acerba.* Another member of the panel of judges that found Cecco guilty, Francesco da Barberino, was likewise a vernacular author who had studied and practiced in Bologna.[96] His *Documenti d'Amore,* a fragment of which was copied in a memoriale in 1319 (Mem. 138), provides one of the earliest pieces of evidence of the reception, influence, and diffusion of Dante's *Inferno* in Italy.[97] But the least expected and perhaps most profound reader of Dante was the inquisitor himself, the Franciscan friar Accursio Bonfantini. According to one early account, Frate Accursio may have been the first public lecturer on Dante, preceding even Boccaccio. An example of his Dante criticism—whether disseminated through oral or written channels—can be found in a gloss on Dante's twofold punishment of the suicides in *Inferno* 13, interpolated into the Ottimo commentary in a manuscript now housed at the Biblioteca Nazionale of Florence (Conventi Soppressi I v 8, fol. 130).[98]

Many factors contributed to the outcome of Cecco's sentence. The Bolognese medical professor was officially accused of promoting astral determinism, for which he had already been suspended from his position at the university several years earlier. But on a personal level, Cecco had also upset certain influential individuals, including Charles of Calabria, the *signore* of Florence for a ten-year period (1326–1336); Dino del Garbo, a rival professor of medicine and commentator on Cavalcanti's philosophical poem "Donna me prega"; and finally, even Accursio Bonfantini himself, whose ancestors Francesco d'Accorso and Accorso da Bagnolo were accused of sodomy in the *Acerba.* Meanwhile, several eighteenth-century scholars found a different motive behind Cecco's condemnation and punishment, namely his anti-*dantismo,* "lo sprezzare le poesie di Dante e di G. Cavalcanti" (his disdain for the poetry of Dante and Guido Cavalcanti.)[99]

While these scholars may have overstated their claims, they nevertheless intuited correctly that Cecco's trial served—albeit never explicitly—as a site for the reception, interpretation, and policing of Dante's poetry. Behind the maneuvering against Cecco, the *Commedia*'s orthodoxy regarding free will and astral influence, revelation and philosophy, was the unspoken authority against the natural determinism and scientific autonomy represented by the defendant. In this view, the trial of Cecco d'Ascoli was the first appropriation of Dante as official Catholic poet, an oddly enduring reception of his poetry, considering Dante's fierce criticism of the church's interests in secular politics and wealth. Indeed, Dante's poem clearly meant something quite different for the inquisitors of Florence than it did for those earlier notaries who had proudly copied Guinizzelli's profane *laudi* or Dante's outburst against Pope Nicholas from *Inferno* 19 (Mem. 143, 1321, fig. 2). At least regarding the boundaries between the religious and secular realms, the reception of Dante through the judge Guinizzelli and the reception of Dante through the judge Cino appear ideologically opposed.

In Cecco's trial and in other inquisitional courts, the censorious editorial policies of Ugolino delle Quercie are disturbingly echoed by the same Tuscan poet-judges who studied in Bologna and whose poems Ugolino recorded in the Memoriali. For this new wave of readers and writers of Italian poetry, the university environment of Bologna seems to have served as a center for the promotion of a restrictive literary and legal hermeneutic. If Ugolino severely limits and eventually wipes out the tradition of transcribing *rime* in the official registers of the city-state, the poet-judges of his circle, with much more serious repercussions, distinguish between orthodox and heterodox scholars and religious leaders. At the root of these changing approaches to legal and literary problems was a common threat to the spirit of nonviolent, rhetorical dispute that had characterized the popular government and was embodied in literary form by the *tenzone*. The representatives of the *scuola ciniana,* in fact, move from a tradition of lively poetic debate, exemplified in the exchanges between Guittone and Guinizzelli, to a public spectacle of punishment. In this light, the execution of Cecco d'Ascoli is only a grim extension of the premature and unnatural elimination, described portentously by Livi, of the *rime* from the Memoriali bolognesi: "la bella tradizionale usanza, tutta bolognese, non passò . . . come una qualsiasi moda, non morì di morte naturale, e neanche ebbe tempo di invecchiare: ma rimase . . . ad un tratto troncata, quasi strozzata" (the lovely tradition [of the *rime*], wholly characteristic of Bologna, did not fade away . . . or die a natural death like other customs, nor did it have time to grow old, but at a certain point . . . it was cut down, essentially smothered).[100]

chapter two

"Apresso che questa canzone fue alquanto divulgata tra le genti"

Vaticano 3793 and the *donne* of
"Donne ch'avete intelletto d'amore"

Dante's inclusion of his *canzone* "Donne ch'avete intelletto d'amore" in the *Vita Nova* (10.15–25) has long been recognized as a turning point in the poet's career as well as a moment of crucial self-definition.[1] Dante would later re-emphasize the historiographical significance of "Donne ch'avete" in the *De vulgari eloquentia* and, of course, in the self-citation of *Purgatorio* 24, where Bonagiunta identifies him and the new poetics of the *dolce stilnovo* through the incipit to his *canzone*. For these and other reasons, much critical attention has been paid to the prose apparatus framing the poem in the *Vita Nova,* to the introductory prose *ragione* and to the concluding gloss of divisions.[2]

The episode of "Donne ch'avete" serves in fact as a pivotal moment within the narrative of the *Vita Nova* because it is here that Dante inaugurates his *stile della lode,* claiming that the only goal of his poetic encomium is disinterested praise itself. He thus attempts to remove his lyrics from the taint of rhetorical persuasion, distancing them from the conventional function of erotic seduction. It is also at this point that Dante establishes a biblical and pentecostal basis for his poetics. Echoing Psalm 29, he explains that his tongue moved as if by itself ("la mia lingua parlò quasi come per sé stessa mossa" [*VN* 10.13]) in composing the incipit for "Donne ch'avete." The hissing s's ("*sé stessa mossa*") in this line acoustically re-perform the sounds of Dante's inspired tongue.[3]

However, after announcing the supernatural origins of "Donne ch'avete," the divinely inspired Dante quickly falls back down to earth. In the sections of the *Vita Nova* directly following the divisions to "Donne ch'avete," Dante confronts the interpretive questions brought out by the public dissemination of his *canzone:* "Apresso che questa canzone fue alquanto divulgata tra le genti" (After this *canzone* had been somewhat disseminated among the people) [*VN* 11.1]. Despite the allegorizing tendencies and shadowy elusiveness generally associated with Dante's first prosimetrum, these lines remain a concrete and historically specific reference to the material circulation of his texts. In fact, the entire discussion surrounding "Donne ch'avete" in the *Vita Nova* is concerned with phenomena of textual interpretation and dissemination. On the one hand, the emphasis on the female audience both in the introductory *ragione* and in the first stanza of the *canzone* testifies to the expanded readership afforded by composing in the vernacular; given that Dante equates the very origins of Italian poetry with the desire to communicate with a woman unlettered in Latin (*VN* 16.6), the *donne* may stand for the new vernacular audience. In a similar spirit of cultural democratization, the gloss divisions that follow "Donne ch'avete" in chapter 10 are particularly detailed and explanatory in an effort to make the poem better understood, "meglio intesa" (*VN* 10.26).

But Dante leaves these divisions only half-finished and ends the section with an expression of interpretive paranoia about his *canzone,* fearing that he has already exposed its meaning to too many people: "certo io temo d'avere a troppi comunicato lo suo intendimento" (*VN* 11.33).[4] In particular, he worries about an uncontrolled circulation of his texts and commentaries, and his anxieties stem from the possibility that "molti le potessero udire" (many might be able to hear them) [*VN* 11.33]. The verb *udire,* recalled twice at the beginning of the next section, evokes the origins in oral culture of the emergent vernacular literature and the mixed oral and written aspects of its transmission. Even the verb *divulgare* itself—a hapax in Dante's corpus— evokes the ambiguous origins of the *volgare* in the crowd, or *vulgus.*

Yet the critical establishment has largely passed over the significance of Dante's comments about the circulation of "Donne ch'avete." Little has been written about the singular fact that Dante incorporates the history of the reception of his text, its *fortuna,* into the formal narrative of the *Vita Nova.* This omission is even more surprising knowing as we now do (thanks largely to Domenico De Robertis's examinations into the tradition of the *rime estravaganti*) that many of the poems eventually collected in the *Vita Nova* enjoyed an earlier, independent circulation. Moreover, two extant transcriptions of "Donne ch'avete," copied when the poet was still alive, demonstrate the importance of the contemporary reception of the *canzone* "tra le genti."

As mentioned in the previous chapter, a rare thirteenth-century transcription of "Donne ch'avete" is to be found in the Memoriali bolognesi; in 1293, the notary Pietro Allegranza copied the first stanzas of the *canzone* among the Latin contracts of his register (Mem. 82). Written out as prose in a hurried notarial cursive, the fragmented text indicates the potentially fragile transmission of Dante's early lyrics. At the same time, despite the frequent instances of textual corruption in this early dissemination of Dante in Bologna, the university-trained notaries who copied his poems were an almost ideal audience. As I have just argued, their poetic selections exhibit a distinctly anti-Guittonian bias and present a vision of the early Italian lyric close to Dante's own.

In this chapter, I will concentrate on the second extant thirteenth-century transcription of "Donne ch'avete," which is to be found in the lyric anthology Vaticano Latino 3793, as well as on its implications for the *Vita Nova.* The poem is written out in prose, largely unadorned, and, most surprisingly, left anonymous; the title "Dante" written above the text was added by a later hand (fig. 10). As in the memoriale, it is copied in a notarial cursive instead of the calligraphic *textualis* script used for literary, scientific, and legal books of the period.[5] Judging from the Memoriali bolognesi and the Vatican anthology, the earliest written circulation of Dante's lyric texts thus appears limited to the cursive documentary scripts usually reserved for archival documents and private bookkeeping.

The transcription of "Donne ch'avete" in the Vatican anthology is especially important because it is followed in the manuscript by a response to Dante's poem in the form of the *canzone* "Ben aggia l'amoroso et dolce chore" (fig. 10).[6] "Ben aggia" (v 307) is a stanza-by-stanza response to "Donne ch'avete" (v 306), written in the voice of the ladies, the *donne,* addressed in "Donne ch'avete," and sharing the same rhymes. The author of "Ben aggia"—usually identified by the misleading epithet "Amico di Dante"—has five other *canzoni* transcribed in the Vatican anthology after "Ben aggia," as well as a *corona* of

sixty-one sonnets in the sonnet section of the manuscript. "Donne ch'avete" and the compositions of the Amico di Dante are copied at the end of the *canzone* and sonnet sections of the manuscript by a second hand contemporary or nearly contemporary to the first hand and primary compiler of the anthology, datable to the end of the thirteenth century or the beginning of the fourteenth.[7] The reliability of the texts is such that scholars have tentatively proposed that the transcriptions are autograph (except, obviously, in the case of "Donne ch'avete"), that is, that the scribe and author of the poems may be one and the same.[8]

In what follows, I propose both that Dante was aware of the reception of his *canzone* in "Ben aggia" and that his framing of "Donne ch'avete" in the *Vita Nova,* especially regarding the question of the female voice, forms part of a complex response to the way in which it was received and anthologized in manuscripts such as Vaticano 3793. In this view, Dante's founding of a new poetics of authenticity and interiority was directly influenced by "Ben aggia"'s transformation of "Donne ch'avete" into a fictional dialogue with a fictional group of ladies. And this turning inward in the *Vita Nova*—toward inspiration, private experience, and even physical interiors—represents a model of lyric poetry at odds with its public function in contemporary Florentine society. As we shall see, members of the mercantile ruling oligarchy in this period preferred the highly conventional, often ostentatiously fictional poetic exchanges popularized by Guittone and his followers, which might have been useful in ritually maintaining social cohesion (at least among male political elites), but which bore with them the specter of fraud.

It may seem incautious, at first, to suggest that Dante was directly influenced by the material circulation of his texts. In the past we have tended to insulate the poet from the murky territory of misreading and historical contingency involved in reception studies. While it is conceded that his readers may misinterpret, appropriate, and even thwart his message, Dante's text itself is often studied as if it were produced in a sort of prelapsarian, pre-public moment. Even analyses of Dante's various palinodes, which deal explicitly with his anthologizing and self-citations, rarely take into account the historical circulation and reception of his texts. Yet if Dante were not concerned with the prior transmission and interpretation of his poems, it is unlikely he would have felt the need to publicly revise his attitude toward them.

The elusive relationship between literary composition and reception can help us better to understand not only Dante's writings, but also Dante the writer. The actual labor behind Dante's literary production, the historicized process of writing and rewriting, elucidates in turn the social backdrop of his revisions. In such an analysis of his retrospective poetics, Dante emerges as not only interested in his earlier poetry morally and existentially, but also as artistically concerned with how his former poetic selves had been received and misrepresented in specific environments by specific social groups. In order better to understand the consequences for Dante of such misreading, I will analyze his self-anthologizing of "Donne ch'avete" in the *Vita Nova* as a response to the *canzone*'s reception in the lyric anthology Vaticano 3793. But before turning specifically to Dante's response, we must first examine the pairing of "Donne ch'avete" and "Ben aggia" within the context of the Vatican anthology as a whole.

The *donne* of Vaticano 3793

Vaticano 3793 is one of the most important literary artifacts of the vernacular middle ages,[9] not least because of its inclusiveness and heterogeneity. Various poets are preserved only in the Vatican anthology, and it alone preserves a great majority of the works of important poets such as Monte Andrea, Chiaro Davanzati, and Rustico Filippi. Vaticano 3793 has also received critical attention because Dante's reception of Italian poetry seems to have been influenced by a manuscript of the Vatican anthology tradition, a so-called "twin" of the codex that has not survived.[10]

In addition, the anthology's internal organization, its *compilatio,* represents a sophisticated and innovative history of the early Italian lyric that has important repercussions in Dante's corpus. Divided into two sections (with *canzoni* occupying quires 2–14 and sonnets quires 18–26), the poems are arranged according to a precise historical and geographical narrative, and each quire is dedicated to a particular school, region, or period of poetry: Sicilian, Bolognese, Florentine, etc. The organization of poems is thus conjoined with the physical structure of the codex.[11] The Vatican anthology's physical structure and its unique appearance further distinguish it from contemporary lyric anthologies; the cursive handwriting, simplified page layouts, and bourgeois reception of the manuscript situate it in a distinctly mercantile and urban environment.[12] These historiographical and codicological features will be treated in detail in chapters 3 and 4, respectively. For the present discussion, I need to focus on two important characteristics of the anthology: first, the conspicuous number of poems written in the female voice; and second, the social and political function of many of the poems, especially evident in the sonnet section.

The quires of the *canzone* section of the Vatican anthology typically begin with the major figures, or *caposcuola,* of the early Italian poetic tradition, and they end with various anonymous poems. Scholars have noticed that in this way the historiographical narrative of the anthology remains intact; the integrity of individual quires—divided chronologically and regionally into various poetic schools—is safeguarded by filling in the remaining pages of booklets with anonymous poems.[13] What has not been noted are how many of these "filler" poems are written in the female voice and what this might mean for the conceptualization of the anthology as a whole.

The first booklet, or quire, in the Vatican anthology, representing the Sicilian-school poets, begins with Giacomo da Lentini's epochal "Madonna dir vo voglio" (V 1) and ends with a single anonymous poem, "Oi llassa 'namorata" (V 26). After twenty-five poems written by despairing male lovers, or *innamorati,* the quire suddenly switches to the voice of a female lover, an "[in]namorata." The betrayed female speaker in the anonymous *canzonetta*—not to be confused with the almost certainly male author—tells how she was deceived by the rhetoric of courtly love: "ché m'era / dolze lo suo parlare, / ed à mi 'namorata" (because his speech was sweet to me and it caused me to fall in love) [41–43]. Her relatively generic lament about the abuses of courtly language gains force when read alongside one of the poems that immediately precedes "Oi llassa 'namorata" in the Vatican anthology, "Donna, audite como" (V 24) by Messer lo re Giovanni; the deceitful lover quoted in "Oi llassa 'namorata" appears, in fact, to echo the flattery and hyperbole used by the male protagonist of "Donna, audite como." Just as the lover in "Oi llassa 'namorata" swears, falsely, that he would prefer the speaker's love to being lord over the entire world—

> Lassa! che mi diciea
> quando m'avea in cielato:
> "Di te, oi vita mea,
> mi tengno più pagato

ca ss'io avesse im ballia
lo monddo a segnorato."
(25–30)

[Alas, that he would say, when he had me in private, "O my life, I consider myself better rewarded by you than if I held the whole world as a lordship.]

—the lover in "Donna, audite como," slightly more modestly, opts for his beloved's favor over the county of Bologna and the dukedom of Gascogne:

"Melglio mi tengno per pagato
di madonna,
che s'io avesse lo contato
di Bolongna
e la Marca e lo ducato
di Guascongna."
(89–94)

[I consider myself better rewarded by my lady than if I held the counties of Bologna and the Marches and the dukedom of Gascogne.]

Both geographical analogies, moreover, are expressed in the imperfect hypothetical subjunctive and share similar phrasing (for example, "mi tengno più pagato" [28] in "Oi llassa 'namorata" and "melglio mi tengno per pagato" [89] in "Donna, audite como").[14]

Although these similarities in language and content are most likely accidental, the sequential placement of the two poems makes it seem that the female voice of "Oi llassa 'namorata" is responding critically to the male voice of "Donna audite como." In a similar fashion, other poems written *in voce di donna* are strategically positioned within the anthology next to poems whose language they seem to echo and thus undermine. These anonymous poems suggest a dynamic and dialogic reading of the manuscript that calls into question the sincerity of the major authors occupying the bulk of the anthology.[15] Coming at the end of sections, the female voice can be seen as skeptically answering the courtly pleas that precede it.[16]

In creating a dialogic and narrative arrangement of lyric poems, the compiler of the Vatican anthology was likely influenced by similar elements in poetic traditions such as the *contrasto* and the *tenzone fittizia*.[17] In the *contrasto,* male and female personae trade off often heated contrapuntal responses within a single poem, while in the *tenzone fittizia* the exchanges between male and female speakers consist of various poems, typically a series of alternating sonnets. Both poetic forms are prominent in Vaticano 3793. For example, the *canzone* section features the most famous *contrasto* of Italian literature, "Rosa fresca aulentissima" (V 54), while the sonnet section contains various examples of fictional *tenzoni*—by Guittone d'Arezzo, Chiaro Davanzati, Monte Andrea, and Messer Ubertino Giovanni del Bianco d'Arezzo—which form mini-narrative sequences within a collection of lyric poems.

The various *contrasti* and *tenzoni fittizie* contained in the Vatican anthology share a form of linguistic skepticism we have already seen in "Oi llassa 'namorata." For example, the female speaker of "Rosa fresca aulentissima" exposes the insincerity of the male protagonist's seductive, courtly rhetoric, telling him "prezzo le tuo parabole meno che d'un zitello" (I trust in your word less than in that of a young bachelor) [78].[18] The entire composition turns, in fact, on a series of metalinguistic critiques of the uses and abuses of poetic language.[19] In a similar fashion, Guittone's two highly influential *tenzoni fittizie* gradually reveal the true sexual motives behind the courtly rhetoric of the male protagonists. Although the exchanges in his first *tenzone fittizia* (V 703–715) maintain a courtly tone, the female speaker soon intuits the duplicitous nature of the lover's language. Guittone's character is accused of being a "falsso amante e 'mfingidore" (false lover and a faker) [V 710.4] whose greatest talent lies in his seductive rhetoric: "sì sotilemente altrui sa' predicare" (you know how to preach to others so subtly) (V 712.4). In the second *tenzone* [V 716–721], all courtly pretenses disappear. Guittone's character, having been rebuked by the lady, now simply addresses her as "villana donna" and proudly declares his hostility toward the courtly lyric tradition: "Ch'io fino nom sono" (That I am not refined) [V 716.3]. He further reveals that his aim all along has been nothing more than sexual intercourse: "volendo ti covrire" (V 716.7).[20] Guittone reverts here to the voice of his *ars armandi*—preserved in its entirety only in the Vatican anthology—in which poetic language and flattery serve only as techniques of seduction.[21]

Rhetorical artifice is inherent, of course, in the very formal structure of the *tenzone fittizia*. Since the same poet authors both the male and female sonnets, any pretense of lyric authenticity is suspect, and individual speakers are easily reduced to theatrical personae. Even the rubrics of the fictional *tenzoni* in the Vatican anthology point to the blatant artificiality of the genre. For example, while the Laurentian anthology labels the male and female protagonists separately as "Guittone" and "La donna," the Vatican anthology ascribes all compositions simply to "Guittone" and "Guittone medesimo." The anonymous compiler of Vaticano 3793 demonstrates, in this way, that he is aware of the degree of contrivance characterizing these poems, just as the female speakers of "Rosa fresca aulentissima" and "Oi llassa 'namorata" convey their distrust in the poetic clichés of their supposedly courtly suitors. If the tradition of impersonating the female voice is central to the conceptualization of the Vatican anthology, it is in part because poems written in this style often manifest a critical, even cynical attitude toward poetry and poetic language.

The second aspect of the Vatican anthology that has direct relevance for understanding the reception of "Donne ch'avete" in the manuscript is the social and political function of the poems it collects, especially in the sonnet section. The social role of early Italian poetry is most evident in the *tenzone*. Whether the argument is poetic, philosophical, or political, the *tenzone*—however divisive in content—enacts a social bond among participants, emphasizing the communicative, even epistolary nature of literary production in late medieval Italy.[22] Scholars have already noted the marked importance of the *tenzone* in the compilation of the Vatican anthology.[23] For example, the sonnet section begins with an exchange between Giacomo da Lentini and the abbot of Tivoli, perhaps the very first *tenzone* of Italian literature, and several quires are dedicated exclusively to this form of poetic debate. In this portion of the Vatican anthology, where poetic exchanges are often arranged by argument and topic instead of collected within the corpus of each poet as in the *canzone* section, the autonomy of the author-figure and the "author's book" is consequently eroded. In this way, the social and socializing role of the early lyric is emphasized over individual authorship.

Many of the poems anthologized in Vaticano 3793 were written by members of Florence's political class, and these prominent magnates and members of the major guilds prove themselves to be amateur poets of surprising sophistication and technical skill. Writing poems in the vernacular was apparently viewed as an important social rite for the merchants-bankers, notaries, and judges who made up the new urban elite of the Florentine oligarchy.[24] Of particular note is a series of heated *tenzoni,* including an impressive chain of seventeen sonnets (V 882–898) debating the outcome of the arrival of either Conradin (1267–1268) or Rudolf of Habsburg (1278–1289) in Italy.[25] The exchanges among the six interlocutors, evenly divided between Guelphs and Ghibellines, represent for Roberto Antonelli "una fotografia quasi collettiva degli scontri ma anche dell'orgoglio del ceto dirigente municipale (le Arti maggiori)" (an almost collective photograph of the conflicts as well as the pride of the municipal ruling class [the major guilds]).[26] This "photograph" not only provides a glimpse of the contemporary Florentine political landscape, it also aesthetically re-enacts and legitimizes the authority of the ruling urban elite by demonstrating their capacity for nonviolent, verbal debate. Although they often functioned as divisive and violent elements within Florentine politics, the magnates and wealthy tradesmen (*popolani grassi*) represented in these *tenzoni* appear as if they were active participants in the fledgling "deliberative democracy" of the popular government.

The correspondence between these two important features of the Vatican anthology—between erotic and political debates—is hardly self-evident. Yet in collecting the *tenzoni fittizie* together in a section of the anthology (quire 23) dedicated to other, "real" *tenzoni,* the compiler of the manuscript seems to have intuited the similar function of both poetic traditions. Instead of including the male-female exchanges in the various corpuses of individual authors as part of their literary autobiographies (as in the Laurentian anthology), he emphasizes the social role of the fictional *tenzone.* As with standard *tenzoni,* these ritual impersonations of the female voice, enacted by socially prominent male authors, are incorporated in this way within the larger contemporary culture of debate. From a similar perspective, Brunetto Latini explains in his *Rettorica*—an adaptation of Ciceronian adversarial rhetoric for the Italian city-state republic—that love poems ("canzoni d'amore"), with their strategic maneuvers, persuasions, and negotiations between lover and beloved, should be understood as an implicit disputation ("tencione tacita").[27] Equating the battle of the sexes represented in vernacular poetry, especially in the *contrasto* and the *tenzone fittizia,* with the political councils and debates of the Florentine *popolo,* Brunetto singles out verbal dispute, which he refers to uniformly as a "tencione," as characteristic of the prevailing zeitgeist. In this light, poets such as Chiaro Davanzati and Monte Andrea, authors of both important political *tenzoni* and *tenzoni fittizie,* are central figures in the Vatican anthology less as autobiographical lyric poets than as active participants in these literary rites.

Further evidence of the link between the erotic and political debates can be found in the arrangement in the Vatican anthology of four "double" (twenty-eight-verse) sonnets by Monte Andrea and Schiatta di messer Albizo Pallavillani. Two of Monte's double sonnets, "Meo sire, cangiato vegio ti il talento" and "Meo sire, troppo vincie vi voluntate" (V 621–622), both *contrasti* in which the male and female personae exchange responses every two lines in the octave and every three verses in the sestet, are anthologized as the last two poems of quire 21. In exactly the same finishing position two quires later, at the end of quire 23, we find, instead, a political *tenzone* in double sonnets between Monte and Schiatta. As in the previous *contrasti,* the debating characters of "Non isperate, ghebellini, socorsso" (V 778) and "Non vale savere a chiu Fortuna à scorsso" (V 779) exchange jibes every two verses in the octave and every three verses in the sestet, but the contrasting male and female speakers have given way to a dialogue between opposing political voices, the Guelph Monte and the Ghibelline Schiatta. Presented in this way, the cultural practice of recording both male and female voices is formally associated with the inclusion of opposing, heterogeneous political views within a single poem.

While there is a clear difference between a real political opponent and an invented female beloved, in the world of the Vatican anthology they are placed on an almost equal footing. In this way, through their association with fictional exchanges between lovers, contemporary political divisions are aestheticized in the Vatican anthology and, at least temporarily, reconciled. Within both the poetic space of the sonnet stanza and the larger structure of the compilation of the manuscript, poetic rivals engage in a highly ritualized literary game, in which they must adhere to the rules of meter, rhyme, and stylistic decorum as if they were the personae of an erotic debate. Bound by the literary "laws" of convention, the authors of both the political *tenzone* and the *tenzone fittizia* demonstrate a willingness to incorporate difference and debate—an essential ideological element of the new Florentine oligarchy. A final example of how imitating the female voice might actively facilitate social cohesion is found in a remarkable sonnet exchange in the Vatican anthology ("Né fu, néd è, né fia omo vivente," "Nesuno pote amare coralmente," and "D'amore sono preso, sì che me ritrarne" [V 685–687]) in which Ser Cione responds to Monte Andrea's love poem in the female voice, as if he were the latter's beloved, his "donna amata" (to whom Monte responds favorably in turn).[28] Although the Guelph banker Monte and the Ghibelline notary Ser Cione appear elsewhere in the manuscript as ideological opponents bitterly divided along social and party lines, here they solidify a masculine political community by writing erotic poetry to each other, with Ser Cione assuming the female voice.

The Amico di Dante and the *donne* of "Ben aggia l'amoroso et dolce chore"

When the Amico di Dante responds to "Donne ch'avete intelletto d'amore" (V 306) with "Ben aggia l'amoroso et dolce chore" (V 307) in the female voice, he is thus perfectly in line with the ideology and poetics of the Vatican anthology. Since "Ben aggia" is less well known than Dante's *canzone,* it may be useful at this point—given its importance for the present discussion—to cite it in full:

> Ben aggia l'amoroso et dolce chore
> che vol noi donne di tanto servire,
> che sua dolçe ragione ne face audire,
> la qual è piena di piacer piagente:
> ché ben è stato bon chonoscidore,   5
> poi quella dov'è fermo lo disire
> nostro per donna voler la seguire,
> (per che di noi ciascuna fa saciente),
> à cchonosciuta sì perfettamente
> e 'nclinato s' a llei chol chore humìle;   10
> sicché di noi chatuna il dritto istile
> terrà, preghando ongnora dolçemente
> lei chui s'è dato, quando fia cho noi
> ch'abia merçé di lui choglі atti suoi.
> Ai Deo, chom' àve avançato 'l su' detto,   15
> partendo lo da nnoi, inn alta sede;
> e cchom' àve 'n sua laude dolce fede,
> che ben à cchominçato e meglio prende!
> Torto seria tal-homo esser distretto
> o malmenato di quell' al chui pede   20

istà inclino, e ssì perfetto crede,
diciendo sì pietoso, e non chontende,
ma dolci motti parla, sì cch' acciende
li chori d'amore tutti, e dolci face:
sicché di noi nessuna donna tace,   25
ma pregha Amore che quella a cchui s'arrende
sia a llui humiliata in tutti lati
dove udirà li suoi sospir' gittati.
   Per la vertù ch' e' parla, dritto hostelo
chonoscer può ciascun ch' è di piacere,   30
ché 'n tutto vole quella laude chonpiére
ch'à cchominçata per sua chortesia;
ch'unqua vista né voce sott' un velo
sì vertudiosa chome 'l suo cherére
non fu néd è, per che dé hom tenere   35
per nobil chosa ciò ch' e' dir disia:
ché chonosciuta egli à la dritta via,
sì cche le sue parole son chonpiute.
Noi donne sén di ciò inn-achordo essute
ch'e' di piacere la nostra donna tria;   40
e ssì l'avemo per tale innamorato,
ch'Amor preghiamo per lui in ciascun lato.
   Audite anchor quant' è di pregio e vale:
che 'n far parlare Amore sì ss' asichura
che cchonti la bieltà, ben a drittura,   45
da lei dove 'l su' chore vol ch ssi fova.
Ben se ne porta chom' om naturale,
nel sommo ben disia ed à sua chura,
né inn-altra vista crede né in pintura
né nonn- attende né vento né plova: 50
per che faria gran bene sua donna, po' v'à
tanta di fe', guardare ai suo' istati,
poichéd egli è infra gl'innamorati
quel che 'n perfetto amare passa, et più gio' v'à.
Noi donne il metteremmo in Paradiso,   55
udendo·l dire di lei ch' à llui chonquiso.

"Io anderò né non già migha in bando;
in tale guisa sono acconpangnata
che ssì mi sento bene assichurata,
ch'i' spero andare e rredir tutta sana.   60
Son cierta bene di nonn ir mi isviando,
ma in molti luoghi sarò arrestata:
pregherò llì di quello che m'ài preghata,
finchéd i' giungnerò ala fontana
di 'nsengnamento, tua donna sovrana.   65
Non sò s'io mi starò semmana o mese,
o sse le vie mi saranno chontese:
girò al tu' piacere presso et lontana;
ma d'esser vi già giunta io amerei,
perch'ad Amore ti racchomanderei."   70
                         (V 307)

[Blessed be that love-filled and sweet heart that so wants to serve us ladies that it has us listen to its sweet poetry, full of pleasing pleasure. Truly he has demonstrated himself a fine connoisseur since he has perfectly recognized and pledged his humble heart to the one whom we firmly desire to follow as our lady, she who makes each of us wise. Because of this, each one of us, maintaining the proper style, will always, whenever she is among us, sweetly beseech the lady to whom he is pledged that she may show mercy to him with her acts.

O Lord, how he has elevated his poetry, carrying it from us toward Your lofty seat! And how he places his faith in his sweet praise which he has begun well and continues better. It would be unjust for such a man to be vanquished or mistreated by the one at whose feet he prostrates himself and whom he entrusts so perfectly, speaking in a merciful manner. And he makes no objections, rather he speaks sweet words, so that he enflames all hearts with love and renders them sweet. Because of this, not one of us ladies is silent, but we beseech Love that she to whom he yields will humble herself wherever she will hear his sighs.

Through the virtue with which he speaks, anyone can recognize him as the true vessel of courtesy because he wants completely to finish the praise he has begun on account of his gallantry. For neither has there ever been nor is there now any woman whose appearance or voice is as virtuous as his pleas, so that one must consider a noble thing what he wishes to say. He has uncovered the proper way, and thus his words are perfect. We ladies are all in agreement that our lady must needs choose to please him, and we hold him for such a lover that we beseech Love for him on every occasion.

Continue to hear how much he is worth. He is so assured in having Love speak that he (Love) bases his evaluation of beauty, correctly, on that lady with whom he wants to warm up his heart. Truly, he behaves like a loyal servant: He desires and places his care in the highest good; he does not believe in any other appearance or picture; and he does not take heed of wind or rain. Seeing that he is so faithful, his lady would do well to take notice of his condition, since among lovers he surpasses all in perfect love and receives more pleasure from it. We ladies would put him in Paradise hearing him speak about she who has conquered him.

"I will go forth—and not at all into exile; I am so well accompanied that I feel confident enough to hope to leave and return safely. I am quite sure that I will not wander off but that in places I will be held up. There I will ask what you asked me to do until I reach the fountain of sapience, your sovereign lady. I do not know if I will stay there for a week or a month, or if my paths will be blocked, but I will go near or far according to your wishes. However, I would love to have already arrived because I would then commend you to Love."]

That the Amico di Dante reductively misreads the philosophical and experimental content of "Donne ch'avete" is evident from even a quick first appraisal of "Ben aggia." Ignoring key innovations of Dante's groundbreaking poem, such as the introduction of a conceptual framework drawn from Aristotelian causality, the author of "Ben aggia" instead constructs a fictional dialogue by answering Dante's praise for the lady with the ladies' praise for Dante. Often, he simply switches male and female pronouns in his stanza-by-stanza response or changes the attribution of a certain phrase. If Dante claims, for example, that the effects of Beatrice's appearance include turning anyone who observes her into something noble, a "nobil cosa" (36), the Amico declares in turn, in the corresponding verse of "Ben aggia," that Dante's speech is itself something noble: "nobil chosa ciò ch' e' dir disia" (36).

The most important misreading in "Ben aggia," however, can be seen in the way the Amico di Dante treats the question of the intended female audience of "Donne ch'avete." For Dante, his address of the female public in "Donne ch'avete" signals a revolutionary shift in poetics vis-à-vis his new, less individualistic relationship to the lady, and he spends the entire first stanza commenting upon this change. For the Amico, on the other hand, Dante's invocation of the *donne* provides the opportunity to impersonate the female voice, to respond, in a highly artificial manner, as the ladies themselves. As highlighted by the contiguous placement of "Donne ch'avete" and "Ben aggia" in the Vatican anthology, the Amico turns Dante's poem into a playful dialogue between male and female protagonists, a "ludus letterario," in the words of one recent critic.[29] In the spirit of other *tenzoni fittizie* in the corpus of the Amico di Dante—most notably the exchange between Madonna and Messer in V 952–955—"Donne ch'avete" is read as an example of the insincere, dialogic poetics characterizing the pre-stilnovist and Guittonian tradition.[30] Within this tradition, the Amico di Dante incorporates Dante's signature *canzone* into the sort of stylized exchanges and female ventriloquism enacted between male poets that we saw in Monte and Ser Cione.

The highly contrived nature of the Amico di Dante's response in "Ben aggia" culminates in the last stanza, where the personified poem "speaks." According to the most recent editor of the Amico di Dante's poetry, the quoted dialogue of this last stanza is spoken by a personification of the *canzone* "Ben aggia."[31] In fact, these verses make sense only as spoken by a personification of the *canzone* "Donne ch'avete," which Dante addresses in the last stanza of his poem:

> Canzone, io so che tu girai parlando
> a donne assai, quand'io t'avrò avanzata.
> Or t'amonisco, poi ch'io t'ò allevata
> per figliuola d'Amor giovane e piana,
> che là ove giugni tu dichi pregando:
> "Insegnatemi gir, ch'io son mandata
> a quella di cui laude io so' adornata."
> E se non vòli andar sì come vana,
> non restare ove sia gente villana:
> ingegnati, se puoi, d'esser palese

solo con donne o con omo cortese,
che ti merranno là per via tostana.
Tu troverai Amor con esso lei;
raccomandami a·llui come tu dêi.
(*VN* 10.25, lines 57–70).

[Canzone, I know that you will go speaking to many women once I
have set you forth. Now I warn you, since I have raised you as a young
and pleasant daughter of love, that wherever you go you say, beseech-
ing, "Teach me the way, for I am sent to that lady whose praise adorns
me." And if you don't wish to go about like a vain one, don't stay
where there are vulgar folk; contrive, if you can, to show yourself only
to ladies or a courtly man, for they will lead you there by a quick road.
You will find Love with her, commend me to him as you should.][32]

When, in this *congedo,* Dante tells the personification of his *canzone* to question the ladies for the way to his beloved,

dichi pregando:
"Insegnatemi gir, ch'io son mandata
a quella di cui laude io so' adornata"
(61–63)

—the last stanza of "Ben aggia" answers, in the voice of Dante's poem,
that she will do just that, until she arrives at the "fontana di 'nsegnamento":

"pregherò llì di quel che m'ài preghata,
finchéd i' giugnerò ala fontana
di 'nsegnamento, tua donna sovrana."
(63–65)

Similarly, when Dante instructs his *canzone* to recommend him to Love ("Tu
troverai Amor con esso lei / raccomandami a·llui come tu dêi" [69–70]), the
personified "Donne ch'avete" speaking in "Ben aggia" assures him that "d'esser vi già giunta io amerei, / perch' ad Amore ti racchomanderei" (69–70).
In the last stanza of "Ben aggia," the Amico di Dante thus ingeniously responds in the voice of the personified feminine *canzone* addressed by Dante in

his own last stanza, just as in previous stanzas he responds in the voice of the *donne* addressed in "Donne ch'avete." By playfully responding to Dante's apostrophes to the ladies and to his *canzone* in this overtly literal fashion, the Amico di Dante erodes the authentic lyric voice in "Donne ch'avete" in favor of a literary game where a ritualized exchange (influenced by the culture of the *tenzone*) takes precedence over the sincerity of the poetic message.

The specter of insincerity raised by the Amico di Dante in the playful nature of his response poses a threat to the actual message of Dante's *canzone* and its supposed purpose. In fact, the fictional *donne* of "Ben aggia" read "Donne ch'avete" as a rhetorical plea to the lady (*argumentum ad misericordiam*), in which praise for Beatrice serves as a means to acquire her favor. Most of their response is concentrated on the apostrophes and entreaties found in the first and last stanzas of "Donne ch'avete"—more easily assimilated into the traditional *petitio* of the love lyric—ignoring the philosophically charged middle stanzas. Instead, the first part of each stanza of "Ben aggia" is almost exclusively concerned with praising Dante's praise—his "dolci motti" (23), "cherére" (34), "parole" (38), "parlare" (44), and above all his "laude" evoked in lines 17 and 31. As a reward for the efficaciousness of this speech, in the tail end, or *sirma,* of each stanza, the ladies promise to intercede on Dante's behalf with his beloved. Persuaded by his language, they will in turn persuade his lady, underlined by the repetition of the verb *pregare* in lines 12, 26, 42, and 63 (twice). By omitting the doctrinal aspects of "Donne ch'avete," the *donne* of "Ben aggia" treat Dante's learned analogies as particularly eloquent examples of self-interested praise; that is, as a means to an end, and thus not unrelated to the praise found in other male-female exchanges in the Vatican anthology.

In part, the last stanza of "Donna ch'avete" justifies this mediating role that the Amico invents for the *donne* in "Ben aggia." As we have seen, Dante envisions in the *congedo* that his future female readers will serve as go-betweens for the *canzone*—which is itself a sort of go-between—and the beloved. The view of "Donne ch'avete" as an erotic request is amplified throughout "Ben aggia" by emphasizing this last section of Dante's poem and especially Dante's imperative "tu dichi pregando" (61). Yet Dante's request to his poem (and, by inference, to the ladies) needs to be understood within the architecture of the entire *canzone,* in which a theory of a single, unifying Love, present at once in the celestial, earthly, and even infernal realms ("e che dirà nello 'Nferno: O mal nati, / io vidi la speranza de' beati" [and one who will say in Hell: "Oh ill-born ones, I have seen the hope of the blessed"][27–28]), is articulated among the stanzas and the parts of each stanza. Robert Durling and Ronald Martinez's discussion of the *divisioni* of "Donne ch'avete" reveals how carefully Dante distributed the implications of his love for Beatrice within a scale of being that is reproduced in the formal divisions and parts of the *canzone* space.[33] In Dante's bold parsing of the hierarchy of causes, his erotic pleas to the lady participate in the same love expressed by the saints, angels, and even God.

Indeed, the rhetorical entreaties that characterize the *congedo* to "Donne ch'avete" reproduce on a smaller scale the use of rhetorical apostrophe that Dante incorporates into the theater of Heaven, as he imagines it, in the second stanza of "Donne ch'avete":

> Angelo clama in Divino Intelletto
> e dice: "Sire, nel mondo si vede
> maraviglia nell'acto che procede
> d'un anima che 'nfin qua sù risplende."
> Lo cielo, che non àve altro difecto
> che d'aver lei, al suo Segnor la chiede,
> e ciascun sancto ne grida merzede.
> Sola Pietà nostra parte difende,
> che parla Dio, che di madonna intende.
> "Dilecti miei, or sofferite in pace
> che vostra spene sia quanto Mi piace
> là ov'è alcun che perder lei s'attende,
> e che dirà nello 'Nferno: O mal nati,
> io vidi la speranza de' beati."
>
> (15–28)

[An angel cries out in the divine intellect and says, "Sire, in the world a marvel appears in the act that proceeds from a soul, a soul that shines back as far up as here." Heaven asks for her from its Lord, since it contains no imperfection except not possessing her, and every saint calls out for her mercy. Only Pity takes our side, as God speaks, having milady in mind, "My beloveds, now suffer in peace that, as long as it pleases Me, your hope be there where someone is who awaits losing her and who will say in Hell: "O ill-born ones, I have seen the hope of the blessed."]

In this passage the dialogue between lover and beloved is transformed into a dialogue between the angel and God (assimilating the genres of the *contrasto* and the *tenzone fittizia*), yet the language, feudal metaphors, and rhetorical pleas of the Occitan and Italian courtly love tradition remain unchanged. God is addressed as "Sire" (16) and replies with "Dilecti miei" (24). Each saint, like a forlorn lover, "grida merzede" (21). Unlike Guinizzelli's "Al cor gentil rempaira sempre amore," where the heavenly court serves as an ironic self-critique, the heavenly court in "Donne ch'avete" legitimizes the erotic motives behind Dante's use of rhetorical persuasion by reproducing them in an atemporal Paradise.

In "Ben aggia," the personified *Pietà* of "Donne ch'avete," who defends humans in love with Beatrice against the angels and saints, is transformed into a clichéd "pietoso" (22), a word used to describe the submissive lover. And the saints asking God for "merzede" are replaced by a traditional request for mercy as a reward for the beloved's service ("abia merçé di lui chogli atti suoi" [14]). In this way, the Amico di Dante effectively omits the key innovation of "Donne ch'avete," its daring experiments in blurring the sacred and profane. Translating the language and commonplaces of the love lyric back into their proper and traditional positions, the Amico reintegrates "Donne ch'avete" into the pre-stilnovist and Guittonian culture exemplified in the Vatican anthology, with its emphasis on rhetorical persuasion and the social uses of poetry. A misreading this blatant might be deliberate, even polemical.[34]

The *donne* of the *Vita Nova*

The response of "Ben aggia l'amoroso et dolce chore" to "Donne ch'avete intelletto d'amore" must have served as a potent reminder for Dante of the hermeneutic instability latent in his new vernacular audience. The gross misreadings of "Ben aggia," in fact, help explain and contextualize Dante's anxieties about the circulation and reception of "Donne ch'avete," expressed in chapters 10 and 11 of the *Vita Nova*. When he worries in the *divisione* about having exposed the *canzone*'s meaning to too many ("di avere a troppi comunicato lo suo intendimento" [*VN* 10.33]), Dante refers not only to a generic intended audience, but to a specific, historical readership as well, one that included the Amico di Dante.[35] For this reason, the overtly philosophical language of the poems and prose in chapter 11 seeks to reestablish the doctrinal basis for "Donne ch'avete" that is ignored by the Amico in "Ben aggia." When Dante mentions that a friend has asked him ("a pregare me" [*VN* 11.1]) to explicate the poem and that he feels obliged to serve him ("era da servire" [*VN* 11.2]), he recalls the emphasis on both *pregare* and *servire* in "Ben aggia," which begins "Ben aggia l'amoroso et dolce chore / che vol noi donne di tanto servire."[36] The ensuing prose and sonnets of chapter 11 appear as additional attempts to serve the public represented by the Amico and to restrain potential misreadings such as that found in "Ben aggia."

Before going any further, it is worth considering another possibility: that the *Vita Nova* influenced "Ben aggia" and not the other way around. When approaching such tricky questions of directionality and influence in medieval vernacular texts, one cannot be too cautious—as we have seen in the recent debate about the contested chronology of "Donne ch'avete" and Cavalcanti's "Donna me prega."[37] Without the advantages of DNA testing, fingerprints, or even autograph manuscripts, scholars of the medieval period must deduce their conclusions from fragmentary evidence and expect the question to remain open to future debate and further contributions. Still, the verbal evidence suggesting that the Amico di Dante was aware of Dante's reframing of "Donne ch'avete" in the *Vita Nova* is thin,[38] and nothing in the text of "Ben aggia" requires, relies on, or is enhanced by a prior knowledge of Dante's *libello*.[39] At the most, one could posit that the very absence in "Ben aggia" of echoes of Dante's prose gloss functions as part of a polemical response. On the other hand, when the interpretive apparatus surrounding "Donne ch'avete" in the *Vita Nova* is examined as a response to "Ben aggia," the results are at once more fertile and economic. As I intend to illustrate, the interpretive gap between the *canzone* "Donne ch'avete" and its staged reading in the *Vita Nova* is beholden linguistically, thematically, and above all conceptually to "Ben aggia." In particular, I will examine the theme of poetic praise, the emphasis on beginnings, and the question of the female voice.

The most evident and significant response of the *Vita Nova* to the contemporary reception of "Donne ch'avete" regards the question of poetic praise.[40] In the prose introduction, or *ragione,* to "Donne ch'avete," Dante encounters a group of ladies, acquaintances of Beatrice—the same audience that supposedly responded to the *canzone* in "Ben aggia." The ladies immediately recognize him from his lovestruck foolishness, his numerous "sconfitte" (*VN* 10.3). After talking and laughing amongst themselves, one of the group steps forward and asks Dante, what, since he cannot bear to be in the presence of his beloved, could possibly be the purpose or end goal, "fine" (*VN* 10.5), of his love. The emphasis on the term *fine* is repeated twice by the lady and picked up twice by Dante in his response. Formerly, he tells the ladies, the "fine" of his love was found in receiving Beatrice's greeting, but now it lies in the very words that praise her: "In quelle parole che lodano la donna mia" (*VN* 10.8).

This new theory of disinterested praise contradicts, in part, the text of "Donne ch'avete" itself. In his introduction to "Donne ch'avete" in the *Vita Nova,* Dante claims to have decided, before composing the poem, to speak only *about* Beatrice and *to* the ladies, "pensai che parlare di lei non si convenia che io facesse, se io non parlassi a donne in seconda persona" (I thought that speaking about her was not appropriate unless I were to speak to ladies in the second person) [*VN* 10.12], contrasting with earlier poems written explicitly *to* his beloved ("Poi che dissi questi tre sonetti nelli quali parlai a questa donna" [After I composed these three sonnets in which I spoke to this lady], "avegna che sempre poi tacesse di dire a·llei" [so that from hereon I ceased speaking to her][*VN* 10.1]). However, in the *congedo* to "Donne ch'avete," Dante hopes that his poem, specifically his praise, will eventually arrive at and influence his beloved: "son mandata / a quella di cui laude io so' adornata" (62–63). The last stanza of "Donne ch'avete" thus makes it clear that while the *canzone* does not explicitly address Beatrice, it is still very directed at her, "a quella."

The apostrophes in the last stanza of "Donne ch'avete" suggest a more traditional function for poetic praise as rhetorical persuasion, a potential use of *laude* as mediator between lover and beloved that was picked up and amplified by the Amico di Dante in "Ben aggia." But while "Ben aggia" continually emphasizes the erotic and objective goal of the *laude* found in "Donne ch'avete," Dante claims and counters in the prose of the *Vita Nova* that the end goal, *fine,* of his praise consists in praise itself. By asserting that the object of his desire is the composition and enunciation of his poems and not what they might accomplish, Dante distances his *canzone* from the rhetoric of seduction that typifies the dialogic poems of Vaticano 3793 as well as from the dialogue created by "Donne ch'avete" and "Ben aggia." In fact, when Dante claims that the goal of his love for Beatrice now lies in his own poetry, "in quelle parole che lodano la donna mia" (*VN* 10.8), the resultant solipsism effectively removes the need for the sort of intercession promised in "Ben aggia."

The announcement of a new poetics of disinterested praise sends Dante's character into an existential and artistic crisis, since, as the ladies are quick to point out, in the past his poetry has been anything but disinterested. Intimidated by the new material he must undertake, his character is unable to write—or, more specifically, unable to begin ("non ardia di cominciare" [I did not dare to begin], "con paura di cominciare" [with fear of beginning][*VN* 10.11])—until, passing by a clear river one day, his inspired tongue moves almost by itself and utters the words: "Donne ch'avete intelletto d'amore" (Ladies who have understanding of love). At the end of the short narrative, Dante now has the incipit to his poem. In fact, there is a pronounced backward movement throughout the introductory passage to "Donne ch'avete," from a discussion of ends, with "lo fine" repeated three times at the beginning of the narration, to a discussion of beginnings, underlined by seven variations on the verb *cominciare* at the end of it.[41] This temporal reversal also contrasts with the forward-moving, goal-oriented ideology of "Ben aggia," which moves quickly from Dante's text, to the reception by the *donne,* to their intercession, to the ultimate hoped-for erotic goal of union with the beloved—from *cominciare* to *compiere*.[42] In the *Vita Nova,* moving in the opposite direction, Dante shifts the erotic goal, or *fine,* back closer and closer to the original moment of composition or even inspiration of the text.

The *donne* in both "Ben aggia" and the *Vita Nova* play an important part in this shift of perspective, underlined in the differences in what they ask for. In "Ben aggia," reacting to Dante's elegant praise in "Donne ch'avete," they promise to intercede with his beloved, emphasized by the repeated use of *pregare.* In the *Vita Nova,* however, the inquiry into Dante's motives by the ladies, "Noi ti preghiamo che tu ne dichi ove sta questa tua beatitudine" (We ask you to tell us where your blessedness lies) [*VN* 10.8], furnishes the initial stimulus for the composition of his *canzone* and for the new poetics of disinterested praise—once again, a movement from reception and uses of a text to its inspiration and composition. Moreover, in the ideal literary trajectory of the *Vita Nova,* the ladies' reprimands of Dante's previously goal-oriented poetry, that is, his poetry before "Donne ch'avete," substitute a fictionalized critique of Dante's poetic past for the actual critique of the *canzone* brought out by its contemporary reception in an unframed and unglossed version.

Indeed, by incorporating the apostrophized ladies of "Donne ch'avete" into the narrative structure of the *Vita Nova,* Dante stages a reception of his poetry that effectively replaces the real public of the Amico di Dante and the Amico's own response in the female voice. In particular, Dante emphasizes the original dictation of the incipit to "Donne ch'avete" from a higher power and its subsequent transcription in his book of memory ("Queste parole io ripuosi nella mente con grande letitia" [I stored these words in my mind with great happiness][*VN* 10.14]). The transcendent narrative of the inspired origins of "Donne ch'avete" is thus the ideal counterpoint to the various misreadings and historical vicissitudes involved in the material circulation of the *canzone,* "divulgata tra le genti."

The importance for Dante of establishing a supernatural basis for his poetics by describing the transcendent origins of "Donne ch'avete" in chapter 10 of the *Vita Nova* has long been recognized and studied especially for the parallels with a similar description of poetic inspiration in the citation of "Donne ch'avete" in *Purgatorio* 24. What is less obvious and less examined is why Dante's poetics of inspiration should be linked to the question of the *donne* in the first place:

> Avenne poi che passando per uno camino lungo lo quale sen gia uno rivo chiaro molto, a me giunse tanta volontà di dire, che io cominciai a pensare lo modo che io tenessi; e pensai che parlare di lei non si convenia che io facesse, se io non parlassi a donne in seconda persona, e non a ogni donna, ma solamente a coloro che sono gentili e che non sono pure femine. Allora dico che la mia lingua parlò quasi come per sé stessa mossa e disse: "Donne ch'avete intellecto d'amore." (*VN* 10.12–13)

> [It happened then that while I was passing along a road, beside which there ran a very clear stream, I was struck by such a desire to compose, that I began to think of the manner I should observe, and I thought that speaking about her was not appropriate unless I were to speak to ladies in the second person, and not to every lady, but only to those who are noble and not just women. Then, I say, that my tongue spoke as if moved by itself, and it said: "Ladies who have understanding of love."]

Why should Dante be inspired to write to a female audience, and why, when his tongue pronounces the vocative "Donne," should it be moved by a higher power? These questions are complicated by the fact that at the same time as Dante presents a foundation myth for a new poetics of authenticity and interiority, his supposed dialogue with the ladies could not have escaped being associated by contemporary readers with the most insincere and artificial genres of the Italian lyric tradition, the *contrasto* and the *tenzone fittizia*. In fact, the rhetorical fraud associated with writing in the female voice raises the stakes for a series of passages in the *Vita Nova*—such as the narrative moments built around the presentation of "Voi che portate la sembianza umile" and "Donna pietosa"—in which Dante engages with a female public. Within the confines of the present discussion, it is not possible to explore the many suggestive connections among these related moments in the text (linked verbally through the apostrophes "donne" and "a voi" as well as through the shared rhyme words *voi—altrui*). Yet in order to understand fully Dante's response to "Ben aggia," it is important to examine, albeit summarily, how Dante associates his new poetics of interiority in the *Vita Nova* with a specific domestic and feminine space—a space that contrasts sharply with the public and political space represented in the Vatican anthology and the accompanying social uses of poetry written in the female voice.

Falling in between the two *canzoni* to the ladies—"Donne ch'avete" and "Donna pietosa"(*VN* 14.17–28)—are two sonnets that form a question and response exchange between Dante and the *donne:* "Voi che portate la sembianza umile" (*VN* 13.9–10) and "Se' tu colui ch'ài tractato sovente." (*VN* 13.12–15). As in the two *canzoni,* in "Voi che portate" Dante addresses the ladies, but here the ladies themselves respond in their own sonnet, identifying Dante as the poet who writes to women: "Se' tu colui ch'ài tractato sovente / di nostra donna, sol parlando a noi?" (Are you that one who has often written about our lady, speaking only to us?) [1–2]. This is the closest Dante will come in the *Vita Nova* to writing a *tenzone fittizia*. In doing so, he evokes the dialogic poetics exemplified in the Vatican anthology and, in particular, the dialogue with the ladies created by the pairing of "Donne ch'avete" and "Ben aggia."[43]

Not surprisingly, then, the prose apparatus accompanying the sonnets is aimed specifically at countering the rhetorical fraud associated with writing in the female voice. Dante contextualizes his dialogue with the ladies within a specific time and place, and he claims that "Se' tu colui" was an act of transcription, not invention. Although not mentioned in the sonnets themselves, the prose *ragione* identifies the mourning in the poems with the rituals surrounding the death of Beatrice's father. Hidden in a strategic "luogo" (*VN* 13.4), Dante overhears the ladies returning from a visit to the grieving Beatrice:

> E con ciò sia cosa che secondo l'usanza della sopradecta cittade donne con donne e uomini con uomini s'adunino a cotale tristitia, molte donne s'adunaro colà dove questa Beatrice piangea pietosamente. Onde io veggendo ritornare alquante donne da·llei, udi' dicere loro parole di questa gentilissima com'ella si lamentava. (*VN* 13.3).

> [And since, according to the custom of the aforementioned city, ladies with ladies and men with men gather together in this sadness, many ladies had gathered there where a pitiful Beatrice was crying. And so, seeing several ladies returning from her, I heard them speak about how this most noble one was grieving.]

The authenticity of the voices Dante overhears and subsequently reports in sonnet form is bolstered by a gendered domestic scene. With an anthropological eye, he refers in particular to the gender separation in these rituals of mourning. In fact, contemporary chronicles, sumptuary laws, and literary texts attest that while important male citizens and kinsmen formed the public funeral procession, the women remained in the home of the deceased in sustained lamentation. This exclusion from the public sphere was both customary and legislated.[44]

For the politically prominent citizens whose writing is contained in the Vatican anthology, impersonating the female voice was an important public ritual of communal identity and consensus. Dante appears, on the other hand, to be carving a different space for the gendered voices of his vernacular poetics: the domestic and the private.[45] He overhears the ladies speaking amongst themselves as they return from a space of private lamentation that is both exclusive and excluded. Even more private and interior, Dante's questions to the ladies in "Voi che portate" were never even pronounced in public, but existed only in the poet's mind, an intended text ("E però che volentieri l'avrei dimandate se non mi fosse stata riprensione" [And since I would have gladly asked them if it hadn't been an indiscretion][*VN* 13.7])

that, unlike the reception of "Donne ch'avete" in "Ben aggia," never participated in the persuasion and seduction that typify the dialogic poetic tradition.

The importance for Dante of this experiment with writing in the female
voice—as well as his anxieties about it—is further demonstrated in two
sonnets, "Onde venite voi cosí pensose?" and "Voi, donne, che pietoso atto
mostrate," that Dante seems to have reworked for the *Vita Nova* to create the
dyad "Voi che portate" / "Se' tu colui."[46] In "Onde venite," Dante asks the
downcast ladies if they have just returned from seeing his *donna,* recalling
the situation of "Voi che portate." The language of the two sonnets is similar, as well.[47] The sonnet "Voi, donne" is a mini-dialogue with the ladies, integrating the questions and responses of "Voi che portate" and "Se' tu colui"
into one poem, as in a *contrasto.* In the octave, Dante asks the ladies to confirm
the identity of Beatrice, transformed by sorrow and almost unrecognizable,
while the *donne* respond in the sestet. Lacking the context of the funeral of
Beatrice's father, "Voi, donne" reads like a highly artificial exercise in writing
in the female voice. In addition, the Aretine rhymes *venta—penta—spenta* (2, 3, 6)
and the antanaclasis in the equivocal senses of *parere* (7–8) lend an uncomfortably Guittonian register to the poem.[48] When Dante rewrites these poems
to construct the episode surrounding "Voi che portate" and "Se' tu colui" in
the *Vita Nova,* he removes the most obvious traces of a Guittonian influence
and re-presents his earlier work within a specific, even intimate, context, head-
ing off the potential for misreading demonstrated all too clearly by the reception of "Donne ch'avete" in "Ben aggia." Yet this very process of revision
betrays the precariousness of Dante's truth claims in this first self-anthology,
especially when he confronts the traditional insincerity involved in writing in
the female voice.

Despite these ambiguities, the female audience in the *Vita Nova* is crucial
for Dante in defining his new relationship to the beloved. In particular, it signals his shift from an individualistic, ego-driven poetry to the collective praise
manifest in the use of "nostra donna" in both "Voi che portate" and "Se' tu
colui." The only other time Beatrice is referred to as "nostra donna" is when
Love indicates her dead body to Dante in the prose and verse describing the
hallucination of "Donna pietosa." With the exception of these uses at the
center of the book, Dante always refers to Beatrice as "la mia donna" or
"donna mia," often in rhyme position and a total of twenty-eight times within
the *libello.* In "Voi che portate" and "Se' tu colui," moreover, the double oc-
currence of "nostra donna," both by Dante in his initial address ("Vedeste voi

nostra donna gentile / bagnar nel viso suo di pianto Amore?" [Did you see our noble lady bathe Love, in her face, with tears][5–6]) and by the ladies in their response ("Se' tu colui ch'ài tractato sovente / di nostra donna, sol parlando a noi?" [Are you that one who has often written about our lady, speaking only to us][1–2]), unites them in the common disinterested concern for the troubled Beatrice. Dante's love for Beatrice is thus instrumental for integrating him into a female community.

In "Onde venite," on the other hand, Dante's concern for "la donna mia" (3) is still very much part of the narcissistic erotic economy of the traditional love poet. "Onde venite" ends, in fact, with a lament about a personified *Amore* ("sì mm'ha in tutto Amore da ssé scacciato / ch'ogni suo atto mi trae a fferire" [Love has so completely banished me that his every act leads me to injury][10–11]) probably left out of the *Vita Nova* because it was inappropriate in light of Dante's new disinterested praise poetry.[49] In "Voi, donne" Dante identifies a transformed Beatrice only as this woman, " 'sta donna" (2). And while the ladies in their response do call her "our lady" (9), the possessive adjective in this case clearly refers only to the ladies themselves and not to Dante: "Se nostra donna conoscer non pòi / ch'è sí conquisa, non mi par gran fatto, / però che quel medesmo avenne a noi" (If you cannot recognize our lady, who is so vanquished, it is no surprise, since in the same way it happened to us) [9–11]. In other words, it is no wonder that Dante cannot recognize Beatrice: neither can the ladies and she is their *donna*. In a similar fashion, the use of "nostra donna" by the ladies of "Ben aggia," instead of indicating a shared community, marks a distance between Dante's and the ladies' Beatrice: "Noi donne sén di ciò inn-achordo essute, / ch'e' di piacer la nostra donna tria" (39–40). Here the *donne* promise to intercede on Dante's behalf with *their* lady, reading his address to the *donne* in "Donne ch'avete" as a rhetorical attempt to bridge the erotic separation between lover and beloved.

By simply identifying Beatrice as "nostra donna" in "Voi che portate," Dante corrects, at one and the same time, the narcissism of "donna mia" in "Onde venite" and the gendered exclusivity of "nostra donna" in "Voi, donne" and "Ben aggia."[50] The linguistic differences are admittedly slight, but they carry with them considerable conceptual weight. For if Dante and the ladies are on the same side, there is no need for him to convince them of anything and no need for them to intercede on his behalf, as they do in "Ben aggia." By taking the desire for possession out of the possessive adjective,

Dante integrates himself into the circle of *donne* in the *Vita Nova* and realizes a poetics of lament that surpasses, in its chorality, the self-interested rhetoric typically associated with poetry written in the female voice.

This shared community made up of Dante and the ladies prepares the way for the "nostra donna" in the episode framing "Donna pietosa," where the iconic vision of the dead Beatrice links Dante's erotic experience with a community of mourning that is at once feminine and private as well as liturgical and universal.[51] In fact, the typological and even Christological significance of Beatrice's death revealed at this point in the narrative contrasts strikingly with the domestic, feminine setting described in the *ragione*. The apocalyptic vision of "Donna pietosa" is part of Dante's feverish dream while he is being watched over by a group of ladies at his sickbed.[52] Dante emphasizes the private/domestic nature of the experience in the particularly detailed introductory *ragione* as well as in the first two stanzas of the *canzone* itself, which detail the setting for the dream and its select audience. The threat for Dante of exposing elements of his erotic and interior life—while partially obscured by the incoherent enunciation of Beatrice's name—is mitigated because the poem is literally framed, in the beginning stanzas and the last verse, as a private speech act intended exclusively for the present ladies: "Donne, dicerollo a voi" (Ladies, I will tell it to you) [28].

Dialogue with a female audience—both real and dreamt—thus plays a central role in the themes and structure of the episode of "Donna pietosa," as emphasized by the rhetorical figure of *sermocinatio* in the last two verses of each stanza of the *canzone*. Yet Dante's insistence on the interiority of his exchanges sharply distinguishes them from the public and political uses of the female voice that characterize the Vatican anthology. First, the dialogue in Dante's dream with the mourning ladies—as well as with Death, Love, and in part, Beatrice herself—belongs to the intimate text of Dante's imaginary, psychic life. This text, in turn, when externalized, is enunciated within the domestic confines of Dante's sickroom. And the enclosed space of this "camera" (*VN* 14.12) mirrors the private room or "camera" (*VN* 14.10) in which Dante, in his dream, finally breaks down and calls his beloved's name, "O Beatrice" (*VN* 14.13).

The invocation of Beatrice is thus enclosed within a private room that is enclosed within Dante's dream-vision, both of which are further enclosed within the "real" sickroom of Dante and the ladies. When Dante's voice does break forth and calls out "Beatrice" *in mundum*—bridging the gap between the poet's subjective vision and the objective reality of the sickroom—the result is fragmented and unintelligible.[53] And Beatrice's response, locked within the dream, is even more qualified. The closest we will come to hearing the voice of Beatrice in the entire *Vita Nova* is when Dante sees a vision of her corpse in his feverish hallucination: "e pareami che la sua faccia avesse tanto aspecto d'umilitade, che parea che dicesse: 'Io sono a vedere lo Principio della pace'" (And it seemed to me that her face had such a semblance of humility that it seemed to say: "I am contemplating the source of peace") [*VN* 14.8]. In this false vision, it only appears that Beatrice speaks, and the double emphasis on "parea" in the vision marks Dante's refusal to construct a fictional female voice for the beloved (a refusal notably shared by the other stilnovists). The failure of Dante's dialogue with Beatrice in "Donna pietosa" is also, in a sense, the failure of the dialogic poetics of the Vatican anthology, with its fraudulent rhetoric and narcissistic erotic economy. At the center of the *Vita Nova* lies the absence of the *tenzone fittizia.*[54]

Of course, the *Vita Nova* is meant to be a publicly circulated text, and the ladies are only one of the represented audiences in the book, which include his poet-friends evoked at the beginning of the work and the pilgrims at the end.[55] Dante's private staging of the genesis of his poems is ultimately conceived for public dissemination, to be "divulgata tra le genti." The enclosed dialogues of "Donna pietosa" are eventually enclosed within a *canzone* space and circulated as "amorosa cosa da udire" (something lovely to hear) [*VN* 14.16]. Dante's prose-poem is not a private journal, nor is it an outpouring of supposedly unmediated sentiment in the romanticist tradition. Dante instead locates the texts of his psychic interiority within gendered spatial interiors as an express response to the exclusively political and municipal uses of vernacular poetry—and of the female voice in particular—in the same way that he removes proper place names and recognizable civic architecture from his representation of Florence. The air of private mourning that dominates the *Vita Nova* is also a public comment about contemporary practices of vernacular poetry.

This movement from private to public in the book of memory marks a final striking contrast to the Vatican manuscript. Although the Vatican anthology may represent the public political sphere, as we have seen, the codex itself remained a private object. As will be discussed in detail in chapter 4, studies of the codicological and paleographic aspects of the manuscript demonstrate that it did not circulate widely and that its use was primarily domestic and private. These contrasting uses of the female voice in the *Vita Nova* and in the Vatican anthology—a representation of private speech for a public text versus a public ritualized exchange in a private book—thus form a chiastic relationship that embodies perfectly the remarkably fluid social "places" of vernacular poetry in the period.

"Quando Amor mi spira, noto"

No doubt the very fluidity in the status of vernacular poetry in this period accounts, at least in part, for Dante's continued efforts to control the interpretations of his work, whether through self-anthologizing, self-commentary, or direct addresses to the reader. Within these various episodes of self-reference, the case of "Donne ch'avete" stands out for the number of times Dante attempts to reframe it, the *Vita Nova* being only the first one. In addition to important citations of "Donne ch'avete" in the *De vulgari eloquentia,* Dante returns to the poem in *Purgatorio* 24, in which the fellow vernacular poet Bonagiunta da Lucca identifies him via the now famous *canzone:*

> "Ma dì s'i' veggio qui colui che fore
> trasse le nove rime, cominciando
> 'Donne ch'avete intelletto d'amore.'"
> (49–51)

["But tell me if I see here the one who drew forth the new rhymes, beginning 'Ladies, who have understanding of love.'"]

In a canto including two specific examples of disinterested praise for female figures (Forese praising Piccarda, Bonagiunta praising Gentucca), Bonagiunta confirms the pivotal historiographical role that Dante sought to establish for his *stile della lode.* In particular, recalling the prose language of chapter 10 of *Vita Nova,* Bonagiunta emphasizes the inspired beginning ("cominciando"), or incipit, of "Donne ch'avete" and the fact that Dante drew it forth ("fore / trasse le nuove rime") from an interior space. When Dante responds with his famous self-definition,

> "I' mi son un che, quando
> Amor mi spira, noto, e a quel modo
> ch'e' ditta dentro vo significando"
>
> (52–54)

["I in myself am one who, when Love inspires me, takes note, and to that measure which he dictates within, I go signifying"],

he will seal this image of internal dictation and transcription that he first evoked in describing the book of memory in the opening paragraphs of the *Vita Nova*.

Purgatorio 24 is one of the most richly allusive cantos of the *Commedia*, and it has inspired a number of significant critical responses, especially regarding Dante's censuring influences as literary historiographer and his construction of a theological poetics based on trinitarian analogies.[56] Although this is not the place to attempt a detailed interpretation of the text and its critical reception, I would like to underline that both the historiographical and theological questions raised by the canto are played out against the backdrop of the material transcription and circulation of texts, especially the transcription and circulation of "Donne ch'avete." Bonagiunta's response to Dante is evidence of the previous dissemination of the *canzone,* that it was "divulgata tra le genti." The Luccan poet thus replaces the ladies of the *Vita Nova,* who had in turn replaced the *donne* of "Ben aggia." And whatever our final interpretation of the tropes of writing in the canto ("noto" [53]; "e' ditta dentro" [54]; "le vostre penne" [your pens/feathers][58]; "dittator" [he who dictates][59]; "stilo" [style/stylus][62]), at least at the literal level Dante is explicitly contrasting contemporary material practices of transcription and publication with an act of interior writing belonging solely to the author. Bonagiunta and Giacomo da Lentini are notaries, moreover, and the word play on *noto / Notaro* (53, 56) sets Love's internal "dictation" and the "book" of memory against the legal writing of the notaries, discussed in the previous chapter.[57]

As in the *Vita Nova,* Dante turns in *Purgatorio* 24 from the uncertainties of historic reception to the original moment of inspiration and composition. This return to the *cominciamento* underlines, once again, the place of memory and the individual psyche as an alternative to the social place of textual circulation. In addition, by textualizing and theologizing the material processes of book production, Dante is able to revisit his ambiguous status in the lyric canon and take aim at his more successful, better-published rivals. Still, while he may have the last word in the anthology of the *Commedia,* where, as a perceptive *compilator,* Dante chose Bonagiunta as a link between old and new schools, it is important to remember that in thirteenth-century manuscripts, it was the *sectatores* of Guittone who overlooked Dante.

In the final framing of "Donne ch'avete" in *Purgatorio* 24, Dante thus perfects two innovative authorial strategies that he first attempted in the *Vita Nova.* First, he suggests that the ultimate authentic text lies in the author's mind and not in the public reception and various material redactions of his texts. This shift in emphasis from reader to writer foreshadows textually what Petrarch and Boccaccio would later experiment with materially when introducing their autographed author's books, and it places renewed importance on authorial intention. Second, Dante presents his dialogue with other vernacular poets as transcending the contingent, contentious "nodo" of contemporary literary production and politics. The success of this last move is obvious when we consider that intertextual studies today more or less reproduce the strictly interpersonal, decontexualized scene represented in *Purgatorio* 24. Yet although Dante suggests, through Bonagiunta, that in the otherworld the historical specificity of poems and poetic styles no longer matters ("non vede più da l'uno a l'altro stilo" [cannot see one style from another][63]), texts are always manifest in material forms laden with specific social, political, and ideological content. In the next two chapters, the spaces of writing and the book will be examined as models for this contradiction between ineluctable historicity and the desire to transcend one's place.

chapter three

"A terrigenis mediocribus"

The *De vulgari eloquentia* and the
Babel of Vaticano 3793

> *The enslavement of language in prattle is joined by the enslavement*
> *of things in folly almost as its inevitable consequence. In this turning*
> *away from things, which was enslavement, the plan for the tower of*
> *Babel came into being, and linguistic confusion with it.*
> —Walter Benjamin, "On Language as Such
> and on the Language of Man"

In the second book of the *De vulgari eloquentia,* as part of his demonstration
of the superiority of the *canzone* form, Dante cites the care taken in preserving *canzoni* in written form, as those who often frequent books ("ut constat
visitantibus libros") can attest.[1] This reference to the material circulation of
texts, along with several others that will be discussed in more detail at the
end of this chapter, have gone unremarked by scholars of the *De vulgari*. Yet
when Dante tries to prove the inherent authority of *canzoni* by pointing to
their manifestations as written artifacts—artifacts inevitably informed by
historical and social forces—he illustrates a tension between textuality and
materiality, rhetoric and history, that characterizes the *De vulgari* as a whole.
As with other philosophical and linguistic discussions in the work, these references to the material status of texts are inextricably tied to the author's

new role as exiled intellectual producer. For this reason, when considering the abstract arguments of the treatise,[2] we also need to take into account Dante's precarious status as exiled vernacular author and the resulting precariousness of his writings—writings also understood in the physical sense as written records of texts.

Recent criticism of the *De vulgari* has facilitated a more historical understanding of the work. Pier Vincenzo Mengaldo, first and foremost, has studied it within specific literary and political contexts.[3] In particular, Mengaldo has demonstrated the extent to which the politics of contemporary vernacular literature and literary historiography lie behind Dante's linguistic discussions of the noble vernacular and Italian dialects. But he does not take the further step of examining how Dante's literary awareness was mediated by contemporary manuscripts and lyric anthologies and Dante's response to this in his Latin treatise. Dante's notion of contemporary vernacular poetry was conditioned by the way it was represented to readers of books, "visitantibus libros." Notwithstanding its undeniable originality and theoretical scope, the *De vulgari* remains enmeshed in the historicized processes of cultural reproduction, a world of vernacular readers and writers.

With this perspective in mind, the present chapter will explore the *De vulgari* as a response to the specific literary practices and literary historiography exemplified in the lyric anthology Vaticano Latino 3793. Although scholars generally agree that Dante's original exposure to the Italian lyric must have been through a manuscript similar to Vaticano 3793,[4] until now no detailed study has been undertaken to analyze the influence on the *De vulgari* of the tradition represented in the Vatican anthology.[5] Yet the two works share a remarkably similar geographical vision in their literary historiographies: both trace the evolution of different centers and schools of the early Italian lyric across the Italian peninsula, mapping the rise of an Italian literary canon from the Sicilian school to Bologna and the central city-states. In fact, if we consider the influence that Dante's literary historiography continues to have on literary critics and textual editors, we can see that, in many ways, Dante's reception of a manuscript similar to the Vatican anthology has formed the basis of our current perception of the early Italian lyric.

When viewed through the lens of the Vatican anthology, moreover, Dante's attack on municipal poetry in the *De vulgari* acquires specific social and political significance, as does his privileging of a poetics of space over one of place. In the previous chapter, we saw how the Vatican anthology, especially in the *tenzone* section, emphasizes the ritualized and performative function of the vernacular lyric, its role in constructing social cohesion among political elites. In the *De vulgari,* Dante turns this social use of poetry on its head, underlining the limits of a localized interpretive community and contrasting his intellectual, political, and linguistic mobility with the sort of regionalisms and regional poetics set forth in the overtly Florentine Vaticano 3793. In addition, by mapping out the literary traditions of his day, by literally putting other contemporary poets in their place, he frees a space for the more elusive "illustrious vernacular" and turns its social and political placelessness—given the poet's exile and the political fragmentation of the Italian peninsula—into an advantage. The rationalized space Dante theorizes for his own poetry and that of his circle contrasts with the confining local political context of municipal poetry.

In articulating this opposition between Italian and municipal poets, Dante relies in particular on the sort of dialogic poetic genres found in the Vatican anthology, especially the *contrasto.* In the traditional *contrasto*—in which male and female personae exchange expressive quips in a rhetorical game of seduction—gender and class differences are often overlaid with differences in language, diction, and literary style. Dante makes use of the sociolinguistic differences highlighted in the *contrasto* in order to draw a sharp distinction between noble vernacular and dialect, written literature and oral performance, abstract *canzone* and concretely localized *ballata.* Not only does he cite important *contrasti* such as "Rosa fresca aulentissima" and the so-called Canzone del Castra, "Una fermana scopai da Cascioli," in distinguishing the illustrious vernacular from local dialects, he also incorporates, as I will argue, the gendered and dialogic structure of the form into the treatise as a whole. In the movement from book 1 to book 2, for instance, Dante plays an increasingly masculine, rule-based Italian against a feminine, spontaneous vernacular. In this way, the aesthetic and social hierarchies enacted within the *contrasto* help Dante organize the emergent vernacular literature into strict categories according to use, content, and style—categories that were elsewhere still in formation and contested among different social groups.

At the same time that Dante makes use, in the *De vulgari,* of the hierarchical structure built into the *contrasto* and other dialogic poetic genres, he distances his own poetry from their more ambiguous aspects. In the Vatican anthology, as examined in the previous chapter, dialogic poems encapsulate the linguistic skepticism of the anthology, where the function of an utterance takes precedence over its veracity and where the author-figure behind a poem is often exposed as a blatantly fictional pose. For Dante, these features are examples of municipal poetics, to be sharply distinguished from his noble vernacular. Indeed, Dante's construction of authorship in the *De vulgari,* his interest in Adamic language, and his exploration of *canzone* space can all be read as responding to the Babelic instability inherent in dialogic genres, as they are represented in the Vatican anthology. From this perspective, the *De vulgari* sets up an opposition between an interior, disinterested "Edenic" poetics and the fallen linguistic world of the *contrasto* and the *tenzone fittizia,*[6] between "Donne ch'avete intelletto d'amore" and "Rosa fresca aulentissima." That Dante's own personal stake in these competing poetic practices and perspectives is even less evident than in the *Vita Nova* attests to his success in reframing contemporary cultural politics within a sacred and transhistorical narrative. As we shall see, in his revisionist accounts of Adam and Eve and of the Tower of Babel, Dante transforms contending aesthetic and political visions into biblical myths and universal linguistic truths.

The *compilatio* of Vaticano 3793 and Dante's Virtual *canzoniere*

The enduring influence of Dante's role as literary historiographer in the *De vulgari* has long been recognized. Modern editions and anthologies continue to reproduce versions of the thirteenth-century poetic canon first articulated in the *De vulgari,* with the same categories—from the Sicilian school to the *stilnovists*—established in that text. And much of our understanding of Dante's own early work stems from the *De vulgari*'s status as a self-anthology,[7] in much the same way that we rely on the self-citations in the *Vita Nova* or the *Commedia* for our understanding of his ideal literary biography. At the same time, at least since the publication of Contini's *Poeti del Duecento,* scholars have begun to qualify and question Dante's editorial choices and his role in the formation of the early Italian canon. The Guittonians have particularly benefited from this new approach to Italian literary history, with new analyses and editions of the texts of Monte Andrea, Panuccio del Bagno, and Guittone d'Arezzo himself.[8]

However, even these recent studies, concerned as they are with demonstrating the literary worth of their neglected authors, tend to overlook the historical meaning of Dante's anthological practices. Instead, his censuring editorial choices are explained psychologically, as part of a competitive and oedipal relationship to his contemporaries.[9] Whether admired or critiqued, Dante remains somehow above history and unaffected by political and social forces. And although a Bloomian "anxiety of influence" no doubt played an important role in Dante's revisionary historiography, it is important to recognize that this anxiety arose within a context of politically influenced canon formation and book production. For this reason, the growing critique of Dante's dominance as literary historiographer should take into account how Dante himself was reacting to contemporary representations and collections of Italian poetry, such as the three extant thirteenth-century *canzonieri,* the Vatican, Palatine, and Laurentian (in which the popularity of Guittone is as evident as the neglect of Dante's early lyrics.) Within this framework, as first recognized by the humanist Angelo Colucci—who, in bold handwriting, noted "Dante cita questa" (Dante cites this) next to the appropriate poems in the Vatican manuscript—the anthology of the *De vulgari* and the anthological tradition behind Vaticano 3793 share an intimate, if elusive, relation.[10]

Dante's critique of municipal poetics in the *De vulgari* is both more incisive and more comprehensible when read as a response to the municipalism of a lyric anthology such as Vaticano 3793. Indeed, the entire "deep structure" of the *De vulgari,* its peculiar geographical-chronological-linguistic narrative, recalls the same spatial-temporal paradigms found in Vaticano 3793. Although Mengaldo takes particular note of Dante's originality in mapping out the power struggles ("gioco di forze") of thirteenth-century poetry according to geographical criteria,[11] the layout of the Vatican anthology, with its allotment of individual quires for each poetic school / region of Italy, provides a literary geography even more complex and articulated than that found in the *De vulgari.* The massive manuscript, containing over a thousand poems, is arranged according to precise historical and geographical criteria (especially in the *canzone* section of the manuscript, quires 2–14), and each quire is dedicated to a particular school, region, or period of poetry. The anthology thus moves from the origins of Italian poetry in the Sicilian school (quires 2, 3, 4, and 5), through Emilia and the Tuscan communes (quire 6), to Guittone and Fra Guittone (quires 7–8), before ending up with the works of the Florentine poets represented primarily by Chiaro Davanzati and Monte Andrea (quires 9–13). The historiographical narrative that emerges from this innovative *compilatio* reproduces the shifts in political and cultural power that had occurred throughout the Italian peninsula and Sicily, underlining

above all the contemporary economic and literary dominance of the Florentine city-state.[12] Or, to put it another way, the Vatican anthology tells the story
of municipal poetics in Italy, with Florence embodying the most prestigious
vernacular of the time.

The discussion of Italian dialects in book 1 of the *De vulgari* is also an
anthology of sorts. Dante names numerous contemporary poets in his examples, and his citations of the languages of Italy often derive from or are
influenced by contemporary poems.[13] Indeed, with their similar geographical perspectives, Dante's "hunt" for the elusive "panther" of the illustrious
vernacular often reads as if he were wandering through the vast, heterogeneous "woodlands" of the Vatican anthology. Yet the shared structural elements between the anthology and the treatise serve only to highlight Dante's
selective rewriting of the historiographical tradition. The revision begins with
a process of exclusion and elimination or, in the words of the *De vulgari,* of
clearing the path and passing through a sieve. Dante first eliminates the most
heterogeneous poetic genres from his Vatican anthology "twin," dialogic
poems such as the Canzone del Castra and Cielo d'Alcamo's "Rosa fresca
aulentissima."[14] Next, Guittone is dismissed—the same Guittone who is allotted two entire quires (7 and 8) for his *canzoni* in Vaticano 3793 and who
plays an even more central role in the Palatine and Laurentian anthologies.
While singling out Guittone, Dante targets other notable Tuscan writers:

> Et in hoc solum plebeia dementat intentio, sed famosos quamplures
> viros hoc tenuisse comperimus: puta Guittonem Aretinum, qui nun-
> quam se ad curiale vulgare direxit, Bonagiuntam Lucensem, Gallum
> Pisanum, Minum Mocatum Senensem, Brunectum Florentinum, quo-
> rum dicta, si rimari vacaverit, non curialia sed municipalia tantum inve-
> nientur. (*DV* 1.13.1)

> [And it is not only the common people who lose their heads in this
> fashion, for we find that a number of famous men have believed as
> much: like Guittone d'Arezzo, who never even aimed at a vernacular
> worthy of the court, or Bonagiunta da Lucca, or Gallo of Pisa, or
> Mino Mocato of Siena, or Brunetto the Florentine, all of whose po-
> etry, if there were space to study it closely here, we would find to be
> fitted not for a court but at best for a city council.]

With that the provincial schools of Lucca, Pisa, and Siena, embodied by the poets Bonagiunta, Gallo, and Mino, are similarly removed from the path; in Vaticano 3793, they occupy the second half of the sixth quire. Finally, in the very same sentence, the minor Florentines (quire 9 in the Vatican anthology), represented solely by Brunetto Latini, are excised. Thus, in a single, viciously concise passage, Dante does away with the literary history spanning quires 6 to 9 in the Vatican anthology.

As Dante defines the illustrious vernacular negatively in book 1 of the *De vulgari*—indicating above all what it is not—he relies on the very municipality foregrounded in Vaticano 3793. More specifically, he appropriates its "topographical" structure to assign these regional poets their limited place in literary history. In this context, it is especially telling, even if it is at first unexpected, that Dante cites Brunetto Latini as the last poet in the list of important Tuscans who mistakenly believe their dialect is the most noble. Brunetto is not typically distinguished, after all, for his lyric production, with just one extant poem, the *canzone* "S'eo son distretto inamoratamente," recorded only in the Vatican anthology (V 181). His vernacular output was largely of a didactic nature, and his major work, the *Tresor,* was in Old French. Yet despite his limited poetic output, Brunetto represents perfectly that fusion of municipal politics and culture from which Dante distances himself throughout the *De vulgari*. Verbal action always serves an ancillary role to local political action for Brunetto, as is evident in his role as Florence's head secretary and laid out explicitly in his *Rettorica*. He even views the sexual politics implicit in love poetry as a subcategory within the culture of debate that characterizes city politics.[15] In the Vatican anthology as well, as we saw in the last chapter, vernacular production often serves a primarily ritualized and social function, building an imagined community among political elites, the "famosi viri" (*DV* 1.13.1) exemplifying the Tuscans in the *De vulgari*. But for Dante, whose very involvement in the Florentine priorate contributed to his exile, vernacular authorship needs to reach beyond the nexus of literature and local politics represented ideally by Brunetto. In constructing his new role as professional vernacular intellectual, Dante tries to free his texts from the overdetermined context of a single place.

When Dante turns to defining positively his illustrious vernacular, he creates a transhistorical narrative emphasizing the formal, thematic, and linguistic continuities among poets and poetic schools—a narrative that, at the

same time, relegates the localized contexts of literary acts. Having chiseled down the lyric canon in his discussion of the inferior dialects, Dante essentially reduces the tradition of the Vatican anthology to the Sicilian school, a few Siculo-Bolognese imitators, and a small circle of innovative Tuscan poets: Cino da Pistoia, Lapo Gianni,[16] Guido Cavalcanti, and himself. Chiaro Davanzati and Monte Andrea, who hold a privileged and concluding position in the Vatican anthology (quires 9–13) and whose poetry Dante must have known, are passed over in silence. The absence of Chiaro and Monte is particularly striking since, in some sense, the entire Vatican manuscript is constructed around presenting them, with their respective *leu* and *clus* styles, as the natural Florentine heirs of the two poetic traditions, inherited from Giacomo da Lentini and Bonagiunta da Lucca in Chiaro's case and from Inghilfredi da Lucca and Guittone d'Arezzo in Monte's. In fact, given his emphasis in the *De vulgari* on the formal experiments of the *petrose,* Dante can even be seen as substituting Cino and himself for Chiaro and Monte as the proper contemporary representatives of the two traditions.[17] In this way, he is also able to ignore the mediating influence of Guittone, evoking a history of the lyric (Siculo-Bolognese-stilnovist) similar to that found in the *rime* from the Memoriali bolognesi.

The substitution of the postmunicipal poets and recent exiles Cino and Dante for the ultra Florentines Chiaro and Monte reveals a fundamental difference between the literary geographies of the Vatican anthology and the *De vulgari.* In the Vatican anthology, literary prestige moves from region to region, quire to quire—continuously appropriated and reproduced within autonomous, self-contained territories (and discrete booklets). The works of Chiaro and Monte are thus meant to represent the currency of Florentine culture and politics, and their love poetry in the *canzone* section of the codex complements their participation in the political debates and *tenzoni* in the sonnet section. Dante's literary historiography, while taking geographical criteria into account, is equally concerned with tracing a diachronic narrative that cuts across different periods and linguistic areas (including France and Provence), instead linking poets by their shared themes (arms, love, rectitude), style, and meter. In exploring these protonational and romance literary traditions, Dante neglects the synchronic elements of the poems he cites, their contextualized place, and the social and political forces involved in their composition.

This is not to say that Dante is unconcerned in the *De vulgari* with the links between politics and culture, but rather that he sets up a clear distinction between the verse of those poets whose output is determined by and only intelligible within the confines of municipal politics and the larger scope, both temporally and spatially, of the texts of the illustrious poets. When it comes to the Sicilian school, for example, Dante establishes a protonational model for Italian poetry that actually has much in common with the representation of Sicilian-school poets in the Vatican anthology tradition: Mengaldo underlines Dante's originality and influence in defining the *scuola siciliana* by its institutional structure and affiliation instead of by strictly geographical or chronological criteria, "come unità omogenea di rimatori non necessariamente siciliani attorno a Federico e Manfredi e alla loro politica culturale" (as a uniform group of poets who, while not being necessarily Sicilian, are associated with Frederick and Manfred and their cultural politics).[18] Yet in the fifth quire of Vaticano 3793, the role of Frederick II's bureaucratic court in the history of Italian poetry is already clearly foregrounded. While the first three quires (quires 2–4, with quire 1 serving as an index) collect native Sicilian poets composing in the high and middling styles, the fifth quire consists of later poets and poets working on and even originating from the continent. The booklet opens with a "homegrown" poet, Mazzeo di Ricco from Messina, who must have been one of the last active Sicilian-school poets since Guittone dedicated a poem to him. Mazzeo is followed by various poets who clearly indicate the eastward movement of the Sicilian school onto the peninsula: King Enzo (Frederick's son imprisoned in Bologna from 1249 until his death in 1274); the Genoese Percivalle Doria (an imperial functionary active late in the Swabian reign); Compagnetto da Prato; and the Florentine Neri de' Visdomini. (The placement of King Enzo at the center of the quire is especially suggestive since his confinement in a prison in Bologna represents, on both a symbolic and practical level, a crucial moment in the *translatio* of Sicilian-school poetry to the central and northern communes.)

With respect to these "continental" Sicilian-school poets, the Vatican anthology shares with the *De vulgari* an almost Dionisottian understanding of the subtle interrelations of institutional power, culture, and geography. Yet even here, where Dante seems most influenced by the tradition of the Vatican anthology, his own geographical imagination diverges notably from it in one respect. The progress of the Sicilian school of the Vatican anthology is fundamentally expansionist, originally centered around Frederick's Sicilian court and then spreading to the central, northern, and Tuscan communes through poet-functionaries such as Percivalle Doria. In Dante's imagining of the Sicilian-school, on the contrary, everything moves toward a center; Sicilian poets and their language are defined by their contact with the royal court ("aula") and seat of empire ("regale solium") [*DV* 1.12.4].[19] The difference between these centrifugal and centripetal movements also reveals different perceptions of the social place of the Sicilian-school poets. Their careful arrangement in the quires of the Vatican anthology illustrates the overriding power of Frederick II's court; the poets themselves represent an expanding bureaucracy. Dante, on the other hand, is careful to emphasize the mobility of those poets who, like the stilnovists, are of noble heart and choose consciously and independently to stick close to the court: "Propter quod corde nobiles atque gratiarum dotati inherere tantorum principum maiestati conati sunt" (On this account, all who were noble of heart and rich in graces strove to attach themselves to the majesty of such worthy princes [Frederick and Manfred])[*DV* 1.12. 4]. If the poet-functionaries of the Sicilian-school are a vital part of the Vatican anthology's literary map, they are transformed in the *De vulgari* into professional intellectuals who are able to move freely upon that map.

Throughout the *De vulgari,* Dante similarly privileges distance and movement while marking place and fixity as negative values. He thus meticulously maps out the dialects of the Italian peninsula and Sicily only to showcase the interregionality of the illustrious vernacular, the swift-moving placeless panther that has left its scent in every city but made its home in none ("in qualibet redolet civitate, nec cubat in ulla" [*DV* 1.16. 4]). In a similar fashion, while the poets of the Sicilian school are described as freely aggregating around a centralized court, and the stilnovists, lacking such a court, are described as wandering the peninsula, the municipal poets are criticized because their language and poetry are overdetermined by their place of origin. Indeed, Dante repeatedly describes the poets of the noble vernacular as having physically departed from their native tongues. The Sicilians and Apulians speak in the noble vernacular only because they have turned away from their own original language ("indigenas ostendimus a proprio divertisse" [*DV* 1.4.6]), and the same formula is used to describe noble Bolognese, Tuscan, Romagnol, and Venetian poets. The use of a metaphor of spatial movement, expressed by the verb *divertere,* in these six distinct contexts casts the adoption of the illustrious vernacular as an act of physical abandonment, a desertion of the mother tongue.[20]

In an extended passage about the inhabitants of Pietramala, whom Dante ridicules for believing that their regional dialect is the original language of Adam, we can see the implications of this rhetoric of movement and distance for Dante himself as a recently exiled vernacular poet:

> In hoc, sicut etiam in multis aliis, Petramala civitas amplissima est, et patria maiori parti filiorum Adam. Nam quicunque tam obscene rationis est ut locum sue nationis delitiosissimum credat esse sub sole, hic etiam pre cunctis proprium vulgare licetur, idest maternam locutionem, et per consequens credit ipsum fuisse illud quod fuit Ade. Nos autem, cui mundus est patria velut piscibus equor, quanquam Sarnum biberimus ante dentes et Florentiam adeo diligamus ut, quia dileximus, exilium patiamur iniuste, rationi magis quam sensui spatulas nostri iudicii podiamus. Et quamvis ad voluptatem nostram sive nostre sensualitatis quietem in terris amenior locus quam Florentia non existat, revolventes et poetarum et aliorum scriptorum volumina, quibus mundus universaliter et membratim describitur, ratiocinantesque in nobis situationes varias mundi locorum et eorum habitudinem ad utrunque polum et circulum equatorem, multas esse perpendimus firmiterque censemus et magis nobiles et magis delitiosas et regiones et urbes quam Tusciam et Florentiam, unde sumus oriundus et civis, et plerasque nationes et gentes delectabiliori atque utiliori sermone uti quam Latinos. (*DV* 1.6.2–3)

> [In this, as in many other matters, Pietramala is a great city indeed, the home of the greater part of the children of Adam. For whoever is so misguided as to think that the place of his birth is the most delightful spot under the sun may also believe that his own language—his mother tongue, that is—is pre-eminent among all others; and, as a result, he may believe that his language was also Adam's. To me, however, the whole world is a homeland, like the sea to fish—though I drank from the Arno before cutting my teeth and love Florence so much that, because I loved her, I suffer exile unjustly—and I will weigh the balance of my judgment more with reason than with sentiment. And

although for my own enjoyment (or rather for the satisfaction of my own desire), there is no more agreeable place on earth than Florence, yet when I turn the pages of the volumes of poets and other writers, by whom the world is described as a whole and in its constituent parts, and when I reflect inwardly on the various locations of places in the world, and their relations to the two poles and the circle at the equator, I am convinced, and firmly maintain, that there are many regions and cities more noble and more delightful than Tuscany and Florence, where I was born and of which I am a citizen, and many nations and peoples who speak a more elegant and practical language than do the Italians.]

Unlike the foolish citizens of Pietramala, Dante's movement through space, his wandering and exile, allows for a more rational and relativist perspective on his native place—a perspective from the outside, as it were, supposedly free from the mystifications of purely subjective experience. While he recognizes his own emotional ties to Florence and Florentine (especially suggestive in this context is the link between breastfeeding, "quanquam Sarnum biberimus ante dentes," and the mother tongue),[21] his traveling and learning have now afforded him a more objective, cosmological perspective on the hierarchy of places, which takes into account measurable, scientific data such as a given site's distance from the equator and the two poles. In part, the journey Dante has undertaken to gain such knowledge is imaginative and literary, accomplished through reading books ("revolventes et poetarum et aliorum scriptorum volumina"), and in the conclusion to this chapter we will see the importance for Dante of the "space" of writing. For now, it is important to note that by making the experience of other places, whether through physical travel or reading, the sine qua non for any balanced judgment, Dante turns his exile into an authorizing strategy for the work as a whole.[22]

Contrasting Voices and the "Place" of Dialect Poetry

In affirming the oppositional categories of the *De vulgari*—illustrious versus inferior dialects, professional versus municipal authors, mobility versus social and geographical fixity—Dante relies heavily on dialogic genres such as the *contrasto*. Many of the examples he gives of regional dialects have characteristics of these stylized genres, including simplified subject-verb phrases, frequent basic interrogatives, vocatives, interjections, and other syntactic affinities evoking conventions of spoken exchange.[23] Two citations are unmistakably *contrasti:* the Canzone del Castra, "Una fermana scopai da Cascioli," and Cielo d'Alcamo's "Rosa fresca aulentissima." In the contemporary manuscript tradition, these two poems are preserved only in Vaticano 3793. In fact, along with other dialogic poems, they play an essential role in the Vatican anthology—although, as we will soon see, framed in a much different light than in the *De vulgari.* For now I want to focus on how the contrasting and often competing voices in genre poems such as "Una fermana scopai da Cascioli" (V 89) and "Rosa fresca aulentissima" (V 54) provide an underlying structure not only for Dante's description of the dialects of Italy, but also for the treatise as a whole.

Scholars typically treat the importance of the *contrasto* in the *De vulgari* within the context of dialect parody—or, as Dante identifies it, the "improperium" (*DV* 1.11.5)."[24] One of Mengaldo's most important contributions is to have demonstrated that, like poems Dante explicitly mentions as *improperia*—the Canzone del Castra and "Enter l'ora del vesper, ciò fu del mes d'ochiover" (*DV* 1.11. 5)—the other citations of inferior dialects in book 1 of the *De vulgari* are similarly informed by an established literary tradition of linguistic parody.[25] This tradition—as Gianfranco Contini, Cesare Segre, and others have noted—evolved largely out of dialogic genres, beginning with the Old Occitan *pastorela.*[26] In the traditional *pastorela,* the aristocratic knight and the peasant woman, seducer and seduced, are armed with distinct and disparate linguistic and rhetorical skills. In Rambaldo di Vaqueiras's "Domna, tant vos ai preiada," the difference in gender and class is explicitly codified linguistically as the contrast between the literary Occitan vernacular and the "popular" Genoese dialect.[27] In many ways, the Italian *contrasto* is a version of this latter variation of the *pastorela,* in which the representation of female and popular voices provides an opportunity to explore the politics of language. Yet in a suggestive development whose relevance will soon become apparent, protagonists in the Italian *contrasto* often demonstrate an increased strategic fluidity in their linguistic choices, switching at will between courtly and popular registers, literary koiné and characteristic regionalisms.

"Rosa fresca aulentissima" and other *contrasti* of the *De vulgari* are typically explained as precocious examples of, in Benedetto Croce's terms, "poesia dialettale riflessa."[28] In this view, the literary use of dialects reflects, integrates, and stems from an already established national literary language. But why should we assume that a noble, literary Italian is a necessary antecedent and departure point ("antecedente e punto di partenza"), in Contini's words, for dialect poetry and not the other way around?[29] After all, critics today are still unsure of the status of Dante's shadowy noble vernacular, whether it really existed for Dante as a functional, spoken language or whether it was an abstract ideal. And, as Dionisotti importantly pointed out, the establishment of Florentine Tuscan as a dominant literary language is possible only *after* Dante and not *for* Dante at the time he composed the *De vulgari*.[30] Given the political and linguistic fragmentation of Dante's Italy, the illustrious vernacular may depend more for its legitimacy on dialect poetry than dialect poetry does on the illustrious vernacular, since a parodied dialect always implicitly points to its counterpart, a more prestigious and transregional koiné.

In a similar fashion, the very nobility of Dante's noble vernacular is defined against, and in a sense depends on, the native female and popular voices evoked in the *contrasto* tradition. An essential part of his definition of the illustrious vernacular proceeds *ex negativa,* demonstrating what it is *not* by citing the popular and feminine voices of the dialogic tradition; only through the expressionist parodies of such voices can Dante posit its opposite, a protonational Italian literary language. Later in book 2, when Dante insists that the illustrious vernacular is not suitable for all, he similarly makes use of cultural prejudices and assumptions associated with the stereotype of the *rusticus:* "nemo enim montaninis rusticana tractantibus hoc dicet esse conveniens" (for no one would suggest that it [the illustrious vernacular] is appropriate for mountain dwellers when they discuss country matters)[*DV* 2.1.7]. In this way, the seemingly natural sociolinguistic distinctions typical of the *contrasto* can be drawn on by Dante in order to accomplish the subtle shift in the *De vulgari* from the dyad Latin/vernacular to illustrious vernacular / inferior vernacular. In order to create a Latinate, ruled-based Italian, the vernacular itself must first be split into two conceptual categories: male and female, noble and popular, protonational and dialect.[31] In fact, if we take a step back and look at the *De vulgari* as a whole, the entire structure could be characterized as functioning like an extended *pastorela* or *contrasto,* with masculine literary citations competing with the feminine and popular dialect voices. Of course, it is difficult to ascertain the extent to which Dante deliberately and consciously borrowed on the *contrasto* in structuring his treatise, yet it seems likely that the fundamentally dialogic (and even dialectical) nature of the work was influenced in some respect by the dialogic aspects of such poems, especially given the examples of *contrasti* cited in book 1.

Dante's approach to the *contrasto* is not, however, without ambivalence and even inconsistency. And his appropriation of the multivocal structure of dialogic poetry in defining his illustrious vernacular should not be taken as an unqualified endorsement of it. On the contrary, Dante carefully distances his poetics of interiority from the more semiotically ambiguous elements of the *contrasto* and the *tenzone fittizia.* In particular, his attempts at establishing a necessary relation between empirical author and lyric voice, especially in his discussion of *convenientia,* or poetic decorum, stand in sharp contrast to the fictional personae and fluid linguistic registers of dialogic poems. Indeed, Dante's engagement in the *De vulgari* with poetic forms such as the *contrasto* may be indicative above all of a problem he needs to resolve or at least contain in constructing his model of poetic authorship. This is especially evident in the way his treatment of the contrasti "Rosa fresca aulentissima" and "Una fermana scopai da Cascioli" differs from their presentation in Vaticano 3793.

In the Vatican anthology, "Rosa fresca aulentissima" (V 54) opens a quire (4) within the Sicilian-school section that emphasizes middling and comic genres such as the *devinalh* by the jongleur Ruggieri Apugliese and the popularizing works of Giacomino Pugliese. Many of these poems showcase the authors' ability to imitate popular and female voices and inhabit different literary personae. In the case of "Rosa fresca aulentissima," critics have noted that the two speakers of the poem (one male, one female) are themselves adept at shifting between literary and popular registers, ranging from the courtly praise of "Rosa fresca aulentissima" (Fresh sweet-smelling rose) [1] to the more pragmatic "a lo letto ne gimo a la bon'ora" (let's go right to bed) [159], and that these contrasting levels of diction are often further overlaid with differences between a Sicilian-school koiné and local-dialect usage.[32] The male character is particularly skillful at switching between literary and linguistic registers—not surprisingly since he is referred to in the poem as a jongleur ("canzoneri" [39]); as a literary performer, manipulating linguistic conventions would form part of his professional expertise.

In Dante's highly selective treatment of the "Rosa fresca aulentissima" in the *De vulgari,* he ignores the possibility that the speakers might be manipulating social and linguistic codes, and instead emphasizes their fixed origins. Dante attributes the text to ordinary Sicilians ("a terrigenis mediocribus"

[*DV* 1.12.6]) for whom he excludes any literary or linguistic self-consciousness. In fact, by quoting the third line of the poem ("Tragemi d'este focora—se t'este a bolontate" [*DV* 1.12.6]) instead of the more literary incipit, Dante underlines regionalisms such as "focora," "este," and "bolontate" that locate the linguistic community behind the *contrasto* to a particular place.[33] These are the socially middling ("mediocribus") inhabitants who lack the mobility and self-determination necessary to turn away from their mother tongue, as did the illustrious first poets of the Sicilian-school tradition. They are confined to and by place, literally born of the earth, *terrigenae,* like the dragon's teeth sowed by Cadmus. No doubt the primary meaning of this curious expression "a terrigenis mediocribus" is simply to single out the ordinary, average natives of Sicily.[34] Yet the constricting sense of physical place evoked by the *terra* of "terrigenis" alongside the *medius* of "mediocribus" is also difficult to ignore; these Sicilian speakers are oddly landlocked.

If the speakers of "Rosa fresca aulentissima" are linguistically and geographically trapped, in Dante's brief discussion of the other *contrasto,* "Una fermana scopai da Cascioli," he instead focuses on the spatial and temporal distance of the poem's author. In the Vatican anthology, "Una fermana scopai da Cascioli" (V 89) is attributed to "Messer Osmano," suggesting that the author is from the town of Osimo in the Marches (Osmano was also a common surname in the Marches in this period). If the poem, which employs several linguistic features characteristic of dialects from the Marches, was really written in Florence by a Florentine, as critics concur, the anonymous Florentine compiler of the anthology is here conflating author with author-figure, empirical poet with fictional persona.[35] As in the other dialogic poems in the manuscript, "Una fermana scopai da Cascioli" thus participates in an act of artifice on two levels. The male protagonist seeks to rhetorically deceive and seduce the *fermana,* while the author of the poem assumes a fictional persona, a sort of poetic mask.

In identifying the author of "Una fermana scopai da Cascioli" with a "Florentinus nomine Castra" (*DV* 1.11.4)—the only attributed citation of a regional dialect in the *De vulgari*—Dante marks an unambiguous distance between empirical poet and fictional persona. Between Messer Osmano and "Florentinus" Castra, he inserts that geographical distance necessary in his view for proper judgment and perspective. The dialect of the Marches is thus pushed to the periphery and viewed from an emergent Florentine center. In classifying "Una fermana scopai da Cascioli" as an *improperium,* a linguistic parody of a popular dialect, Dante creates a further distance between author and subject matter, since the authorial perspective in parody is always posited from an external, and supposedly superior, vantage point. Finally, by calling attention to the poem's studied metrical structure—it is perfectly bound, "recte atque perfecte ligatam" (*DV* 1.11.4)—he introduces a temporal distance between the fictional enunciation of the dialogue and its carefully crafted written form. As we shall soon see, this spatial rendering of acoustic speech, as a metrical form, is crucial for Dante's conceptualization of the canzone space and speaks to the essential notion of place and space in the *De vulgari*.

In his contrasting presentation of "Rosa fresca aulentissima" and "Una fermana scopai da Cascioli," Dante continues to valorize distance and perspective in poetic expression, with the middling Sicilians and the Florentine Castra at diametric ends of the spectrum. At the same time, his need to clarify—even at the risk of overdetermining—the social, geographical, and authorial origins of both poems, albeit in opposite ways, betrays a deep-seated anxiety about the potential ambiguities inherent in the *contrasto* form. Indeed, the same fluidity among authorial personae and linguistic registers that characterizes the *contrasto,* making it (and "Rosa fresca aulentissima" in particular) central to the ideological and aesthetic structure of the Vatican anthology, potentially undermines both Dante's new role as exiled poet and his new autobiographical poetics. Beginning with the *Vita Nova,* as we have seen in the previous chapter, Dante constructs a poetics of interiority, in which the representation of the psychic life of the poet outweighs the conventional social functions of vernacular texts. In the *contrasto* and the *tenzone fittizia,* on the other hand, linguistic registers are conventions to be appropriated at will for the ultimate goal of erotic seduction. The fictional personae themselves are also mere conventions, stock characters that may have little to do with the authors who created them. In the Vatican anthology, this sort of conventionality reaches an apex with the imitation of popular, female, and political voices, all serving to hold together an often-divided community of poet-functionaries. But once exiled, Dante had even less to do with this ritualized civic function of vernacular poetry. He instead needed to create a space where poetic authorship was no longer ancillary to one's social position but identical to it. Whatever else we make of Dante's contradictory treatment of "Rosa fresca aulentissima" and "Una fermana scopai da Cascioli, " he was clearly interested in fixing their attribution, in answering the question, who wrote it?—a question that now had fundamental socioeconomic and existential repercussions for him.

In this light, Dante's innovative treatment of poetic decorum, *convenientia,* in the second book of the *De vulgari,* can be seen as responding to the literary tradition of the *contrasto,* viewed by Dante as a threat to his construction of vernacular authorship. While the importance of matching language, style, and subject matter belongs to a long-standing rhetorical tradition, Dante introduces an almost metaphysical link between individual author and poetic expression, between the personal character of the poet, namely his "scientia" and "ingenium" (*DV* 2.1.8), and the language, style, subject matter, and even metrical form employed.[36] His insistence on a nonaccidental connection between the inner conceptions of the mind and the exterior form of the poem ("optimis conceptionibus optima loquela conveniet" [the best language is suited to the best conceptions][*DV* 2.1.8]) is incompatible with the interchangeability of linguistic registers and authorial personae of the *contrasti* cited in book 1. This interiorization of poetic decorum coincides in the treatise, moreover, with Dante's most explicit attempt at establishing poetic labor alongside other recognized social estates and professional occupations such as merchants, knights, and rulers ("mercari, militare ac regere" [*DV* 2.1.7]). When, in this section, Dante compares the illustrious vernacular, for example, to the best horse of the best knight,[37] he seeks to naturalize his professional status as vernacular author and, at the same time, to lay claim to an autonomous sphere of literary production that is not subordinate to its social uses. To do so, his theory of *convenientia* needs to counter the mere conventionality of poetic discourse characterizing dialogic poems and the Vatican anthology.

Dante's Genesis and the Babelic Language of Vaticano 3793

With the contrast between his poetics of "conceptiones" (*DV* 2.1.8) and the authorial masks of "Rosa fresca aulentissima," Dante returns to a literary and ethical problem that has troubled him from the very beginning of his poetic career. Already in the *Vita Nova,* he had attempted to distance his poetics of interiority and disinterested *laude* from the blatant fictionality and insincerity of the *contrasto* and the *tenzone fittizia.* However, while in the *Vita Nova* the dialogic tradition remained an unnamed pressure lurking outside the text, in the *De vulgari* Dante directly confronts and even cites examples of *contrasti*. If in the *Vita Nova* the reframing of "Donne ch'avete intelletto d'amore" responds implicitly to the dialogic aspect of "Ben aggia l'amoroso e dolce chore," in the *De vulgari* the discussion surrounding "Donne ch'avete" instead responds explicitly to the dialogic tradition informing "Ben aggia"—the sort of *contrasti* evoked in book 1 of the treatise.[38] At the same time, Dante masks his personal stake in these competing literary practices by reframing them as universal and even biblical truths. In his discussions of the *primiloquium* of Adam and Eve and the construction of the Tower of Babel, Dante creates a sacred and mythic allegory of contemporary poetic practices that foreshadows the totalizing perspective of the *Commedia*. While in the *Commedia* Dante views contemporary political and literary questions from the perspective of the end of time, in the *De vulgari,* as we shall soon see, he reads them from the perspective of the beginning.

Recent scholarship has begun to address the highly idiosyncratic retelling of Genesis in the first section of the *De vulgari*—previously neglected in lieu of the more analytical sections of the treatise. Zygmunt Barański, in particular, has signaled the important ethical aspects of Dante's personalized biblical poetics.[39] What has gone largely unexamined is the degree to which the·biblical exempla Dante recounts are enmeshed in contemporary politics and poetics. Critics have rightly noted, for example, that Dante emphasizes the linguistic nature of the sins behind the Fall and the Tower of Babel.[40] I propose, in addition, that Dante's treatment of these two linguistic sins—which frame the biblical narrative and, to an extent, the *De vulgari* as a whole—is specifically aimed at his poetic rivals as well as at the political and economic forces that led to his exile.

Dante's biblical revisionism focuses first on the question of Adamic language and the *primiloquium*. And as with his search for an illustrious vernacular, his investigation of humankind's original language and first utterances begins with an act of exclusion: Dante initiates his discussion by eliminating the possibility that Eve spoke first. With unfortunate misogynist reasoning and questionable philological methods, he insists that, in spite of the evidence found in scripture, "in scriptis" (*DV* 1.4.3), a woman could not have been the first to speak. While the slight to Eve and female speech is obvious, the question remains: Why bring up the case of Eve in the first place? After all, despite Dante's claims about the evidence of scripture, Adam, and not Eve, was first to speak when he named the animals—an episode that is curiously glossed over in the treatise. Critics have typically explained away this apparent *lapsus* on Dante's part by concentrating on the generic and grammatical status of Adam's speech, arguing that, as an example of monologic versus dialogic speech or of unrelated words versus syntactically constructed meaning, the naming of the animals was excluded.[41] In an original contribution, Barański has instead suggested that the entire question of who spoke first is a false problem, with Eve serving simply as a "smokescreen" to call attention to Dante's real interest in the moral origins of human speech in Adam.[42] Yet when Dante's discussion of the *primiloquium* is viewed from the perspective of contemporary poetics instead of biblical exegesis, many of these contradictions no longer appear as such.[43] I believe that Dante's ranking of Adam's first words above Eve's conversation with the serpent has to do less with his interpretation of the Bible than with the relation of the biblical speech acts to a contemporary hierarchy of poetic styles, in which Dante was himself implicated. In this context, even the naming of the animals, as we shall see in the last section of this chapter, is not completely elided but rather displaced.

Eve's sin is certainly one of language, but it occurs within a very specific form of speech, a disputation, which Dante foregrounds by identifying it as the source of all fallen language. It is important to remember that in Dante's account there are two actors involved in the linguistic travesty of the Fall: a male seducer, the "diabolus" himself, and a female seducee. His only direct citation, moreover, of the biblical text comes with Eve's initial attempt to counter the serpent's blandishments, when she objects that eating from the Tree of Knowledge is forbidden by God ("precepit nobis Deus").[44] Dante thus focuses on the moment in the dialogue when Eve is still resisting the serpentine speech of the Great Seducer—reproduced onomatopoetically in "dyabolo sciscitanti" (*DV* 1.4.2)—the moment, in other words, when she is still "contrasting" with him. In the linguistic deception and seduction of the episode as well as in the use of the female voice, we can see the outline of the first, archetypal *contrasto* in human history. Dante thus posits as the cause of Man's Fall a deceptive linguistic exchange reminiscent of the dialogic poems found in the Vatican anthology and cites it in his discussion of inferior dialects. Even the peculiar discussion about whether it is the serpent or the Devil who is speaking here recalls the ambiguity in dialogic genres between author and fictional persona. When Dante fixes the Devil as the true author of the speech (*DV* 1.2.6), he effectively establishes a precedent for his unmasking of the Florentine Castra as the true author of "Una fermana scopai da Cascioli."

In a pattern we encounter repeatedly in the *De vulgari,* Dante uses the negative example of Eve to define better his own poetics, in this case represented by Adam's speech. In Dante's biblical narrative, Adam was the first to speak, praising his Maker, and the first human word was the Hebrew word for God, "El," countering the "Heu" of the children of Eve (*DV* 1.4.4). Guglielmo Gorni has already noted the similarities between the *primiloquium* of Adam and the *cominciamento* of "Donne ch'avete" in the *Vita Nova,* between the spontaneous expression of "gaudium" (*DV* 1.4.4) by the first man and the *poesia della lode* of the new poet.[45] In fact, Dante frames Adam's praise of God within a socially insular space in a manner similar to that in which he situated his disinterested praise for the lady within private rooms and feminized locales; he places Adam's speech within the safe confines of the Garden of Eden before the Fall, where there are no other human beings to persuade or deceive: "non oportebat illum loqui, cum solus adhuc homo existeret" (there was no need for him to speak since he was the only human being yet in existence) [*DV* 1.5.2]. The lack of human community, combined with God's foreknowledge of Adam's mind ("licet Deus sciret, immo presciret" [*DV* 1.5.2]), effectively makes the *primiloquium* unnecessary on a rhetorical level, distinguishing its purpose from the normally goal-oriented and functional uses of language. Adam's praise can thus remain disinterested, an example of Edenic language that participates in a pre–market economy of the gift: "voluit tamen et ipsum loqui, ut in explicatione tante dotis gloriaretur ipse qui gratis dotaverat" ([despite his foreknowledge,] God still wished that Adam should speak, so that in the employment of such a great gift, He who had freely given should be glorified) [*DV* 1.5.2].

In the divergent first utterances of Eve and Adam, Dante thus mythologizes the origins of two contending poetic traditions which he first delineated in the *Vita Nova*—on the one hand, the fraudulent rhetoric of the *contrasto* and the *tenzone fittizia* and, on the other, the new interiority of the *poesia della lode.* As the *De vulgari* continues, these models of speech take on ever greater resonance, encompassing the differences between municipal poetics and illustrious *canzoni;* "Rosa fresca aulentissima" and "Donne ch'avete"; and the Guittonians and the stilnovists. While in the *Vita Nova* Dante's personal involvement in these polarized traditions gradually acquires typological and even Christological significance, in the *De vulgari,* conversely, sacred narratives and biblical types provide the interpretive framework in which to read the subsequent discussions of literary historiography and contemporary poetics.

When considered as a similarly organizing foundation myth, Dante's retelling of the construction of the Tower of Babel stands out for its significance within the text as a whole.[46] Dante infuses his innovative rendition of the exemplum with a quality of detail and visual immediacy that, as critics have noted, provides a striking glimpse of contemporary Florentine building construction, even as it draws on the literary precedent of Dido's Carthage from the *Aeneid*.[47] Nevertheless, this remains one of the most misunderstood passages in the entire treatise:

> Presumpsit ergo in corde suo incurabilis homo, sub persuasione gigantis Nembroth, arte sua non solum superare naturam, sed etiam ipsum naturantem, qui Deus est, et cepit edificare turrim in Sennaar, que postea dicta est Babel, hoc est 'confusio', per quam celum sperabat ascendere, intendens inscius non equare, sed suum superare Factorem. O sine mensura clementia celestis imperii! Quis patrum tot sustineret insultus a filio? Sed exurgens non hostili scutica sed paterna et alias verberibus assueta, rebellantem filium pia correctione nec non memorabili castigavit.
>
> Siquidem pene totum humanum genus ad opus iniquitatis coierat: pars imperabant, pars architectabantur, pars muros moliebantur, pars amussibus regulabant, pars trullis linebant, pars scindere rupes, pars mari, pars terra vehere intendebant, partesque diverse diversis aliis operibus indulgebant; cum celitus tanta confusione percussi sunt ut, qui omnes una eademque loquela deserviebant ad opus, ab opere multis diversificati loquelis desinerent et nunquam ad idem commertium convenirent. Solis etenim in uno convenientibus actu eadem loquela remansit: puta cunctis architectoribus una, cunctis saxa volventibus una, cunctis ea parantibus una; et sic de singulis operantibus accidit. Quot quot autem exercitii varietates tendebant ad opus, tot tot ydiomatibus tunc genus humanum disiungitur; et quanto excellentius exercebant, tanto rudius nunc barbariusque locuntur. (*DV* 1.7.4–7)

[Incorrigible humanity, therefore, led astray by the Giant Nimrod, presumed in its heart to outdo in skill not only nature but the source of its own nature, who is God; and began to build a tower in Sennaar, which afterward was called Babel (that is, "confusion"). By this means human beings hoped to climb up to heaven, intending in their foolishness not to equal but to excel their creator. Oh boundless mercy of the kingdom of heaven! What other father would have borne so many insults from his child? Yet, rising up not with an enemy's whip but that of a father, already accustomed to dealing out punishment, He chastised His rebellious offspring with a lesson as holy as it was memorable.

Almost the whole of the human race had collaborated in this work of evil. Some gave orders, some drew up designs; some built walls, some measured them with plumb lines, some smeared mortar on them with trowels; some were intent on breaking stones, some on carrying them by sea, some by land and other groups still were engaged in other activities—until they were struck by a great blow from heaven. Previously all of them had spoken one and the same language while carrying out their tasks; but now they were forced to leave off their labors, never to return to the same cooperative endeavor, because they had been split into groups speaking different languages. Only among those who were engaged in a particular activity did their language remain unchanged; so, for instance, there was one for all architects, one for all the carriers of stones, one for all the stone-breakers, and so on for all the different operations. As many as were the types of work involved in the enterprise, so many were the languages by which the human race was fragmented; and the more skill required for the type of work, the more rudimentary and barbaric the language they now spoke.]

Scholars have long recognized Dante's originality here in structuring the punishment of Babel by professional group;[48] just as the various professionals and artisans collaborated ("coierat" [*DV* 1.7.6]) on the prideful tower, now they are punished, divided into numerous mutually unintelligible tongues. Dante's elaboration on the biblical story has customarily been read as evidence of his wholesale condemnation of Florentine urbanism and the values of the guild system on which it was based.[49] In this view, Dante rejects the polis as representative of the Augustinian earthly city.

Yet, when compared to the building of Carthage in the *Aeneid,* it is not at all clear that Dante is describing the building of a city in the aforementioned passage—at least not a city-republic. While in the *Aeneid* (1.418–444) the citizens of Carthage build roads, gates, a theater, and a citadel, the inhabitants of Sennaar are not interested in civic architecture. Even less are they interested in instituting laws and electing judges and a hallowed senate, unlike

the Carthaginians described in the *Aeneid* ("iura magistratusque legunt sanc-
tumque senatum" [1.426]). Instead, under the antisocial influence of the
giant Nimrod, they build a tower. As a work of architecture, the tower was
antithetical to civic buildings such as the Palazzo del Popolo and the Palazzo
Comunale; it provided the nobility with a military advantage over the popu-
lace and was seen as the ultimate symbol of magnate arrogance and lawlessness. Dante's critique thus seems directly to target Florence's ruling oligarchy,
that alliance of nobles and international banking elites, and not simply the
concept of the city.[50] In the promotion of the Ordinances of Justice, the *popolo* government attempted to outlaw the construction of towers and punish
the magnates,[51] and here, at the beginning of human society, God Himself
seems to sanction this class-based legislation when he marginalizes the most
prominent social groups by assigning them the lowest languages.

Of course, the exiled Dante was hardly a card-carrying member of the
popolo at this point, and one cannot forget that his political allegory of Babel
also strikes at the actions of the professional guilds. But the guilds of Dante's
Babel are not so much attacked in themselves as they are charged with abandoning the guiding principle of their *popolo* government—the principle of
lawful self-determination, of *universitas*. Along with the rest of society, they
are seduced by ("sub persuasione"[*DV* 1.7.4]) the individual will of Nimrod
and his vision of the Tower of Babel—the scope of which projects a vision
of expansionist, protocapitalist Florence ("pars mari, pars terra vehere inten-
debant"[*DV* 1.7.6]) that threatens to swallow up the *libertas* of both city and
guild. Indeed, it is this cooptation of municipal politics by the ruling elites and
the forces of international finance that Dante saw as leading to the events of
his exile.

For the rest of the *De vulgari,* Dante attempts, in his analysis of *grammatica* and the illustrious vernacular, to recuperate, at least aesthetically, the
principles of law and *universitas* promulgated by the experimental government
of the *popolo*.[52] In contrast to the factional justice of the magnates (symbolized
most brutally by the violence of the *vendetta*), the *popolo* represented themselves as a self-regulating and self-determining association based on law and
consent, a political vision derived from the experience of the guilds. This associational form of polity is elegantly expressed in the Ordinances of Justice: "that is considered most perfect which consists of all of its parts and
is approved by the judgment of all."[53] In the same spirit, Dante presents the
stability of Latin not as stemming from a transhistorical and transcendent

authority, but as the historical product of consent and law: "Hec cum de comuni consensu multarum gentium fuerit regulata, nulli singulari arbitrio videtur obnoxia, et per consequens nec variabilis esse potest" (Its rules having been formulated with the commom consent of many peoples, this [*grammatica*] can be subject to no individual will; and, as a result, it cannot change) [*DV* 1.9.11]. He blames the mutability of the vernacular tongue across time and space on unregulated will, on the isolated, lawless expression of "singulari arbitrio"—as in the archetypal example of the giant Nimrod. In order to counter the tendency of human nature toward fragmentation, man created *grammatica* by a process of common accord, "de comuni consensu." These comparisons between language and the law—first with reference to Latin and later, especially in book 2, to the illustrious vernacular—demonstrate a continuity in Dante's postexilic imagination with the rhetoric and ideology of the *popolo*. True, Dante distances himself throughout the treatise from provincial municipal politics, but even his imagined Italian court and protonationalist state can be viewed as a way of reclaiming, in a new form, the principles of the *popolo* rather than as a wholesale rejection of them.

The construction of the Tower of Babel thus represents nothing less than an ideological betrayal on the part of the nonaristocratic citizens. Only God, as mentioned above, seems not to have forgotten the spirit of the *popolo* and of the Ordinances of Justice, as evident in the class bias of his punishment: "Et quanto excellentius exercebant, tanto rudius nunc barbariusque locuntur" (And the more skill required for the type of work, the more rudimentary and barbaric the language they now spoke)[*DV* 1.7.7]. God's solution for the prideful builders of Babel is also notable because, in its ironic symmetry, it can be seen as a prototype for the style of punishment in the *Inferno,* the *contrapasso,* where worldly status and power are often turned on their head. And yet, at this point in his career, Dante's social mythmaking also signals a retreat from direct political engagement, coinciding with the antidemocratic victories of Florence's ruling elite and his own forced exile from politics. In this context, the "now," *nunc,* referred to in the imagined social punishment of Babel is both loaded and ambiguous, standing somewhere between the social justice formerly possible through legislative means and the retributive wish fulfillment that will characterize the *after*life of the *Commedia*.

One function of this temporally ambiguous *nunc* is to bring to the forefront the significance of the story of Babel for contemporary literary practices. As with Dante's descriptions of the speech of Adam and Eve, the story of Babel sheds light on his discussion of contemporary poets and poetry. Namely, as Dante illustrates in the rest of book 1 and as demonstrated in the Vatican anthology, the most prominent citizens of Dante's time—the "famosi viri" (famous men) and not only the "plebeia" (common folk) [*DV* 1.13.1]—were indeed speaking the lowest languages, in a sense, when they imitated the popular and female voices in genres such as the *contrasto* and the *tenzone fittizia*. By associating Guittone and the Guittonians, in particular, with the builders of Babel, Dante thus ingeniously turns their present-day popularizing, their "plebescere,"[54] into a sign of an original divine punishment. The speech of the builders of Babel, moreover, like the Babelic poets of Vaticano 3793 and the municipal poets of the *De vulgari,* is primarily functional and goal-oriented. With the scattering of languages, they are forced to abandon their labors and with them an expansionist project fueled by market forces. Nowhere else does Dante draw a stronger line between his supposedly self-contained Edenic poetics and the fallen, utilitarian "prattle" described by Walter Benjamin in the epigraph to this chapter. The distance between the *nunc* of Babel and the *nunc* of the *De vulgari* finally collapses with the description of those few individuals ("minima pars"[*DV* 1.7.8]) who continued to speak in Hebrew because they stood aside and refused to participate in the building of Babel, "those who had neither joined in the project nor praised it, but instead, thoroughly disdaining it, had made fun of the builder's stupidity (sed graviter detestantes stoliditatem operantium deridebant)" [*DV* 1.7.8]. Amongst those chosen few who stood apart, observing and deriding Babel's builders, we can recognize the author of the *De vulgari* himself, who has just represented his exile as providing him with valuable physical and intellectual distance, and who will enact, in his use of the *improperium* throughout book 1, the same ridicule of contemporary society exemplified by that "minima pars."

The Space of the *canzone* and the Place of Writing

In his examination of Babel, Dante underlines the foolish pride, the "superbam stultitiam" (*DV* 1.7.3) of Nimrod and his followers. The construction of the tower, like the presumption of Eve, is motivated by the arrogant desire to surpass the creation of the divine architect, "suum superare Factorem" (*DV* 1.7.4). Missing from Dante's account are the more vexed questions of memory and place. For, in the text of the Vulgate, the inhabitants of Shinar are quite explicit about their reasons for building the tower. They want to leave a record of their existence, a mark of their name, before being scattered to the ends of the earth: "Et celebremus nomen nostrum antequam dividamur in universas terras" (Gen. 11:4). The attempt by humankind's first exiles, the "filii Adam"(Gen. 11:5), to counter the flux of time through the stability of place, could not have left the newly exiled Dante unaffected. The desire to mark one's place before the inevitability of temporal oblivion is a fundamental aspect of Western civilization, from the ill-fated Tower of Babel to the transcriptions in the margins of the Memoriali bolognesi. Although in his derision of the tower Dante signals his distance — both spatial and intellectual — from the worshippers of place, no other biblical example comes closer to describing the impetus behind the never completed *De vulgari*: Dante's overriding desire, exacerbated by political and geographical instability, to ensure the proper place for his texts in literary history.

In part, Dante counters his complicity with the phallic and ego-driven creation of Babel, with its inscription onto a specific topographical place, by insisting on a spatialized microcosmic poetics. Dante's description, in book 2 of the *De vulgari,* of the metrical form of the *canzone* identifies the spatial demarcation of the stanza as the locus of poetic creation, evoking the original act of creation of the divine architect. As Durling and Martinez have argued, Dante's technical explanation of contemporary poetic practices (especially regarding the division [*diesis*] of a stanza into *frons, sirma, pedes,* and *versus*) reproduces in microcosmic form the Neoplatonic principles involved in the divine creation and ordering of the universe, the contrasting forces of Same and Other.[55] Seen in this light, Adam's naming of the animals — the human act in Genesis corresponding most closely to divine creation — is not so much elided in Dante's discussion of the *primiloquium* as relocated, in its essential form, to the discussion of *canzone* space. For our purposes, it is especially important that the microcosmic *canzone* space, with its vertical correspondences between poem and universe, individual soul and God, offers an alternative to the limits of horizontal topographical place.[56] The harmonious arrangement of verses within the metrical stanza establishes a relationship between God-creator and poet-creator that, like Adamic language, is meant to exist outside the rhetorical and interpretive circle of fraud. The metaphysics of poetic form thus supplants, in a sense, the tainted placeness of the contextualized speech act.

The contrast between space and place in the discussion of the *canzone* stanza also provides a final illustration of the tension between poetic authority and history in the *De vulgari*.[57] Through a poetic theory based on microcosmic space, the exiled Dante attempts to remake himself, to be poetically reborn outside his current historical conditions. While the illustrious vernacular, like Dante himself, may currently be without a court palace ("palatium"), home ("domus"), or dwelling ("habitaculum") [*DV* 1.18.2], the poet can construct within the *canzone* space his own abode, or "mansio," complete with individual rooms, or stanzas ("stantia").[58] Dante's discussion of *canzone* space thus also signals, on a metaphoric level, both a return home and a rebirth, as most dramatically suggested in the word play on forms of gremium ("gremium," "ingremiat," "congremiatio" [*DV* 2.9.2–3])[59]—literally lap or bosom—in describing the metrical container of the poem. In his new poetic home, which is self-made, abstract, and cosmological, Dante distances himself and his texts from the social and intellectual limits of physical place constricting the citizens of Pietramala, the builders of Babel, and those inhabitants "a terrigenis mediocribus" behind "Rosa fresca aulentissima." Ultimately, then, the poetic "mansio" and metrical "gremium" bespeak a desire for self-determination, a desire to be free from the circumstances of birth, place, and birthplace.

Of course, despite these rhetorical strategies, Dante can no better avoid the reality of place than he can the vicissitudes of history. Even as he attempts to separate his vernacular production from the contingencies of historical context, his references to the written circulation of texts illustrate the inevitable place dependency of all verbal communication. Throughout book 2, Dante tries to distance the uses of the *canzone* from the explicitly performative aspects of vernacular poetry. In his discussion of active versus passive authors (*DV* 2.8.3–4), for example, he explains that the authorship of a text belongs to the poet rather than to the performer. He distinguishes *canzoni* from the *ballate* because the latter were written for and are in need of dancers (*DV* 2.3.5). And he specifies that the term *canzone* refers to a poetic text and not to music (*DV* 2.8.5–6). In distancing his poetry from the contextualized place of oral performance, Dante relies in particular on images of the materiality of writing. Writing on a page ("verba in cartulis" [*DV* 2.8.5]) proves that a *canzone* need not have a performer, and the careful preservation of *canzoni* in contemporary books demonstrates that the *canzone* is the noblest metrical form: "que nobilissima sunt carissime conservantur, sed inter ea que cantata sunt, cantiones carissime conservantur, ut constat visitantibus libros" (the noblest things are preserved with the greatest care; but, among the things that are sung, *canzoni* are preserved the most carefully, as is clear to anyone who often frequents books) [*DV* 2.3.7]. This insistence on written texts, on the visual form over the acoustic message, allows Dante to frame his poetry within a sort of social parenthesis, removed from the functional uses of municipal poetry and the local horizon of oral performance.

At the same time, in attempting to deduce the inherent superiority of the *canzone* form from its material transcription in contemporary books, Dante reveals how even his microcosmic poetics are subject to the social forces of book production and dependent on public opinion and taste. Within the pages of the book, the *canzone* space intersects with the historically specific place of writing, and the results, both visual and temporal, are far from assured. The compiler of the Vatican anthology, for example, is notably insensitive to metrical form, and Dante's own *canzoni,* except for the special case of "Donne ch'avete," are not preserved in contemporary anthologies. In the end, as Dante clearly understood, the written reception of texts is just another form of contextualized performance, despite his (and our) attempts at polarizing written and oral communication. Dante scholars nevertheless continue to neglect the manuscript page, the social place where textuality and historicity are ineluctably linked. This oversight is especially regrettable since Dante remains one of the most important medieval "frequenters of books" and his texts are informed throughout by manuscript culture. For this, if for no other reason, we need to put Dante's texts back in circulation among contemporary book production—rethinking, at the same time, our current approach to medieval intertextuality. We need to be able to look at a *canzone* in the Vatican anthology with the fresh eye of an Angelo Colucci and wonder again why "Dante cita questa."

chapter four

Merchant Bookkeeping and Lyric Anthologizing

Codicological Aspects of Vaticano 3793

The previous three chapters presented a re-examination of Dante's literary historiography and intertextual citations through the lens of contemporary manuscript culture, revealing the social tensions behind the poetic debates of the period. In each of these chapters, manuscript evidence has helped to contextualize the early Italian lyric, historicizing and localizing it as a social practice. Yet manuscripts and documents do more than simply provide the place where vernacular discourses are preserved and experienced. The physical page is itself a meaningful text. The space of the page contains its own economy, its own language or codes, and serves as a historically specific symbolic act, just like the verbal text it presents. The container, in short, is as significant as what it contains. And we have already seen how seriously Dante treats the material text, from the book of memory, to the problematic dissemination of "Donne ch'avete intelletto d'amore," to the written preservation of *canzoni* evoked in the *De vulgari eloquentia*. With these observations in mind, and having discussed in the last two chapters the historiographical importance of the Vaticano 3793, in this chapter I will discuss the codicological aspects of Vaticano 3793, that is, its status as a physical book. Although Dante may not have had direct contact with the Vatican manuscript, it conveys crucial information about contemporary changes in vernacular writing practices, changes that must have affected him in some way.

In order better to understand the role of urban readers and writers in the early reception of Dante and his contemporaries, the Vatican anthology will be examined in the context of contemporary documents, especially mercantile books of account.[1] To a surprising extent, Vaticano 3793 resembles the account books of the Florentine banking supercompanies. Since Armando Petrucci's groundbreaking identification of the primary hand of the Vatican anthology as a proto-*mercantesca*,[2] numerous scholars have confirmed the mercantile provenience of the manuscript, evident in features as varied as page layout and handwriting, parchment quality and orthography.[3] My own discussion will provide further evidence of the Vatican anthology's resemblance to an account book, as well as suggest, more provocatively, that the various merchant-writers of the anthology treated it as if it were an actual ledger of poems. Specifically, I will propose that the merchant-copyists of Vaticano 3793 re-interpreted the cultural practice of transcribing vernacular verse, integrating the preservation of Italian poetry with their methods of keeping accounts. The Vatican anthology provides evidence, moreover, of a radically new perception of blank page space on the part of merchants in this period, which was influenced by their daily accounting practices and their growing familiarity with blank bound books.

Vaticano 3793 is not, however, a mere reflection of contemporary accounting books. Nor is it simply the deterministic outcome of changing economic conditions. In fact, the Vatican anthology remains a suggestively hybrid cultural artifact, demonstrating a variety of writing practices as well as perceptions of and uses for books. Most importantly, as I will discuss below, the book enjoyed both a private reception and at least a limited public circulation. In order better to understand the ways in which the Vatican anthology was enmeshed in evolving and contending perceptions, not only of literature and writing but also of self and society, it is important to analyze both the original composition of the manuscript and its subsequent reception and history as a book.

Merchant Accounting and the Scribal Practices behind Vaticano 3793

The Vatican anthology is transcribed in a variety of notarial and mercantile hands. The primary hand is a neat, orderly *mercantesca,* an emergent handwriting used at this time by the more advanced and powerful merchant-bankers.[4] This primary copyist was responsible for copying the majority of poems in the manuscript and is generally considered to be the original compiler of the codex. Hands 8, 9, and 11, also in *mercantesca,* demonstrate various degrees of competence in professional handwriting. The important second, third, fourth, fifth, sixth, seventh, and tenth hands, however, are all indicative of the dominant cursive handwriting of the period, the notarial and chancery script known as *minuscola cancelleresca.* Yet even among these notarial hands, the increasing importance and influence of mercantile graphic culture is evident. In fact, the *cancelleresca* hands 2 and 6 have certain elements in common—especially in the ligatures—with the new *mercantesca* script.[5] Examined as a whole, the handwriting of the codex is evocative of the cursive world of documents rather than of Scholastic and courtly book production. As in contemporary account books, moreover, the Vatican anthology lacks ornamentation, rubrication, and page lining, lending it an overall rough appearance. Combined with the sheer size and length of the manuscript and the progressive serialization of poetic entries, these elements make the Vatican anthology an example of a "register-book" as opposed to the "courtly-reading" books (copied by professional scribes in high-quality scripts and often illuminated as well) represented by the Palatine and Laurentian *canzonieri.*[6] In fact, the copyists of Vaticano 3793 created a new physical container for their lyric anthology, based on the documentary model with which they were most familiar and that typified their social accomplishments: the accounting ledger.

In this light, the layout of the poems in the Vatican anthology is especially significant. The poems are transcribed as prose with the beginning of each stanza marked by a simple, built-up capital letter in black ink. The visual effect mirrors the various short prose paragraphs or accounts in Florentine merchants' books, each begun with a similar crude, black-ink capital. Furthermore, each poetic entry in the Vatican anthology is preceded by its appropriate Roman numeral and by the name of the respective author. These editorial indications are separated off from the body of the poetic text by square pen lines or brackets, and they are indented or centered within the manuscript page. Once again, in the merchants' books of account, each financial entry is preceded by the date in Roman numerals, centered, and isolated by the same square brackets. The physical similarities between these two types of books are thus immediately evident. Most strikingly, the metrical divisions in the sonnet section of the Vatican anthology are indicated in the right margin by curved lines or brackets—the same technique used in merchants' books to isolate individual financial transactions (figs. 11 and 12). In this way, sophisticated poetic knowledge and everyday mercantile accounting practices are combined in a distinctive transcription style.

Several of these features of the Vatican anthology are not specific only to merchants' account books, but also to documentary culture in general, especially notarial documentary culture. The immense cultural importance of notaries in late medieval Italy led to the adoption of many of the characteristics of their private protocols in the documentary and practical writing of other professions. Merchants' books of account are no exception. In fact, the hybrid nature of the Vatican anthology demonstrates the contiguity and complexity of social and cultural relations between notaries and merchants. And yet, in others ways, Vaticano 3793 quite clearly recalls an account book, not a notarial register.

One striking example is the peculiar abbreviation for the Florentine poet Monte Andrea: *Mo* (figs. 11 and 13). Monte's poetry concludes both the *canzone* and sonnet sections of the Vatican anthology and scholars have rightly noted the significance of both the placement of Monte's poetry in the anthology and the use of this abbreviation. For Monte was a Florentine banker as well as a poet—a representative of the same social class as the anonymous compiler of the Vatican anthology. In fact, according to Antonelli, the abbreviated rubric demonstrates a marked familiarity with the Florentine banker-poet on the part of the compiler of Vaticano 3793, an extremely suggestive "vicinanza" between poet and editor.[7] Still, while Monte Andrea is a central figure in the collection, I would suggest that this "closeness" between poet-banker and merchant-compiler, rather than being indicative of personal familiarity, reveals a shared cultural and ideological vision.

In fact, the abbreviation *Mo* is not unique to the Vatican anthology. In contemporary merchants' account books, we find the abbreviation at the end of each individual account. In these books, *Mo* stands for *Monta,* or the final sum or balance of transactions undertaken with each party—each debtor and each creditor (figs. 12 and 14). In addition, this mercantile abbreviation, *Mo,* along with the relevant numerical sum, is centered below each entry and separated from the rest of the text by the same type of brackets surrounding the abbreviation for Monte Andrea in the Vatican anthology.[8] Hence, the account book's characteristic series of prose paragraphs, separated by the indented and bracketed *Mo* abbreviation—with its *M* written in a distinctive

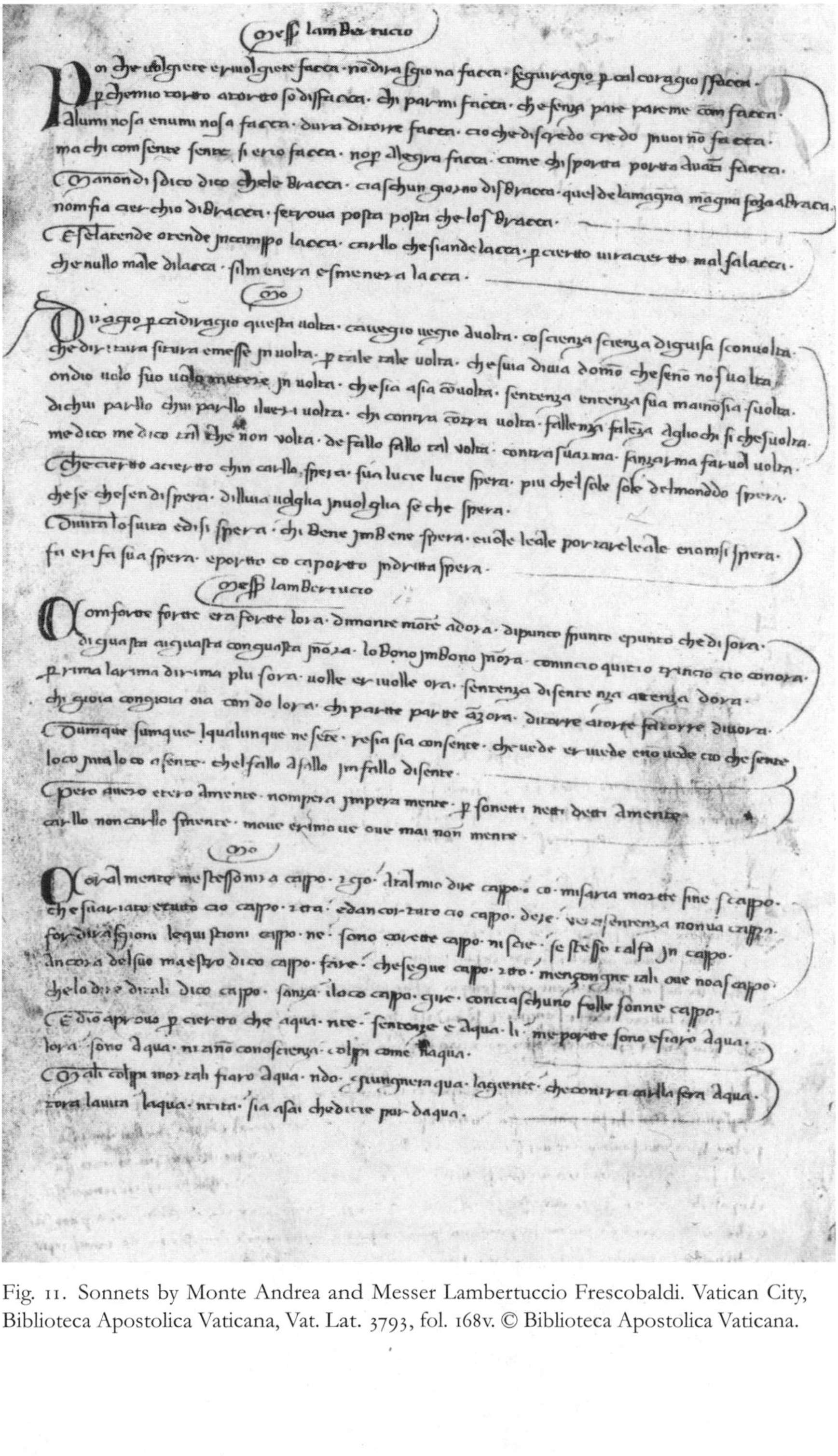

Fig. 11. Sonnets by Monte Andrea and Messer Lambertuccio Frescobaldi. Vatican City, Biblioteca Apostolica Vaticana, Vat. Lat. 3793, fol. 168v. © Biblioteca Apostolica Vaticana.

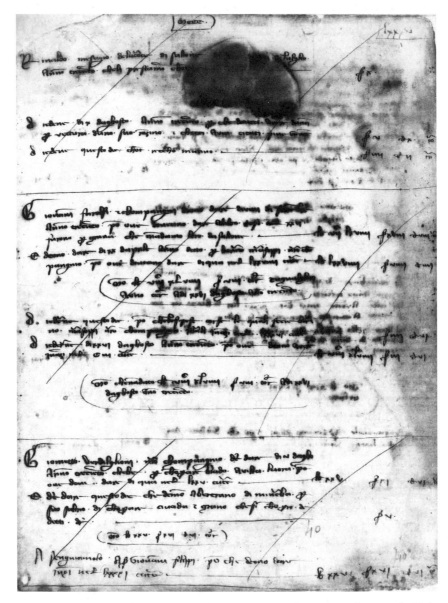

Fig. 12. A sample page from an account book of the Farolfi Company. Florence, Archivio di Stato, Carte Strozziane, s. II, n. 84bis, fol. 85r. © Biblioteca Apostolica Vaticana. Reproduced by permission of the Ministero per i Beni e le Attività Culturali, Biblioteca Nazionale Centrale.

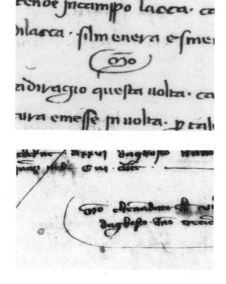

Fig. 13. Detail of figure 11. The abbreviation *Mo* for Monte Andrea.

Fig. 14. Detail of figure 12. The abbreviation *Mo* for *Monta.*

mercantesca—are mirrored almost perfectly in the section of Vaticano 3793 dedicated to Monte Andrea, where poems written out as prose paragraphs are divided by an indented, bracketed rubric *Mo* (figs. 13 and 14).[9]

The frequent use of blank space in the Vatican manuscript also recalls features of contemporary books of account. For example, scholars have noted that the compiler, presumably hand 1, left a blank area at the bottom of every *canzone* less than five stanzas long. He may have considered these poems incomplete and intended to finish them by examining other sources. This editorial practice may well have been informed by the compiler's mercantile and documentary training. In contemporary merchants' books, a blank space was left at the end of each account and before the next entry. In this way, the merchant-bookkeeper could go back at a later date and update the running account, adding the appropriate debit or credit before calculating the final sum. The compiler of Vaticano 3793 treats his lyric anthology in a similar manner, both spatially—with respect to the relation of blank space to the poetic entries—as well as temporally, in the successive, ongoing compilation. Once again, his literary consciousness seems inseparable from his professional training.

Blank space and the blank page are even more conspicuous in the *modi scribendi* of the subsequent copyists of Vaticano 3793. This is particularly the

case for copyists of apparent mercantile background. For example, hand 4—
a "borghese cittadino" according to Petrucci—leaves a blank space before
transcribing his personal selection of poems. He leaves a blank half page on
101r before copying down a *canzone* and a similar, but smaller, blank area before the sonnet on 179r. How are we to reconcile this leniency toward the
blank manuscript page with a professional culture supposedly gripped by the
horror vacui?

At this point it comes as no surprise to learn that similar phenomena can
be observed in the major account books of the merchant-banking elite in
Florence. Looking through these ledgers, one is immediately struck, not only
by the blank spaces left at the end of each account, but also by the numerous
blank pages left between sections and even by entire blank quires. One explanation for the disregard for blank space in these account books is their lack
of legal authority and their primarily private, internal function. Unlike the notarial protocol, the account book did not hold the status of official public
truth, *veritas* and *publicitas*. Although merchant books would gradually acquire
greater legal standing during the course of the fourteenth century, at this time
monetary transactions, contracts, and trade agreements needed a separate
notarization in order to be recognized as legal proof.[10]

The merchant-copyists of Vaticano 3793—educated in and accustomed
to the documentary world of merchants' books—demonstrate a similar disregard for blank space in their transcribing methods. The innovations of these
writing practices are in part evident because of their difference from other
graphic norms represented within Vaticano 3793. The copyists of the anthology who were trained as or by notaries tend to fill in every possible blank
space with poetic compositions, recalling the *modi scribendi* found in the Memoriali bolognesi. The second and third copyists, for instance, writing in orderly
notarial scripts, demonstrate legally influenced approaches toward the page
in their progressive entries of poems and use of available blank space. The
high level of notarial training of hand 2 is evident in both his elegant *minuscola
cancelleresca* as well as in his unique layout of a poem by Panuccio del Bagno.[11]
Panuccio's sonnet "Amore s'à il meo volere miso disovra" (V 305b) is copied
as a complex, logical diagram—consistent with a copyist of an academic,
even Scholastic background and at odds with the mercantile habits characteristic of hands 1 and 4.

The multiple functions of merchant books help further to explain the
copious blank spaces found within them. The important ledgers of the major

companies contained a variety of different records and were divided into discrete, independent sections. In a single book, the accountants for a company would record contracts, annual dividends, salaries for employees and partners, cash accounts, profits, and, especially, separate debit and credit accounts. Since the accounting functions within a given book were largely autonomous, bookkeepers often began a new section at some distance from previous ones, separating it from other categories of records by pages and even entire quires. The blankness of the pages and quires then served as an important border between different kinds of record keeping. While notaries either consolidated their entries into a single serialized and dated progression or separated different categories (contracts, wills, etc.) into separate books or booklets, the merchant bookkeepers entered each financial transaction simultaneously in appropriate sections of the register, which were then meticulously crossreferenced. The sophistication of these accounting methods has led financial historians to identify the most advanced of these registers as precocious examples of double-entry bookkeeping.[12] Whether or not these methods contributed to the Weberian rationalism necessary for the growth of capitalism or to the shift in Tuscany from itinerant to resident mercantilism[13]—as has been claimed—they do reveal a complicated, advanced method of recording, ordering, and calculating the external world.

The merchant-copyists of the Vatican anthology appear to have been influenced by the multi-functional, divided account book in their composition of the anthology.[14] Several of the later copyists leave a blank space between previous sections and their own autonomous poetic sections, as if they were opening a new category of accounts. These "accounts" were then cross-referenced with the other poems in the index. In this way, the later copyists re-interpreted the traditional separation of poetic compositions by genre, the distinct *canzone* and sonnet sections created by the primary copyist, as functioning in the same fashion as the running accounts in their merchant books. It is important to underline, in fact, that many of the distinguishing aspects of the Vatican anthology, including its open-endedness and use of blank space at the end of sections, recall similar phenomena in manuscripts such as the Laurentian *canzoniere* or certain anthologies of Troubadour poetry, where blank space was left at the end of sections in order to allow for further entries.[15] Yet these anthologizing methods receive special emphasis, and in some cases are transformed, by the merchants' professional experience with writing and reading. The multiple copyists of the Vatican anthology do not so much expand on the original plan of the manuscript, which is the case in the Troubadour anthologies, as create heterogeneous, mini-anthologies, *piccoli canzonieri*. Instead of being used to continue the original plan of the anthology, blank space also serves in the Vatican manuscript as a border to mark off discrete sections of the book, which may differ markedly from one another in content, language, handwriting, and layout.[16] For copyists working in such a mode, the overall unity of the anthology apparently depended more on the physical space of the book than on the consistency of a single organizing plan (*compilatio*).

The Emergence of the Blank Bound Book

There is another, related, material cause for the blank spaces scattered among contemporary merchant books at this time, especially in ledgers: the increasing use of the blank bound book. The most sophisticated accounting of the powerful merchant-banking corporations was performed in books that were—quite singularly for the period—already bound. Notarial protocols, on the other hand, were transcribed entry by entry in loose quires, and in each quire a notary would include a title and subscription, often noting the number of pages in the quire, or *quaternus*. If the quires were then collected or bound, he would include a new title and new subscription, now specifying the number of quires as well as pages in this *liber*.[17] The university book was also put together as individual quires, which were at times farmed out to independent scribes in the oft-discussed *pecia* system.[18] In order to ensure that the various *quaterni* were then bound in proper sequence, the lower margins in the last pages of these quires often contained "catchwords" (the first word of the following quire).

The merchant-banking account books, however, were complete, intact, and bound even before coming into contact with ink. Indeed, their binding became an important marker in the various cross-references among books used in the same company; contemporary books in one company often refer to each other by their particular binding, such as "libro rosso," "libro nero," or "libro dell'asse." This technical innovation in the uses of bound books revolutionized the way in which merchant-bankers perceived writing space. The century-old and ubiquitous centrality of the quire in conceptions of the book gave way in merchants' books to the independence of the single page.

Already bound, the merchant books lack both the catchwords of university books and the system of numbered quires often found in notarial protocols and state registers.[19] In fact, the merchant-bankers demonstrate a complete disregard for the autonomy of quires in their bookkeeping techniques. A new accounting section almost never coincides with a new quire, and accounts often begin in the middle of one quire and end in the middle of the following one. As mentioned above, merchant bookkeepers often skip entire pages and quires before starting a new part of the book, even beginning on the last page of a blank quire. Obviously, the fundamental unit of the book for the merchant was no longer the various divisions furnished by *quaterni,* but now the single, blank page.

The shift from articulating the book in leaves and quires to a homogenous series of blank pages is confirmed in a new method of page numbering in selected merchants' books. Some of the most important merchant supercompanies—such as the Peruzzi company—adapted a method of page numbering based on the open-page face instead of the leaf.[20] In other words, the same number was repeated on the left-hand corner of an open book and on the right-hand side of the facing page. The book was thus articulated in a series of open-page faces, with the left- and right-hand pages together considered a single unit.[21]

The visual immediacy of the open-page face thus took precedence over the material structure of the book, assembled and bound in quires and leaves. Traditionally, books were numbered by leaves, marked in the right corner of the front, or *recto,* side. In this conception of the book, the autonomy of the individual, physical leaf is more important than the visual page, since the back side of a numbered leaf is maintained as a single unit even if one side of it is always out of view of the reader. But this new, mercantile form of page numbering breaks down the traditional division of a manuscript book into quires, sheets, and leaves. A single page could span two different leaves, two different sheets, and even two different quires. Paradoxically, the economic resources that allowed merchants to purchase prebound blank books led to a diminished awareness of the actual physical make-up of books, their structure and binding. The merchant elites no longer perceived a book as several sewn-together quires that formed a continuity of physical leaves, but as a homogenous collection of visible pages—a concept of the book still with us today.[22]

It is difficult to imagine the magnitude of this technical and conceptual shift in approaches to the book. We have become accustomed to the facility and naturalness of purchasing a blank, bound book such as a diary, agenda, or notebook.[23] We take for granted the pre-existence of that stable, bound white space. Tellingly, the term "book" in English now refers ambiguously to both a substantive text (for example, "I just finished my first book") as well as to a physical container of empty bound pages awaiting composition. But the technical and ontological shifts that allowed for this ambiguity must have held tremendous import in the late thirteenth century, considering the centrality of the book (and the various divisions within books) in medieval culture.[24] As E. R. Curtius has amply demonstrated,[25] language and thought in the time of Dante was permeated by the idea of the book. Dante himself imagines the cosmos as made up of scattered quires, only united in God's volume ("Nel suo profondo vidi che s'interna, / legato con amore in un volume / ciò che per l'universo si squaderna" [In its depth I saw ingathered, bound with love in a single volume, that which is dispersed in quires throughout the universe] [*Par.* 33.85–87]) For the Florentine merchant elites, however, their quires were always already united in one "volume," and the fragmentary autonomy of the booklet thus gradually ceased to be of much relevance.

In part, the innovative appearance of Vaticano 3793 depends on its being received, used, and appropriated as if it were an already bound, blank book. Many of the later copyists transcribed their selections in an already bound, or at least structurally complete, book. Perhaps still under the supervision of the anonymous compiler, the Vatican anthology was assembled with two extra blank quires at the ends of the *canzone* and sonnet sections, the fifteenth and twenty-sixth quires, respectively. Besides resembling the blank quires in merchants' books, these extra sections allowed for the expansion of the Vatican anthology's collection—a comprehensiveness that at the same time violates the integrity of the original collection. Consistent with this vision, hands 5 through 9 copy down their selections in the extra, fifteenth quire of the *canzone* section, while hands 11–14 utilize the extra, unnumbered twenty-sixth blank quire following the sonnet section. It is possible that the missing sixteenth and seventeenth quires were also included, blank, in the original collection, but were excised in subsequent bindings. This same phenomenon occurs in the transmission of medieval books of account. In the account books of the Peruzzi company, for example, several presumably blank quires are now missing.[26]

The transformation of Vaticano 3793 into a private, open-ended anthology conflicts with the original internal-textual and external-codicological divisions of the manuscript. Although it is difficult to say with absolute certainty when the Vatican anthology became a bound book, we can identify the points at which its careful articulation into separate quires breaks down. For example, the inclusion, at a later moment, of an appendix of chronologically and geographically miscellaneous poets (quire 14)—still by the first hand of the anthology—already interferes with the fundamental temporal-spatial arrangement of poets in the anthology. Moreover, the last two quires in the sonnet section are not numbered and are clearly appended to the original editorial and codicological project of the Vatican anthology.

Even more striking, a subsequent fifth hand transcribes a poem that begins in the fourteenth quire and ends in the fifteenth, violating an essential norm of the anthology and eroding the autonomy and boundaries of the quire. In fact, all of the copyists of this quire ignore the original numbering and division of the manuscript into distinct quires. Even before transcribing his poems, the primary copyist numbered each quire with Roman numerals placed in the lower margin of the first page of each quire. In the fifteenth quire, however, the copyists overlook this Roman numeral on the first page and transcribe the quire instead in an inverted, flip-flopped position; they turn the bottom of the last page into the top of the first page of the current quire. The disregarded Roman numeral *XV* thus appears upside down on the top of the last page of the quire. Finally, many of these Roman numerals identifying the quires have been rubbed out, deleted by a subsequent possessor of the Vatican anthology.[27] In this way, the continuous pages of the manuscript (marked by page numbering) take precedence over its divisions into quires.

The numerous additions, revisions, and alterations to the already complete selection in Vaticano 3793 turn the manuscript into a private, continuous work in progress. To a certain extent, the original text laid down by the anonymous compiler yields to the Vatican anthology's importance as a physical blank book. While a medieval manuscript often represents only one manifestation of a text in its public or semi-public transmission, the Vatican anthology turns inward and remains a private, never-ending working draft. In other words, the physical container of the manuscript is no longer only fashioned for the individual text, but it becomes in itself an important blank space awaiting future transcriptions and revision. The emphasis shifts from a published text to a private book. This private reception of Vaticano 3793 is further confirmed by the various scribblings and marks of bourgeois ownership found throughout the manuscript.[28]

The Fragment BN 2.3.492 and the Mixed Reception of the Vatican Anthology

On the other hand, the Vatican anthology once again reveals a startling heterogeneity even in its ambiguous public and private reception. A fragment of a lyric anthology now housed in the Florentine Biblioteca Nazionale (MS 2.3.492) suggests that Vaticano 3793 was quite possibly copied and circulated at the same time that it remained a private book and a work in progress.[29] (Unfortunately, only two sheets—four leaves and eight pages—remain of the former collection, recuperated from their use as end pages in a later manuscript.) The similarities between the Vatican anthology and the roughly contemporary Florentine fragment have long been noted.[30] The fragment reports a selection of sonnets from Guittone and several *canzoni* of Monte Andrea and his interlocutors in exactly the same order as in the anthology. Furthermore, Monte's *canzone* "Ancor di dire non fino" is preceded by a title with the same Roman numeral as in the Vatican anthology: "CCLXXXVIII" (fig. 15).

A new paleographic and philological analysis of the two manuscripts suggests that the Florentine fragment not only resembles Vaticano 3793, but very possibly derives from it.[31] For example, under ultraviolet light, one can see in the left-hand margins bordering "Ancor di dire" (fol. 6r) and "Amoroso volere ma comosso"[32] (fol. 3r) the same Roman numerals corresponding to the numbering in the Vatican anthology. Hence the number in the title before "Ancor di dire" does not result from a later, subsequent contact with the Vatican anthology, added after the completion of the independent fragment, as has been suggested.[33] Instead, the identical numbering was part of the original plan of the anthology, for these minuscule, penciled numbers in the margins are the original notes to the rubricator of the manuscript. Moreover, the fragment repeats all of the scribal "errors" and variants found in the Vatican anthology, adding its own scribal mistakes. Most importantly, many of these mistakes are paleographic errors and can be traced back to material difficulty in reading passages in the Vatican anthology in which the handwriting is particularly confusing and ambiguous.[34]

The importance of this "publication" of the Vatican anthology cannot be overstated. For one thing, the fragment demonstrates that Vaticano 3793 participated in an actual manuscript tradition—a tradition responsible, in part, for Dante's historical vision of the lyric. The Nazionale manuscript also suggests the geographic and social breadth of the reception of this

merchant's anthology. The fragment shows signs of non-Florentine and even non-Tuscan linguistic and phonetic variations,[35] pointing in particular to a copyist from the region of Romagna. In the sixteenth century, the codex can already be traced to Siena.[36] Furthermore, the manuscript was transcribed by two professional hands in a careful, calligraphic Gothic *textualis,* complete with rubrics, red capital letters, and red paragraph marks dividing the text (fig. 15). This more traditional layout for a vernacular book suggests that its public was not the same as — or at least not limited to — that of the Vatican anthology.

Even the few remaining pages of this anthology indicate that the poetic compilation assembled in the Vatican anthology was able to transcend its documentary and cursive roots and travel though Italy in an official *textualis* container. Indeed, the philological and chronological closeness between the two manuscripts suggests that the anonymous compiler might even have been behind this official version of his compilation — a published, *textualis* copy of his cursive, working draft. Whether or not this was the case, the Vatican anthology apparently operated simultaneously on two distinct cultural fronts: copied and transmitted in the socially recognized and established public sphere, at the same time as it was continually elaborated in the emergent private sphere of writing practices.

The contending prestige in this period between the public and private spheres of writing is amply demonstrated by a manuscript dating slightly later than the Vatican anthology, the famous codex containing Domenico Lenzi's *Specchio umano* (Biblioteca Medicea Laurenziana, MS Tempi 3).[37] Between 1335 and 1340, Lenzi, a Florentine grain merchant, composed his unique miscellany of moral prose and verse, market prices and conditions, historical chronicle, and social commentary on phenomena such as famine.[38] The manuscript containing this text (ca. 1344–1347) has been studied primarily for its nine spectacular illuminations, executed by the so-called "Maestro del Biadaiolo."[39]

The first illumination (fol. 2r) of the manuscript, which is of direct interest for the present discussion, serves as a sort of title page (fig. 16). The rectangular illumination is split by a frame into two scenes. The image in the upper section of the frame depicts a merchant speaking with several clients, presumably discussing the price of the grain contained in the barrels next to the interlocutors. In another scene below this one, Domenico Lenzi sits in his store, surrounded by the tools and materials of his trade. He is portrayed dealing with customers while writing figures, visible Roman numerals, in his thick, bound, merchant's book. The illumination thus links the prices, figures, and market quotes in the finished *Specchio umano* with the accounting recorded in Domenico's personal merchant's book. Indeed, the miniature book depicted on the first page of the *Specchio* reflects in microcosmic form the layout of the entire manuscript (fig. 17). In this way, the final, published form of the *Specchio umano* begins with an illustration of its private inception.

Despite this attempt at associating Domenico's private writing with the content of the *Specchio,* in actuality the author is rigorously impersonal throughout the work.[40] While he does report the market prices for each year, his own financial and private dealings are omitted from the text. He distances himself from the diaristic, mercantile *ricordanze,* and the emergent practices of private autobiography and historiography. Domenico aims rather at an impersonal, public authority. Yet whoever produced the final version of the manuscript, perhaps one of the major guilds, clearly wanted to showcase a private, mercantile form of writing.[41] The illuminated, costly manuscript is a public portrayal of private writing—possibly contrary to the intentions of Domenico Lenzi.

In a similar fashion, Vaticano 3793 courts the prestige of both public and private writing. For example, the allotting of individual quires to major authors in the Vatican anthology simulates a recognized structure already found in several anthologies of Troubadour poetry; the Vatican anthology participates in the established editorial practices of other "published" contemporary collections of lyric poetry. Indeed, the fragment in Florence's Biblioteca Nazionale, copied in a professional Gothic *textualis* script, reveals at least a limited public success for the anonymous merchant's compilation. At the same time, Vaticano 3793 remains a prestigious object in its own right, a private bound book continually elaborated and expanded.

The Vatican anthology's dual private and public functions attest, perhaps better than any other element, to the manuscript's striking modernity. In the manuscripts of a later poet such as Petrarch, for example, we see the same tension between published collections—exposed to the hazards of misreading and interpolation—and continually elaborated, private working drafts.[42] Yet already with Dante's book of memory, as we have seen in the *Vita Nova,* internal and private communications are transformed into a "published" text. What Petrarch achieved in material form with private and public manuscripts (anticipated in Vaticano 3793 and the Biblioteca Nazionale fragment), Dante incorporated into the textual structure of his hybrid narrative, where private

Fig. 16. Domenico Lenzi at the market and writing in his account book. Florence, Biblioteca Medicea Laurenziana, MS Tempi 3, fol. 2r. Reproduced by permission of the Ministero per i Beni e le Attività Culturali, Biblioteca Medicea Laurenziana.

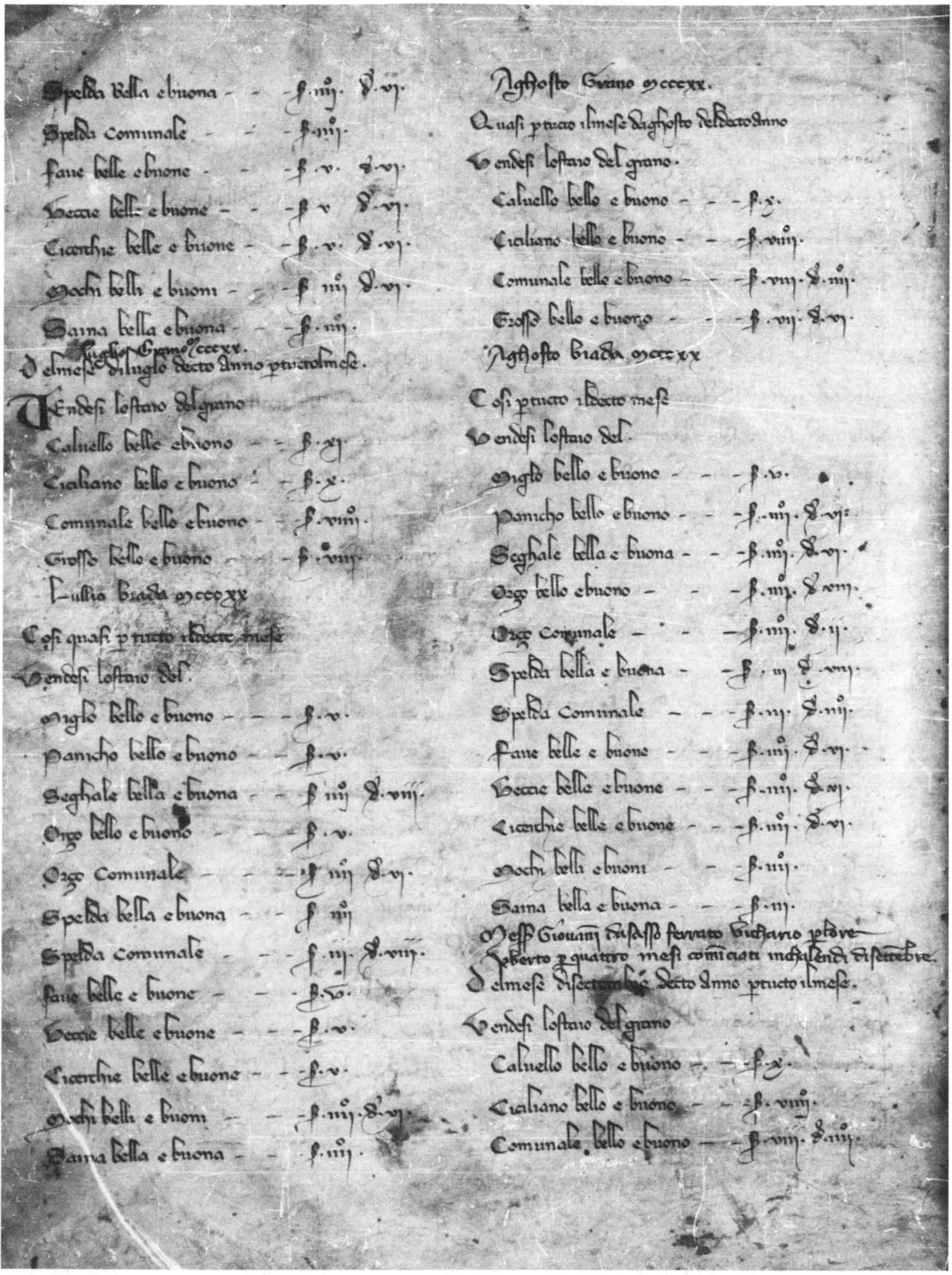

Fig. 17. A sample page from the final, "published" version of Lenzi's *Specchio Umano*. Florence, Biblioteca Medicea Laurenziana, MS Tempi 3, fol. 3v. Reproduced by permission of the Ministero per i Beni e le Attività Culturali, Biblioteca Medicea Laurenziana.

speech and interior monologues are contextualized and glossed for the new vernacular public.

The notion of the book as surrogate for the self (Petrarch) or the self as constituted by a book (Dante) may owe more than we have heretofore recognized to the bound blank books of Italian merchant-bankers. Paradoxically, the merchant's blank accounting book, despite eventually being filled with records of interpersonal and economic exchanges, evokes the sort of socially autonomous realm that Dante seeks for his poetry (although he would never imagine his own work inhabiting such a debased container). For, like the microcosmic *canzone* space described in the *De vulgari,* the blank book allowed for a visual re-ordering of experience that was at least aesthetically protected from the vagaries of time and the unpredictability of external conditions. The world methodically reconstructed within the leather and wooden covers of "red books" and "black books" in the merchant's archive was as real and often more satisfying—at least when the books balanced—than what they recorded. In discussing the standardized visual reproduction of verbal language in modern printed books, Ong goes a step further, arguing that these books, removed from the historical and social contexts of their inception, permit "human beings to think of their own interior conscious and unconscious resources as more and more thing-like" and discrete.[43] But centuries before the advent of printing, the blank merchant's book was already the ideal container for collecting, organizing, and accounting for the human psyche as if it were an inventory of items. The heterogeneity of the self, fundamental in different ways for both Dante and Petrarch, maintains its integrity only between the borders of the book. Indeed, the modern era is commonly identified with the rise of this hermetic subject, with a new concept of the autonomous, integral, and bounded self. Despite such interest in the emergence of the bounded subject, the contemporary and related emergence of the bound, blank book has yet to be explored.

chapter five

Bankers in Hell

The Poetry of Monte Andrea in Dante's *Inferno* between Historicism and Historicity

Whether it was experienced primarily as a private or public document, Vaticano 3793 illustrates how early vernacular texts were experienced in specific social "places." The manuscript was produced by merchant elite writers for merchant elite readers, and later possessors of the manuscript were also drawn from the mercantile and bourgeois classes. Many of the poets collected in the anthology were representative of the political elite in thirteenth-century Florence, and their participation in the culture of the *tenzone,* attested to in various *tenzoni* in the sonnet section, underlines the importance of Italian poetry for maintaining political and social cohesiveness. Ultimately, the Vatican anthology demonstrates the municipality of contemporary poetry, how it portrayed, served, and reinforced specific social groups. Yet current scholarship about the *duecento* lyric, ignoring its anthropological uses, rarely explores the implications of class. Most studies view Dante and his contemporaries as divided by psychological, doctrinal, and aesthetic concerns, not by economic ones. As a result, Dante remains the last flame of High Scholasticism, untainted by the emergence of the *marchands écrivains.*

While erudite commentaries on the *Commedia* increasingly help us to understand the medieval world behind its creation—a world split between church and empire, Guelph and Ghibelline, Guittonians and stilnovists—the social divisions that underlie such categories and that informed the politics and culture of Dante's time are often overlooked. The numerous studies by social historians, for example, on the class rivalries between the magnates and the *popolo* have had little influence on Dante studies. We have, in a sense, obliged Dante's nostalgic, reactionary Cacciaguida—who wishes that the "gente nuova" and "subiti guadagni" (*Inf.* 16.73) had never violated the original Roman walls of a precapitalist Florence—by keeping the urban classes out of the interpretive parameters of our studies. While the works of near-contemporary Boccaccio are readily analyzed within the context of Florentine and Italian mercantilism, Dante, by obfuscating the class tensions underlying his literary historiography, still dictates his own cultural background. Yet the mercantile worldviews underlying contemporary cultural artifacts such as the *Novellino* and Vaticano 3793 suggest that Boccaccio's world overlaps in significant respects with Dante's (though of course there are important differences). For all that Dante incorporated into the *Commedia,* it may thus still be useful to study what he left out.

At first glance, it might seem that he left out the most popular poet of the Vatican anthology, the Florentine banker Monte Andrea. Reproducing Dante's judgment, critics have also tended to neglect Monte and his texts.[1] There has, however, been a recent reassessment of his work, aided by the publication of an important critical edition. Still, restoring censored poets such as Monte to their rightful place in the literary canon is only the first step in addressing Dante's acts of exclusion. We also need to examine the motives behind these exclusions (as with the exclusion of Guittone from the Memoriali bolognesi) and recognize the accompanying social and cultural backgrounds suppressed with every omission. Numerous reasons exist to explain why Dante would not have mentioned Monte Andrea in his work, including his exaggeratedly difficult *trobar clus* style and obvious debt to Guittone. When we examine Monte's reception in Vaticano 3793, however, it becomes clear that Monte's poetry was especially unsettling for Dante for the same sociological and ideological reasons that made it popular for the Florentine merchants who assembled the manuscript.

In this chapter, I will examine the importance of Monte in the Vatican anthology and argue that in fact his poetry plays an important, if problematic, role within the *Commedia.* It is not surprising, of course, that the merchant elites behind the compilation of the Vatican anthology favored one of their own, a Florentine banker, in their own version of the history of Italian poetry.

In addition to this professional affinity, Monte's poetry elaborates a strikingly materialistic perspective on society and history, in line with a mercantile worldview and consistent with the skepticism characterizing the rest of the anthology. Monte's unforgiving realism is thus clearly at odds with the transcendent vision of history and providential view of Fortune that Dante portrayed in the *Commedia*. For the exiled poet, as he reviewed his socially fallen state from the more generous perspective of eternity, Monte's laments over his personal misfortunes and his insistence on the truth of wealth must have seemed weighted down with a dangerously un-transcendent materialism.

Thus, whenever Dante confronts his own vision of Fortune and personal history in the *Commedia,* Monte is in the background, even when he is not directly alluded to. Although scholars have noted that Dante borrowed a series of difficult rhymes from Monte's corpus (*rimas caras*), especially in *Inferno,* they have interpreted his influence as strictly formal.[2] I will suggest, instead, that passages recalling Monte's expressive poetics—in particular in *Inferno* 7, 17, and 30—are informed by the latter's competing treatment of Fortune and history and by the social meaning his texts held for the public of Vaticano 3793. When read against the context of Monte's poems in the Vatican anthology, Dante's excursus on Fortune takes on specific sociopolitical connotations: his sacred history is historicized.[3]

At the same time, Dante's allusions to Monte in the *Commedia* are faint and indirect. And even with the material evidence of Vaticano 3793, their relevance has faded over time. Dante may have intended it that way, since his engagement with the class-biased poetry of Monte reveals his own socially compromised place, his own inescapable historicity. The second part of this chapter examines how the mercantile context of Monte's poetry and his materialistic analysis of society challenges Dante's efforts to write himself out of history by exposing the social origins of Dante's work. The historicization of a text in the first section—the study of Monte's corpus in the material container of Vaticano 3793—will therefore serve in the second section to illustrate Dante's attempts at textualizing history.

The Poetry of Monte Andrea and Vaticano 3793

As we have seen in previous chapters, the poetry of Florence is clearly emphasized in the Vatican anthology, both in the number of anthologized poems and their placement at the conclusion of the historiographical narrative. In the *canzone* section, for example, all five of the final quires (9–13) are dedicated to Florentine poets, and the entire section concludes with the poetry of Monte Andrea (quire 13).[4] Besides being a poet of considerable metrical and linguistic daring, Monte, as a banker by profession,[5] was also a member of the same mercantile class that produced, read, and owned the Vatican anthology.[6] Indeed, several scholars note a pronounced familiarity with Monte on the part of the merchant compiler,[7] a familiarity due no doubt in part to Monte's organic status as both Florentine merchant-banker and producer of vernacular lyrics; he nicely represents the convergence of Florence's mercantile successes and growing cultural prestige. In the banker Monte, the Florentine merchant elites found a natural heir to a tradition that began with a notary, Giacomo da Lentini.

Even more pertinent, the content and themes of Monte's poems are informed by an emergent mercantile worldview. Monte presents a vision of society in his work that is relentlessly materialistic. Most of his *canzoni* are either odes to wealth and money or laments on poverty. In poems such as "Tanto m'abonda matera, di soperchio," "Ancor di dire non fino, perché," and "Aimè lasso, perché a figura d'omo," he praises the personified and all-powerful *Tesauro* and *Ricore,* and he berates the evil *Povertà* and *Povertade.* For Monte, money makes the world go round and his paeans to wealth echo certain goliardic compositions such as "In terra summus rex est hoc tempore Nummus" (Money has become today the supreme king of the world).[8] But instead of betraying an undercurrent of moral indignation and reformist sentiment as goliardic poetry often does, Monte's poems express a cynical resignation to the workings of the world.[9]

Indeed, Monte's poetry is defined by a continual attempt to demystify, without moralizing, the foundation of contemporary power and values. For Monte, both moral virtue and social prestige and power are simply the result of an accumulation of wealth and not of any innate qualities of the individual:

> Qual savio, largo, di bontà compiuto?
> Chi s'à podere, dico ch'è tenuto!
> Chi bestia, chi sgraziato, chi cativ'è?
> Chi scioco, chi 'nodioto sempre vive?
> Chi abassa, d'aver secondo il quanto![10]

[Who is considered wise, generous, and of perfect goodness? He who has wealth. Who is beastly, uncouth, and wretched? Who is foolish and always despised? He who loses his possessions, according to how much is lost.]

In "Ancor di dire non fino, perché," he goes even further and attacks the very structure of medieval society and its hierarchical power relations: "Impero, rege, prencipe ë duca, / marchese, conte: ciascunö è nomo!" (Emperor, king, prince, duke, marquis, count; each one is a name) [27–28]. Monte rejects any fetishized belief about natural social superiority or virtue. Social rank is no more than a name. Only "richezze di tesauro" (abundance of wealth) [66] distinguishes one man from another. Even knowledge is based on wealth, as Monte recognizes in his discussion about the acquisition of "divisate scïenze" (various sciences) [79]: "[Ch]e divien valoroso / sapete, s'e' non fosse poderoso / di tesauro?" (Who becomes worthy [learned] without financial holdings?) [86–88].

After all, getting an education and becoming knowledgeable "valoroso" costs money. Monte further explains that wealth and the cultural capital of education are the real basis of power even within the ecclesiastical hierarchy:

Parlato, di grado in grado, vene Papa
perch'ello sapa?
Sì vertudioso il fa solo Tesoro!
(96–98)

[Does a cleric rise through the ranks to become pope on account of his wisdom? Only wealth has made him so virtuous!]

In this view even the pope's authority ultimately derives from monetary advantage.

The emphasis in Monte's poetry on economic value as well as his own professional and social status thus make him a prime candidate to finish an anthology of Italian poetry produced by the Florentine merchant-banking class. But there is another possible reason that explains why the compilers of Vaticano 3793 selected the Florentine banker-poet to conclude this collection: his name. The copyists of the Vatican anthology never actually write out the name "Monte Andrea" in full—as in the contemporary Laurentian *canzoniere*—but rather simply identify the poet with the abbreviation *Mo,* centered in the middle of the page and further set off from the rest of the text by curved brackets (as are all the authors' names in the manuscript). As we saw in the previous chapter, we find the same abbreviation in contemporary account books, similarly indented and bracketed, where *Mo* stands for *Monta,* the final sum or balance of transactions undertaken with each debtor and each creditor. Even in this verbal and visual pun on his appropriately mercantile name, Monte Andrea turns out to represent, indeed he is almost a synecdoche of, the vernacular community responsible for Vaticano 3793; he is positioned in the manuscript as the sum, the *monta,* of their cultural values.[11]

Competing Visions of Fortune in *Inferno* 7

Monte's place in Vaticano 3793 demonstrates the centrality and social significance of his work for representatives of a particular community of readers and writers. The anthology tells us not only what Monte's poetry says, but also what it does and how it was used in late thirteenth-century Florence, that is, its social place. Dante's own reading of Monte's poetry did not occur in a vacuum. He worked with a manuscript similar to Vaticano 3793 and must at least have recognized the popularity of the latter's poetry and its symbolic status for certain of his contemporaries. And, as Dante was no doubt also aware, not all early readers were equally sympathetic to Monte's poetry. For example, in a letter to Monte, Guittone d'Arezzo, most likely influenced by the mendicant friars, extols the virtues of poverty while critiquing Monte's pessimistic vision of Fortune and praise for wealth. When we consider the contrasting worldviews behind the Vatican anthology and Guittone's letter, the allusions to Monte's poems in the *Commedia* take on new significance and can be seen as taking part in a larger contemporary debate about the interpretation of personal misfortune and economic success or failure. Indeed, I will argue that the allusions to Monte in the *Commedia,* especially the rare rhymes and rhyme words found in *Inferno* 7, 17, and 30, are elements of a focused, class-based polemic against the ideology of the merchant-banker poet and his merchant-banker readers—a polemic that targets, in particular, Monte's attitude toward money, fortune, and poverty.[12] The social and ideological conflicts surrounding these topics are especially vital for Dante in light of his attempts in the *Commedia* to turn the unfortunate circumstances of his exile into an authorizing trope for his work.

In the seventh canto of *Inferno,* Dante describes the punishment of the avaricious and prodigal, whose sins he views as contributing to the larger corruption of Florentine society. Accordingly, those who are guilty of "mal dare e mal tener" (bad giving and bad keeping) [58] receive a *contrapasso* that, because of its geometric and elemental design, is particularly effective and incisive as a memorial image. The two groups of sinners, moving in opposite directions to each other and on opposite sides of their infernal circle, must each move a boulder back and forth in their allotted semicircles. When the two groups collide, they reproach each other for their opposing sins with cries of "Perché tieni?" (Why do you grasp?) and "Perché burli?" (Why do you throw away?) [30]. The antagonistic symmetry of this exchange, what Dante refers to as a "shameful meter" ("ontoso metro" [33]), follows the model of quick, contrapuntal responses found in contemporary comic *tenzoni,* especially the *sonetto dialogato.*[13]

In this canto Dante also treats most directly his vision of Fortune and, subsequently, his philosophy of history. He explains how the apparently casual blows of Fortune are actually ruled by divine Providence. The twin themes of Fortune and Providence are introduced in the canto by Virgil's description of heaven as "là dove Michele / fé la vendetta del superbo strupo" (where Michael avenged the proud onslaugt) [11–12]. These lines allude to the fate of Lucifer—the reversal of his fortune, his just punishment, and his physical fall from the heavens. (The cosmological and topographical repercussions of this fall are described in *Inferno* 34 and *Purgatorio* 12.)

Dante presents his cosmological and transcendent view of the role of Fortune on earth more explicitly in Virgil's description of Fortune and her wheel. Virgil incorporates the circling of the wheel of Fortune and the continuous permutation of the sublunary world into the greater, divinely ordained circling of the heavens and the stars. In fact, the canto contains repeated images of concentric circles, from the circular punishment of the damned at the center, to the celestial spheres ("li cieli" [74]) and Fortune's own sphere (96), to the final glance at the falling and rising movement of the fixed stars: "già ogne stella cade che saliva" (already every star is falling that was rising) [98]. In the Boethian tradition, Virgil explains how the tribulations inflicted by Fortune help us to understand the ephemerality of worldly goods, "la corta buffa / d'i ben che son commessi a la Fortuna" (the brief mockery of the goods that are committed to Fortune) [61–62], and to view them from the much larger perspective of providential and sacred history. The avaricious and prodigal, who fail to see the transcendent divinity of Fortune, the all-encompassing circle, are punished for their shortsightedness with having to perform an eternal semicircular movement, reminiscent of the rise and fall of earthly circumstances.[14]

The Boethian conception of Fortune is especially important for Dante because he employs a suprahistorical and providential viewpoint as one of the central tropes of the entire *Commedia*. Part of the fiction of the *Commedia* is that Dante is writing outside of temporal history, from the vantage point of eternity. Through his providential view of Fortune, Dante attempts to re-interpret and recuperate the problematic personal history that results from his exile and that threatens his literary standing and authority. In canto 17 of the *Paradiso*, Dante's ancestor Cacciaguida finally reveals to the pilgrim the hard-ships that he will endure in exile, the ineluctable "colpi di ventura" (24):

> "Tu proverai sì come sa di sale
> lo pane altrui, e come è duro calle
> lo scendere e 'l salir per l'altrui scale.
> E quel che più ti graverà le spalle,
> sarà la compagnia malvagia e scempia
> con la qual tu cadrai in questa valle."
>
> .   (58–63)

["You will see how bitter another's bread tastes, and what a hard road it is to descend and climb another's stairs. And what will weigh most heavily on your shoulders will be the evil and senseless company with whom you will fall into this valley."]

Dante's exile will leave him even more vulnerable to the whims of Fortune, the constant "scendere" and "salir" of her wheel. He will be beholden to the hospitality and favor of others, and he will fall so far on this wheel ("cadrai in questa valle" [63]) that he will be forced to associate, for a time, with other exiled White Guelphs. Yet, echoing Boethius, Cacciaguida explains that all is ruled by a divine, providential order; all is just and harmonious in the "cospetto etterno" (eternal vision) [39]. Dante's decline in worldly fortune is part of the same plan that allows for his divine journey, his "visïon" (128), and for the writing of his sacred poem, his "grido" (cry) [133].[15] Written in a culture that privileged the impersonal author, Dante's *Commedia* nevertheless acquires authority by representing his personal misfortunes from a viewpoint supposedly above and beyond history.[16]

At the same time, Dante's allusions to the banker-poet Monte Andrea in canto 7 and in other passages in *Inferno* dealing with the themes of Fortune and history illustrate his engagement with the class struggles of late thirteenth-century Florence. Monte's presence in *Inferno* 7 is first noticeable in the marked accumulation of harsh-sounding rhymes, beginning with Pluto's clucking voice, "la voce chioccia" (2). These "harsh" rhymes, such as *-erchio, -etro, -ostra, -ulcro,* are reminiscent of the poetics of Dante's *rime petrose* as well as Monte's poetry written in the *trobar clus* vein. Various derivative rhymes such as *punto–compunto* (32, 36) or *pulcro–appulcro* (58, 60) and the "broken" rhyme *pur lì–burli* (28, 30) are especially characteristic of Monte's poetry, and several of the rare rhymes and rhyme words in the canto evoke crucial passages in his corpus. The rhyme words *ripa–stipa–scipa* (17, 19, 21) closely recall the Montian rhymes *ripa–scipa* (131, 6) in "Ancor di dire non fino, perché"; the rhymes *intoppa–troppa–poppa* (23, 25, 27) echo *troppo* and *rintoppo* in "Ai doloroso lasso, più, nom posso" (66–67); and *cerchio–coperchio–soperchio* (44, 46, 48) appear drawn from the rhyming pair *soperchio–coperchio* in the incipit of "Tanto m'abonda matera, di soperchio" (1, 5). Apart from in Monte's *canzoni*, these rhymes and rhyme words are almost unknown in the extant corpus of thirteenth-century poetry.[17]

By alluding to the poet and poems that best typify the growing cultural prestige and worldview of the Florentine mercantile oligarchy, Dante adds an additional element of class-based, social commentary to his condemnation of human greed. Moreover, through Monte, Dante counters a contemporary materialistic vision of Fortune and history with his own providential explanation of Fortune. The rhyme words cited above are drawn, as we shall see, from places in Monte's corpus where he sings the praises of wealth and condemns ill Fortune. Fortune is, in fact, a fundamental theme in Monte's poems, but unlike Dante he is unable to believe in a providential order beyond the cruel and arbitrary rise and fall of earthly possessions and power.

In a series of poems concluding the Vatican anthology's *canzone* section, Monte continually bemoans his ill fortune, whether amorous or economic.

H. Wayne Storey has identified in this series an original authorial collection (author's book), which he calls a "Book of Misfortune."[18] These thematically and verbally linked *canzoni* conclude with poems such as "Tanto m'abonda matera, di soperchio" and "Ancor di dire non fino, perché" that explicity describe Monte's materialistic and nontranscendent concept of Fortune. He dwells on the tragedy of his economic misfortunes while railing against "disaventura," "ventura," and, of course, his sudden fall on Fortune's wheel:

> Ancor di dire non fino, perché
> la rota di Fortuna m'à congiunto
> non mai esser digiunto
> dal basso stato e perilglioso punto.
>
> (1–4)

[I still have not finished speaking because the wheel of Fortune has imposed on me that I will never be freed from its dangerous low point.]

Like the avaricious and prodigal, Monte is solely concerned with the circle of the sublunary world—a limited vision of Fortune's wheel, in Dante's conception. Indeed, Monte seems to be implicated in Virgil's outburst:

> Quest' è colei ch'è tanto posta in croce
> pur da color che le dovrien dar lode,
> dandole biasmo a torto e mala voce.
>
> (*Inf.* 7.91–93)

[This is she who is so crucified even by those who should give her praise, wrongly blaming her and speaking ill of her.]

Not only do Monte's poems conform to this "mala voce," they are present in the canto through shared rare rhyme words, effectively singling him out as the epitome of the "ontoso metro" reproduced and critiqued in the canto.

Indeed, the passage from "Ancor di dire non fino, perché" alluded to in canto 7 contrasts not only with the themes of the canto, but also with one of the basic themes of the entire *Commedia,* the interpretation of suffering and punishment:

Non poria dir com' Povertà traripa!
Bene foll'è chi le pò star da lunga,
di guisa che no.l punga,
e pur conduce sé ch'essa lo giunga,
per viver, poï, ä l'altrui mercé!
Serv'è d' servi chi così si scipa!

(131–136)

[I could never express the precipice of Poverty! He is indeed a fool
who could stay far away from her, so that she may not harm him, and
nevertheless acts in such a way that she catches him, so that he lives,
afterward, dependent on another's mercy. Servant of servants is he
who thus causes his own ruin.]

For Monte, an individual's economic status gives meaning to his life, and a
loss in wordly success is seen as the worst possible fate. Only a fool then (or,
implicitly, a mendicant friar) would actively seek out poverty. In the perspective of the *Commedia,* on the other hand, Dante replaces poverty—a temporal hardship—as the cause of one's ruin, "così si scipa," with the eternal
punishment of the damned: "e perché nostra colpa sì ne scipa?" (*Inf.* 7.21).

Dante's revision of Monte in canto 7 suggests that he was aware of the
latter's materialistic view of society and that he recognized its persuasiveness.
In fact, Monte's skeptical worldview challenges Dante's attempt in the *Commedia* to transcend his historical circumstances. After all, the passage quoted
above could very well have described the exiled Dante. From a certain perspective, Dante did indeed fail in the world, cause his own downfall, and end
up at the bottom of the wheel; for better or for worse, he was, as Dante has
Beatrice point out, no friend of Fortune ("l'amico mio, e non de la ventura"
[*Inf.* 2.61]).[19] As is clear in *Convivio* 1.3.5, Dante was particularly conscious of
the public disgrace of involuntary poverty, "dolorosa povertade," and in addition to Monte's poetry, several thirteenth-century poems attest to a growing
societal taboo against the indigent.[20] Given contemporary attitudes about economic and social failure, it was only by viewing his personal circumstances ret-
rospectively, from outside of history, that Dante could assert that his worldly
misfortunes and outsider status authorized his otherworldly journey and sacred poem. As Nick Havely has recently argued,[21] Dante also drew on Franciscan ideals of poverty, ideals clearly at odds with the new profit economy and

the values expounded by Monte and his peers,[22] in order to legitimize his prophetic voice. Yet I would claim that even as Dante attempts rhetorically to transcend his own historicity in climactic moments of the *Commedia,* Monte's materialistic vision of Fortune and history remains uncomfortably in the background.[23] At least for contemporary readers coming from the class that produced and read the Vatican anthology, the "pane altrui" and "l'altrui scale" that Dante will have to depend on must have seemed all too close to Monte's dreaded "l'altrui mercé."

Monte Andrea and the Usurers in *Inferno* 17

The most obvious and critically recognized allusion to Monte in the *Commedia* comes in *Inferno* 17, with the rhyme words *scroscio* and *stoscio:*

> Io sentia già da la man destra il gorgo
> far sotto noi un orribile scroscio,
> per che con li occhi 'n giù la testa sporgo.
>   Allor fu' io più timido a lo stoscio.
>
> (118–121)

[I could already hear at my right hand the torrent making a horrible roar beneath us, and so I stuck out my head, and looking down, became more afraid of the fall.]

Dante is riding on the monster Geryon's back at this point, and the sound or uproar, "scroscio," of the River Phlegethon cascading into the pit of Malebolge makes him look down and suddenly fear a deadly fall, a "stoscio." Both of these *rimas caras* are uncommon in Italian, and "stoscio" is a hapax in the *Commedia*. Indeed, the term *stoscio* is rare enough in medieval Italian that its meaning has been the object of critical discussion.[24] Within the thirteenth-century lyric corpus, *scroscio* and *stoscio* are found only in the poetry of Monte Andrea. In fact, Monte uses the terms as rhyme words in two different poems—in the sonnet "Intenda, 'ntenda, chi più montat'è alto!" and the *canzone* "Ancor di dire non fino, perché."[25] Moreover, although the readings "scroscio" and "stoscio" in canto 17 are now generally accepted for stylistic and philological reasons, there are variants for both words in some of the early manuscripts.[26] These variants reveal both the difficulty and rarity of the terms even for contemporary and near-contemporary readers and their almost exclusive associations with Monte.

The generally acknowledged stylistic ties between Dante and Monte in this canto take on a renewed significance when read together with the episode of the usurers.[27] Before Dante's flight on Geryon, he observes a group of seated usurers, fending off their punishment of fire like dogs fighting off insects during the summer. They gaze fixedly at moneybags tied around their necks that display their coats of arms, proof of their nobility. In describing the usurers—all Florentine except for one Paduan—Dante directly attacks the Florentine mercantile and banking elite of his time.[28] In an example of explicit, class-based social criticism, he compares the animal emblems of the representatives of Florence's mercantile oligarchy with their own bestial characteristics. The conspicuous use of rhymes from Monte's corpus thus takes place in a canto that attacks members of Monte's social group, the ideal readership for his poetry, and the milieu that produced, read, and conserved the Vatican manuscript. Through Monte, Dante condemns not only the mores of an entire social group, but also a representative of their literary community.

As in canto 7, the theme of Fortune in canto 17 further develops a subtext with Monte's poetry. In both Monte's sonnet and *canzone,* the rhyme words *scroscio* and *stoscio* refer to a sudden fall in worldly Fortune due to the loss of riches or the onslaught of dreaded poverty. In "Ancor di dire non fino, perché"—Monte's most elaborate treatment of Fortune and her wheel—the passage alluded to in canto 17 serves as a turning point and climax of the *canzone:*

> Povertà tuto disface.
> Qual è più alto, se gli dà lo stoscio,
> òdesi ben lo scroscio,
> sì è mortale il colpo, e ciò conoscio!
> (110–113)

[Poverty destroys everything. That one who is positioned highest, if she makes him fall, you will hear the roar. The blow is so fatal: And that I know!]

While in preceding stanzas Monte eulogizes the power of wealth without any reference to his own circumstances, he turns in this passage to his own experience of falling from high on Fortune's wheel into poverty. He justifies his praise for riches and his attacks against poverty at this point by citing autobiographical evidence: he knows personally ("ciò conosco" [113]) what a blow from Fortune feels like. In the sonnet "Intenda, 'ntenda, chi più montat'è alto," Monte reprises his fall on Fortune's wheel:

> Intenda, 'ntenda, chi più montat'è alto!
> E pensi ben, ciascun, chent'è lo scroscio,
> facendo, di caduta, poi, lo salto!
> Non si trova rimedio in tale stoscio!
> Fa, dico, l'or, e[h], chente vuo', lo smalto;
> mantengnendolo bene, puo' dir poscio:
> "Tutto'ò piacere, ë non mai difalto.
> Oro fa om valere (e' ciò conosco).
>
> (1−8)

[Listen up, listen up, whoever has ascended highest! And consider well how loud the roar sounds when you slide into the abyss. There is no remedy for such a fall. Make gold, I say, and, as much as you want, other ores. Manage them well and you will be able to say afterward: "I have all pleasures, and never lack." Gold makes the man (and that I know).]

In counseling those riding high on Fortune's wheel to amass and protect their wealth, Monte not only recalls the dangers of a sudden fall, a "stoscio," as in "Ancor di dire," but also again refers to his own personal knowledge of such misfortune, "e ciò conosco"(8). It is as if Monte wanted to ensure in these two parallel passages—linked by the rhyme words *stoscio, scroscio, conosco, alto,* and *salto*—an association between his signature lyric persona and an unfortunate fall from Fortune's graces. Not surprisingly then, as we will see below, his contemporaries, including Guittone, Chiaro Davanzati, and Tomaso da Faenza, consistently identify Monte as that poet no longer mounted high on Fortune's wheel.

Like Monte's poem, *Inferno* 17 is structured around a series of images of rising and falling. Most obviously, the usurers, who are still concerned only with their fallen social status, have fallen much more seriously from divine grace. The canto also contains, in the allusions to the myths of Phaeton and Icarus (106–111),[29] two traditional images of the futile rise and inevitable fall that result from earthly ambition. The theme of Fortune and the myth of Phaeton's fall link canto 17 of *Inferno* with canto 17 of *Paradiso,* where Dante examines, as we have seen, the role of Fortune in his life and explicitly compares himself to Phaeton in the opening verses of the canto. The most important fall in this canto, of course, is the descent of Dante and Virgil on Geryon's back. John Freccero has argued that the downward spiral of Geryon's flight recalls the movement of the sun, which, in turn, represents the Neoplatonic principles of Same (in the sun's daily rotation) and Other (in its yearlong trajectory through the ecliptic).[30] Whether or not it contains such cosmological significance, Dante's circling descent on Geryon's back adds another perspective on Fortune's wheel to that provided in canto 7; in his gradual downward flight, Dante can first hear, in the "scroscio" (119), then see the punishments of Lower Hell in their totality, from a bird's-eye view. When compared to the permanent fall of the damned that Dante witnesses below him, both Monte's financial fall and Dante's exile seem mild. In fact, it may be more than coincidence that Dante swears to the veracity of his poem at this point in this same episode (*Inf.* 16.124–132). Not unlike Monte providing testimony ("e ciò conoscio") in "Ancor di dire" for his skeptical vision of society, Dante bases his contrasting perspective on the direct experience of his journey, on what he witnessed as a result of his political and spiritual fall.

Maestro Adamo / Monte Andrea and the Ethics of Lament in *Inferno* 30

The themes of Fortune and Fall bring us to Dante's most important allusion to Monte's poetry in the *Inferno,* namely canto 30 and the figure of Maestro Adamo. Here, Dante witnesses the punishment of the falsifiers in the last and worst *bolgia* of Malebolge. In particular, he encounters the quintessential representatives of fraud, Maestro Adamo and Sinone. Maestro Adamo, a counterfeiter of Florentine coins, is paralyzed with dropsy—his body swollen and deformed by impure humors. The once slippery and treacherous Sinone, the arch-perjurer who facilitated the Trojan Horse deception, is also now immobilized in Hell, struck down by a putrid fever.

The figures of Maestro Adamo and Sinone represent the culmination of Dante's exposition of the metaphorics of deceptive signifiers. Throughout his exploration of the workings of fraud in Malebolge, he examines the potential disparity between container and contained, external appearance and internal contents, sign and signifier.[31] Adamo and Sinone embody—literally in Adamo's case—the fraudulent semiotics of Malebolge. Sinone's Trojan Horse, Maestro Adamo's counterfeit coin, and the dropsical and misshapen body of Adamo himself are all examples of an incongruity between the external "face" of a sign and its internal "belly" ("'l viso non risponde a la ventraia" [54]).[32] At the same time, while Adamo's counterfeit coins, stamped with the authenticating image of John the Baptist, disguised the impure dross of their internal contents, Adamo's swollen belly cannot hide, but actually reveals, the sickly humors that lie within.[33]

The problem of poetic fraud is also never far from the surface in Dante's *Commedia*. Not surprisingly, Malebolge—the infernal web of fraud—climaxes with the presentation, in canto 30, lines 106–129, of a *tenzone* between Maestro Adamo and Sinone. In this way, Dante associates his discussion of semiotic deceit with a specific, contemporary vernacular tradition. As has long been known, the concreteness and vividness of the language of Adamo and Sinone's exchange—combined with learned schemes, allusions, and tropes—places their argument firmly within the literary practice of thirteenth-century comic-realistic poetry. Of particular note are the rare and difficult rhymes (*epa–crepa–assiepa* [119, 121, 123]; *marcia–squarcia–rinfarcia* [122, 124, 126]) and the studied linguistic and syntactic counterpoint of the disputants, such as the structures "S'io . . . , e tu," and "Quando . . . , non l'avei," "Ma . . . l'avei quando" (115, 126–127,109–111).[34] Critics generally point to Dante's own comic *tenzoni,* both with Forese Donati and Cecco Angiolieri,[35] as precedents for the vehement and masterful exchanges between Adamo and Sinone.

Although Dante's continual self-critique is a crucial element of the *Commedia,* he is also criticizing in the *tenzone* of Adamo and Sinone a competing literary tradition with specific social meanings and associations. Namely, in some cases, the rare, difficult, and even broken rhymes (*rime frante*) in the canto recall the *trobar clus* school of Guittone and the Guittonians more than Dante's own comic output.[36] Many of these characteristic rhymes in the canto, when compared to what we know of thirteenth-century uses, find precedents only in poets of the Guittonian tradition, including Panuccio del Bagno and Bacciarone di Messer Baccone da Pisa.[37]

Among the circle of Guittonians alluded to in this passage, Monte Andrea stands out for the conspicuous number of rhymes drawn from his corpus. Of particular note are the rhyme words *conio* and *demonio* (115, 117) in the canto, found in "Più soferir no.m posso ch'io non dica" (80, 85), as well as *arno* and *indarno* (65, 66), drawn from Monte's "Tanto m'abonda matera, di soperchio" (83, 84). Both passages will be discussed below. In the context of the present discussion, an even more important intertext is evoked by the rhyme words *oncia–sconcia–non ci ha* (83, 85, 87), recalling a passage from, once again, "Ancor di dire non fino, perché":

> Ma, se sentenza o rima alcuna ò guasta,
> o c'ag[g]ia il vero in alcun loco sconc[i]o,
> i' spero in ciò
> che, da cui vaï, ti pulisca, e tolla
> via d'ongni solla:
> puro ne facc[i]a ë dritto raconcio.
>
> (193–198)

[But if I have broken any rhymes or sense or deformed the truth in any place, I hope that you will be cleansed of any stains by the one who receives you, so that you will be made pure and correct.]

By addressing the *canzone* itself in these lines, Monte indirectly asks Chiaro Davanzati—the most important Florentine poet in the Vatican anthology, next to Monte—to correct the content and form ("sentenza o rima") of his poem. Dante, in picking up and playing on the rhyme *oncio–oncia* in these passages, competes with Monte's bravura in *rimas caras,* especially in offering his own thrice-split rhyme "non ci ha" (*Inf.* 30.87) for Monte's already daring and singular "spero in ciò" (195). More important, at the center of his condemnation of fraud and fraudulent language, Dante alludes to the moment in Monte's poetry where the banker-poet admits that he may have deformed and twisted the truth: "c'ag[g]ia il vero in alcun loco sconc[i]o" (194).

The tit-for-tat exchange between Adamo and Sinone also resembles the rhetorical mirroring of Monte's frequent political *tenzoni* with other members of the Florentine ruling class. In a series of sonnet exchanges placed in prominent positions in the Vatican anthology, the Guelph Monte debates other prominent Florentine citizens, such as the fellow banker-poet Messer Lambertuccio Frescobaldi, about their Ghibelline politics.[38] The sarcastic blow-for-blow exchanges in these *tenzoni,* combined with the high number of *rimas caras* and *rime frante,* sound much like the useless squabbling of the falsifiers. Monte's sonnets "Non isperate, ghebellin', socorso" and "Non val savere a cui Fortuna à scorso," co-authored with Schiatta di messer Albizo Pallavillani, and the sonnet "I baron' de la Mangna àn fatto impero," written with Ser Cione, are of particular note because the *battute* of the participants occur within, instead of between, sonnets, alternating every two or three lines, as in canto 30.[39] As we have seen in chapters 2 and 3, in the Vatican anthology these political debates bind together a community of political elites, overriding class and professional divisions through cultural means. In *Inferno* 30, through the futile bickering between Adamo and Sinone, Dante instead represents these political *tenzoni* as manifesting social contradictions and self-destructive factionalism.

As in cantos 7 and 17, the presentation of Monte's contentious poetics in canto 30 is framed by the themes of Fortune and history. The canto begins with an image of Fortune's wheel, "E quando la Fortuna volse in basso / l'altezza de' Troian che tutto ardiva" (And when Fortune wheeled to the ground the pride of the Trojans) [13–14], and ends with another explicit evocation, "se piú avvien che Fortuna t'accoglia" [if it happens again that Fortune find you] [146]. Moreover, the lengthy allusions to the transformed destiny of Troy and Thebes that introduce the canto are mythic illustrations of the mutability of Fortune and of her command over collective as well as individual fate. Dante explores in particular in this canto the consequences of a sudden fall on Fortune's wheel: like Icarus and Phaeton, Troy has fallen from its proud "altezza" (14) and the Trojan queen, Hecuba, is now "trista, misera, and cattiva" (sorrowing, wretched, and a captive) [16].[40] Prefiguring Dante's fall among "la compagnia malvagia e scempia" (the evil and senseless company) [*Par.* 17.62] immediately after his exile, Maestro Adamo himself is reduced to "miseria" (61) and has fallen among "sì fatta famiglia" (such a household) [88]—in life, Adamo had all he needed; now he longs in vain for a drop of water: "io ebbi, vivo, assai di quel ch'i' volli, / e ora, lasso! un gocciol d'acqua bramo" (62–63). Critics have recognized in Adamo's yearning for a drop of water an allusion to the New Testament story (Luke 16:19–31) about a fall from worldly fortune, the parable of the rich man, Dives, who spurned the beggar Lazarus.[41] After his death, Dives, from his low point in Hell, sees the beggar Lazarus exalted in the bosom of Abraham and begs him, in vain, for a drop of water. Finally, in his recollection of the undefiled waters of the Casentino, Adamo, like his namesake, recalls for readers the most important fall, the archetypal Fall of mankind from the Garden of Eden.

Ironically, Maestro Adamo seems unaware of the typological significance of his name and the multivocal meanings of his fall. Even in the afterlife, he remains concerned only with Fortune's wheel—who is on top and who has fallen to the bottom. Adamo envies Dante's and Virgil's privileged status in Hell, "'O voi che sanz'alcuna pena siete, / e non so io perché, nel mondo gramo'" (O you who are without any punishment, and I know not why, in this grim world) [58–59], and still blames others and seeks vengeance for his own fall, "Io sono per lor tra sì fatta famiglia" (Because of them, I am among such a household) [88]. Although he acknowledges the "rigida giustizia" (unbending justice) [70] of his fate, he fails to see any providential meaning in his fall; it is a stroke of bad luck, a bad turn of the wheel. He lacks the vision from outside history, or rather from the end of sacred or universal history, that serves as the basis for Dante's narrative. Rather, like the avaricious and the prodigal, and like the class-obsessed usurers, even in Hell Adamo interprets history and Fortune through material eyes and discerns only the smallest circle of Fortune's wheel.

With Maestro Adamo, concerned solely with his personal, worldly fall, Dante creates a parodied image of Monte Andrea. Adamo, as we have seen, shares Monte's wholly secular vision of historical events, a vision the latter confesses to in "Tanto m'abonda matera, di soperchio":

> Ora, s'alcun la mia canzon corregge,
> da l'una parte la Divina Legge
> pongar, però ched io 'n essa nom parlo;
> ché, se ciò fosse, poria, .l mio detto, isfarlo:
> secondo il corso del mondo mess'ò ['n] rima!
> (142–146)

[Now, if anyone wanted to correct my *canzone,* let him set aside Divine Law—since I am not speaking according to it. If it were so, he could undo my poem: for my rhymes have followed the course of the world!]

Similarly, Adamo is clearly still interpreting his punishment "secondo il corso del mondo." Furthermore, when Maestro Adamo laments the worst aspect of his eternal punishment in Hell—the memory of the waters of the Casentino that torment his feverish state—Dante recalls, through the rhyme words *Arno—indarno—discarno* (*Inf.* 30.65, 67, 69), another key passage from "Tanto m'abonda matera":

> Ché tal colpo sì 'l cor de l'ommo squatra,
> dir non si puote bene co' tal latra!
> Ché 'l suo lavoro è sempre pur in darno:
> come 'l molino è che ne va per Arno.
>
> (81–84)

[Because that kind of blow gashes a man's heart, it is not possible to say in words how he wails. But his efforts are always pointless; like a milling wheel moving down the Arno.]

The "colpo" (81) Monte refers to in the passage is the mortal blow of poverty, the worst possible fall one can endure. For Monte, the individual who suffers the fate of irreversible *Povertà* resembles the unmoored milling wheel crashing downstream—another image of the violent revolutions of Fortune's wheel.[42]

Dante was not the first to critique the limited perspective of Monte's laments. The Florentine banker-poet's contemporaries parodied the self-pitying rhetoric of his poetry in their *tenzoni* with him. For example, in "Amoroso voler m'àve commosso," Tomaso da Faenza mimics the weak-willed poet who "immantenente dice: 'Ora languisco!'" (immediately says, "Now I languish") [35], and Chiaro Davanzati ends his "A San Giovanni, a Monte, mia canzone" reprimanding Monte for his pessimism and self-pity: ché quegli è de lo pregio disïoso / che 'l si fa sposo—e non dice 'Io doloro!'" (because that one who desires honor makes it his own, and does not say "I suffer!") [87–88].[43] In the same poem, Chiaro, playing Lady Philosophy to Monte's melancholic Boethius, makes use of the image of the wheel of Fortune to encourage Monte to re-evaluate his circumstances:

> Ché 'l mondo à d'una ròtta asimilglianza
> che volge per usanza:
> che 'l basso monta e l'alto cade giuso.
>
> (73–75)

[Because the world is similar to a wheel, and it has always turned so that those on the bottom ascend and those on top fall down.]

According to Chiaro, just as those on top must fall, those on the bottom must rise again. In particular, Chiaro cites the redemption and salvation of Adam and Eve after the Fall as a reason to hope and evidence of the ultimate justice behind Fortune's turns: "Pilgli d'Adamo e d'Ev'asempro e miri / di gran martiri,—in gioi fuor trambondui!" (Take the example of Adam and Eve and observe. From great suffering they both came unto joy) [59–60]. In Monte's response to Chiaro, however, he fails to see the correlation between the hope and potential for redemption offered by Adam and Eve's exemplum and his own personal misfortune and failure. In this sense, Monte is already an ironized version of the first fallen man, as Dante brings out by giving his voice to a fallen Adam in *Inferno* 30.

The question of exemplarity—suggested in Chiaro's *tenzone* and further highlighted in *Inferno* 30—is particularly germane to Monte's poetry since the failed banker draws continuously from the example of his own personal history in order to justify his materialistic worldview and to link thematically the poems in his "Book of Misfortune." His major *canzoni* are a mixture of private lament and invective, typical of the vernacular plaintive tradition. In "Più soferir no.m posso ch'io non dica," for example, the first poem in the *tenzone* with Chiaro, only stanzas 5 and 6 of the seven stanzas and three *congedi* of the poem are dedicated to Monte's analysis of contemporary society. The rest of the poem is an autobiographical lament of his fall into poverty. Surrounded by descriptions of his own personal experience, Monte's vehement, cynical vision of the world is particularly effective:

> Quello cotale è tenuto idonio,
> se, 'l suo tesoro, troppo no.n gli duole;
> parenti, amici, grandez[z]a à quanto vuole:
> a ciascun piace moneta di suo conio.
> E 'n ciò poria cernire assai asempro,
> ma or non volglio ch'um poco mi tempro.
> Ma si consilglio c'ongn'uom procacci avere,
> e, quanto può, mantenerlo a podere:
> chi no.l fa, più 'nodiato è che domonio.

(77–85)

[That one is considered becoming, if his riches do not weigh too heavily on him, he will have friends, relatives, and esteem—as much as he wants. Everyone likes the money of his coinage. And I could cite many examples of this, but now I do not want to, I am restraining myself a bit. But I strongly suggest that every man procure wealth and, as much as he can, maintain it in his possession. He who does not will be hated more than the devil.]

The explicitly wealth-based philosophy in these lines is based on personal experience, on knowledge acquired *per experimenta*—Monte could "cernire assai asempro." At the close of the second *congedo,* he offers his own history in support of his demystifying view of contemporary social structure: "c'oro ed argento è de l'omo corona! / Chi 'l vero asempro ne vole: ëchi'io!" (for gold and silver crown the man! Whoever wants an example of this: Here I am!) [136–137]. The exemplarity of Monte's constructed persona serves here a distinctly modern function: instead of participating in a mythical, culturally recognized narrative for all Christians to imitate or avoid, it simply legitimizes and lends credence to his own statements. That Dante was struck by the mixing of social invective and personal narrative in this passage is suggested by his use of the rhyme words *conio* and *domonio* in canto 30 (115, 118), as well as Monte's images of coining and of the *monetier:* "a ciascun piace moneta di suo conio" (80).

However, in *Inferno* 30 Dante raises the stakes of rhetorical exemplarity. As scholars have noted, Maestro Adamo suggests not only the exemplum of a post-Edenic Adam, but also the second Adam, Christ, in an ironic representation of the crucifixion.[44] Like Maestro Adamo, the crucified Christ is described in the literature of the time as being strung like a musical instrument. Adamo is also bound, thirsting, tormented, and flanked by two liars as Christ is bound, thirsting, tormented, and flanked by two thieves. In addition, in order to elicit sympathy, Maestro Adamo appropriates a crucial passage from Lamentations:

"O voi che sanz'alcuna pena siete,
e non so io perché, nel mondo gramo,"
diss'elli a noi, "guardate e attendete
a la miseria del maestro Adamo."

(58–62)

["O you who are without any punishment, and I know not why, in this grim world," he said to us, "gaze and attend to the wretchedness of Master Adam."]

In the literature of devotion to the Cross, Christ utters the same passage from Lamentations echoed by Maestro Adamo: "O all ye that pass by the way, attend, and see if there be any sorrow like to my sorrow" (1:12). This and other texts from Lamentations were often associated in the liturgy and in contemporary iconography with the humility of Christ's sacrifice.[45] Yet Maestro Adamo and, by association, Monte Andrea, remain tragically unaware of the irony of the implicit references in their accounts of their personal misfortunes to the exemplary narratives of Adam and Christ.

When the *monetier* Adamo cites Lamentations 1:12, moreover, Dante is both calling attention to his own first-person plaintive rhetoric and distinguishing it from the autobiographical laments of Maestro Adamo and Monte Andrea. Throughout his corpus, Dante often associates his historical circumstances with contemporary interpretations of Lamentations. In this way, his plaintive rhetoric for Beatrice or for the divided city of Florence point to and participate in the literal and allegorical meanings medieval readers saw in the biblical text: the mourning for the destruction of Jerusalem, for the crucified Christ, and for man's pilgrimage on earth.[46] By associating his private mourning with the sacred and typological meanings of Lamentations, the exiled Dante reinterprets his problematic autobiography in light of the authoritative prophetic and Christological narratives of his time—a textual apotheosis. Maestro Adamo, on the other hand, incorporates Lamentations into his private narrative, and not the other way around. In direct opposition to Dante's centrifugal intertextuality, Adamo's allusion to Lamentations collapses inward, pointing only toward his own story, his own hopeless historicity.

For Dante, the distinction between a narcissistic fixation ("lo specchio di Narcisso" [the mirror of Narcissus] [128]) on one's historical circumstances and the transformation of an individual life into an autobiographical exemplum lies in the perspective from which one views the self. The questions of vision and self-reflection are central to the last vivid metaphor of the canto, the analogy of the dreamer:

> Qual è colui che suo dannaggio sogna
> che sognando desidera sognare
> sì quel ch'è, come non fosse, agogna,
>
> tal mi fec'io , non possendo parlare,
> che disïava scusarmi, e scusava
> me tuttavia, e nol mi credia fare.
>
> (135–141)

[Like one who dreams of harm, and, dreaming, wishes he were dreaming, so that he yearns for what is as if it were not, so I became, unable to speak, wishing to excuse myself, and I was excusing myself all along, though I did not think so.]

In this passage, Dante's character has just been reprimanded by Virgil for fixating on the violence and brutal materiality of the exchange between Maestro Adamo and Sinone. Many commentators have interpreted Virgil's censure as part of a palinode written by a mature Dante for his earlier comic-realistic poetry, a last goodbye to the sort of burlesque *tenzone* he engaged in with Forese Donati.[47] In any event, the shame demonstrated by Dante's character pardons him immediately in his guide's eyes. Just as the dreamer of a bad dream wishes to be dreaming, Dante's character desires to be forgiven and already is.

In the labyrinthine predicament of the dreamer, Dante emphasizes the split between a subjective viewpoint and a more encompassing, objective reality, a reality visible only from outside the self. The dreaming self is not able to get outside of consciousness, to view himself sleeping. In a similar fashion, the Christian *viator* strives in vain to view himself critically, to judge the present life on earth from a larger perspective—both from above, from the vantage point of God and the heavens (as in Dante's retrospective vision of the threshing floor in *Paradiso* 22), and beyond, from the end of time and within an economy of salvation. Recalling the split between subjective vision and objective reality in the dream of "Donna pietosa" in the *Vita Nova*,[48] the analogy of the dreamer at the end of canto 30 can even be seen as representing *in nuce* the global historical trope of the *Commedia*, the totalizing vision beyond time and subsequent objectification of the self. In this view, the dreaming self stands for Dante pilgrim and the dreamer for Dante poet, who has woken up and recognizes the dream for what it is. The same split of the self enables the frequent use of the palinode in the *Commedia*, since, having been "woken up" by his otherwordly journey, Dante now witnesses the dreamlike inconsistency of his previous literary incarnations.

Of course, Dante the poet remains, throughout the *Commedia,* very much a part of time and history. He engages with the poetics of Monte Andrea from a distinctly temporal perspective, enmeshed in the contentious discourses of literary prestige and canonicity. As we have seen, Monte's importance — at least among representatives of the powerful Tuscan mercantile class — is demonstrated by his highlighted position in Vaticano 3793. Dante's poetry, on the other hand, is excluded from the thousands of poems collected in contemporary manuscripts and the great lyric anthologies — an uneasy historical reality essential to, and at the same time obfuscated by, the rhetorical strategies of his work. By writing the self-authorizing *Commedia,* the exiled Dante seeks to reverse the circumstances of contemporary manuscript culture, condemning Monte and the merchant readers and writers who championed him. In Dante's re-ordering of the social world, Monte's poetry culminates the final circle of Malebolge, the infernal anthology of fraud. In this way, Dante sends Monte on his final ironic fall, disparaging the poet on his way to creating the *poema sacro.* On the wheel of poetic legitimacy and literary authority, Dante is Lazarus to Monte's Dives.

Still, Monte is never named directly. The allusions to his poetry remain submerged in the *Commedia,* visible only to readers already familiar with his corpus and his representation in manuscripts such as the Vatican anthology. In a sense, Dante treats Monte's poetry the same way he treats the avaricious or the usurers. They are punished in Hell but remain faceless, nameless: "la sconoscente vita che i fé sozzi / ad ogne conoscenza or li fa bruni" (the undiscerning life that befouled them makes them dark now to all recognition) [*Inf.* 7.53–54]. In this way, Dante can both be in history and continue the rhetorical trope of writing outside of history. Our increasing distance (spatial, temporal, social) from the milieu of Vaticano 3793 further obfuscates the intertext with Monte's poetry in the *Commedia.* The Monte Andrea behind Maestro Adamo gives way to the larger, transhistorical questions of Fortune and Truth, and Dante's providential history becomes the only narrative possible. As modern readers of Dante, we are at risk of missing the rich, heterogeneous, and competing literary histories and narratives of his time, histories and narratives expressed in manuscript culture and latent in the *Commedia* itself. Despite the difficulties inherent in any historical inquiry into a fragmentary and fading past, we still have much to gain from trying to name names.

"Dante"

Purgatorio 30.55 and the Question of the Female Voice

What's in a name? Or rather, what's in a proper name? What changes when we identify Dante's treatment of Fortune, and specifically his use of *rimas caras,* with the name Monte Andrea? In part, as I have argued, Monte's name stands for the politics, values, and beliefs of the Florentine mercantile oligarchy in *Inferno.* His name functions as a placemark for a specific class and culture. Monte's name is also easily turned into a common noun, through a pun; he is literarily the sum, the *monta,* of the Vatican anthology, evident in the reproduction of the abbreviation *Mo* as in contemporary account books. Yet the author's name, whether found within the text as a signature or without as an attribution, also resists being turned into just another signifier. As with other proper names, it still promises full presence, direct reference (or "rigid designation" in Saul Kripke's formulation), singularity—wistfully expressed by Emmanuel Levinas in his forward to *Proper Names*:

> Perhaps the names of persons whose saying *signifies* a face—proper names, in the middle of all these common names and commonplaces—can resist the dissolution of meaning and help us to speak. Perhaps they will enable us to divine, behind the downfall of discourse, the end of a certain *intelligibility* but the dawning of a new one.[1]

With the proper name, we still expect a gold standard, a guarantee behind the chain of signifiers, a face.[2] On tombstones and war memorials, proper names are not meant to be easily absorbed into language and interpretation; they denote rather than connote. Indeed, the link between memory, loss, and proper names is especially strong, demonstrating that even if a naming event is not necessarily linguistic, it remains social and conventional. Dante clearly understands this social aspect of naming when he avoids naming the avaricious and the usurers, including Monte Andrea. Effectively exiled from the place of memory, they are exposed to the obliviating elements of time.

Among many other things, Dante's *Commedia* is also a memorial for the dead. Within this monument, acts of naming and being named function as crucial re-inscriptions of individual identities within a social realm. For example, Emperor Justinian's insistence on his Christian name ("Cesare fui e son Iustinïano" [I was Caesar and I am Justinian] [*Par.* 6.10]) elegantly synthesizes the radical social leveling of Christian community. On the other hand, the simple female name "Pia" introduced by the familiarity of the definite pronoun in "ricorditi di me, che son la Pia" (remember me: I am Pia) [*Purg.* 5.133] has haunted readers for the very loss of reference implied in her speech. Due to her compromised socioeconomic position and patronymic anonymity, we cannot oblige her request to be remembered. Despite the valiant work of commentators, "la Pia" remains a voice locked within the text.

The most important act of naming occurs in *Purgatorio* 30, where Beatrice names Dante.[3] Although poetic signatures were not uncommon in medieval literary texts,[4] Dante still felt he had to justify the intrusion of his name, claiming it was necessary in order to maintain fidelity to the narrated events: "quando mi volsi al suon del nome mio / che di necessità qui si registra" (when I turned at the sound of my name, which of necessity is recorded here) [62–63]. Dante is therefore named in the text because he was named by Beatrice in the journey; he simply records what transpired, what he heard. At the same time, the deictic "qui" in his justification is ambiguous, for "here" could refer to a point in the narrative, a place on the page, the moment of writing, or the moment of reading.[5] In a similar fashion, Dante's signature authenticates the text from the outside at the same time as it forms part of the text that needs to be authenticated. To put it another way, the character of Beatrice in the *Commedia* purportedly declares the existence of an empirical "Dante" outside of the text who, in turn, bears witness to the supposed encounter with Beatrice and the calling of his name. The desire to resolve this ambiguity between internal and external in the naming event, text and context, likely influenced an exegetical tradition beginning with the commentary of Dante's son, Pietro, in which the poet's Christian name is resolved as a common name, "dante," the giver.[6] Considering the etymological interpretations of names found in the medieval *accessus ad auctorem*,[7] Dante most likely expected similar interpretations of his shortened name ("Dante" for "Durante").[8] Yet significantly he refuses to gloss it within the text, allowing its interpellative function to remain intact, along with its promise of rigid designation.

When Beatrice calls out to Dante at the top of Mount Purgatory, she is hailing—within the fiction of the narrative—a singularity, a unique individual at a moment of profound transformation. The pronouncement of Dante's name comes at a horizon in the cosmology of the *Commedia,* the narrative of conversion, and the journey to God. Dante is called into a new social identity, a baptism of sorts,[9] while he is between heaven and earth, sin and repentance, Virgil and Beatrice. Much of the recent scholarship on the canto has concentrated on this shift between Virgil and Beatrice—expressed through an especially dense web of allusions to Virgil's poetry—as a statement of Dante's implicitly superior Christian or theological poetics. In these readings, Christian *caritas* replaces the doomed *eros* of Dido (*Aeneid* 4) and the resurrection of and reunion with Beatrice trumps Orpheus's failed recovery of Eurydice (*Georgics* 4).[10] According to John Freccero's influential analysis of the episode, Dante inscribes his name into the narrative while simultaneously effacing Virgil's text; this is evident in the movement from citation to translation to allusion in the canto.[11]

This is not the place to begin a detailed analysis of canto 30 or to reexamine the influential critical tradition surrounding it. The philosophical implications of proper names alone deserve a separate treatment beyond the scope of the present work. At the same time, considering the centrality of Dante's signature both within the text and for the critical tradition, it is worth considering, however briefly, a few of the questions raised by the episode that stand out in light of the previous chapters. For example, why does Dante choose Beatrice, the beloved object of his lyric poetry, to call out his name? What is the significance in this context of the female voice? And what does it mean that Beatrice finally speaks? For all their simplicity, I believe these questions—contextualized within the historical practice of writing in the female voice—are crucial for understanding the name games in this canto. In addition, I want to touch upon these issues because they illustrate how a material text peripheral to the world of the *Commedia,* such as the mercantile, municipal Vatican anthology, can make its presence felt at the very core of Dante's masterpiece.

The reunion of Dante's character with Beatrice is also a return for the poet to the literary tradition of writing in the female voice. Indeed, the entire first part of Dante's otherworldly voyage, his "journey to Beatrice," can be seen as climaxing in a violent and realistic *contrasto* with his beloved, a heated exchange in Eden. At the end of canto 30 and at the beginning of canto 31 of *Purgatorio,* Beatrice reprimands Dante for his transgressions, for abandoning her and the spiritual path for what he confesses are false, earthly pleasures: "Le presenti cose / col falso lor piacer" (Present things with their false pleasure) [*Purg.* 31.34–35]. The moment is particularly effective because the encounter is foreshadowed throughout the *Commedia*; finally, we see the reason and cause of his voyage, the interceding, beatified Beatrice. Even more striking, after having prepared us with an entire poetic career centered around Beatrice, Dante finally has her speak. Up until this point he has studiously avoided the rhetorical fraudulence inherent in writing in the female voice. Even at the center of the *Vita Nova,* for instance, when Dante calls out to Beatrice, her iconic visage only seems to speak. Her utterance of "Dante" in *Purgatorio* 30.55, also coming at the cosmological center of the work, can be viewed in this respect as the long-awaited response to Dante's broken "Beatrice." As in the *Vita Nova* episode, Dante is once again surprisingly inarticulate. At the end of *Purgatorio,* Dante not only writes in the voice of the *donne,* the female public of the *Vita Nova,* but daringly, and at long last, in the voice of his *donna.* And his lady is not happy.

Beatrice is surprisingly concrete and realistic in her first first-person appearance—especially surprising if we consider the abstract quality of her representation in Dante's stilnovist output. In contrast to the latter, here in Earthly Paradise she recalls the lady with whom Guittone matched wits in his fictional *tenzoni,* especially in her biting, sarcastic tone. Undermining the literary idealization of adulterous love, Beatrice's accuses Dante directly of betraying her with another: "questi si tolse a me, e diessi altrui" (this one took himself from me and gave himself to another) [*Purg.* 30.126]. The language and syntax of Beatrice's discourse are reminiscent, moreover, of the sort of colloquial forms found in contemporary poetic exchanges involving female personae. In order to convey spontaneity and familiarity of speech,

Dante has Beatrice use direct and uncomplicated phrases—imperatives ("Guardaci ben!" [*Purg.* 30.73], "dì, dì" [*Purg.* 31.5], "Rispondi a me" [*Purg.* 30.11], "alza la barba" [*Purg.* 30.68]); simple interrogatives ("Come degnasti" [*Purg.* 30.74], "Che pense" [*Purg.* 31.10]); and frequent repetition ("non piangear anco, non piangere ancora" [*Purg.* 30.56], "Ben son, ben son Beatrice" [*Purg.* 30.73], "dì, dì" [*Purg.* 31.5]).[12] While in the *De vulgari eloquentia,* Dante employed similar language to mimic municipal poetry and distance it from his own literary output, here these simplified rhetorical and grammatical structures form part of the critique itself, distinguishing—by its directness and transparency—Beatrice's voice from Dante's inflated lyric persona. Finally, Beatrice's critique—as usual with the female speakers in dialogic poems— is directed at metaliterary and linguistic sins taken from Dante's early lyrics and *Vita Nova.* Whether the ultimate target of her condemnation is a dalliance with the *donna gentile,* with Lady Philosophy, or with the *pargoletta,* Beatrice embodies the linguistic skepticism characteristic of writing in the female voice in her demystification of the courtly tradition. In this way, just as Guittone ends his sonnet sequence with the lady revealing his previous poetic deceit and several quires of Vaticano 3793 finish with female speakers critical of the language and practices of the love lyric, Dante finishes the lyric anthology of *Purgatorio* with a self-critique *in voce di donna.*[13]

By framing Beatrice's metaliterary critique within the tradition of writing in the female voice, Dante also exposes his project to the associations with fraud that accompany dialogic poetic genres. Indeed, the fact that Beatrice speaks at all underscores the potential fictionality of his poem. In his early works, as we have seen, Dante carefully disassociated himself from the blatant artificiality of writing *in voce di donna.* Neither he nor the stilnovists pretend to have their ladies speak or respond to their entreaties. Yet at the top of Mount Purgatory, Dante not only has his literary beloved speak, he embeds his signature in her voice. In doing so, he daringly conflates the externally authenticating function of the authorial signature with the mark of the text's potential inauthenticity, the fictional female voice.

An important precedent for this game of mirrors in which creator and created mutually authenticate or delegitimize each other is found in the love poetry of Guittone. As part of the exchange of sonnets with "la donna," Guittone's character is addressed by name by his invented female persona in "Certo, Guitton, de lo mal tuo mi pesa." In this way, the poet inscribes the empirical guarantee of the authorship and integrity of his sonnet sequence within the voice of a female other who contemporaries must have recognized as Guittone himself ("guittone medesimo" according to the rubrics in the Vatican anthology). Within Dante's own corpus, the closest parallel occurs in the episode of Geryon, where Dante swears by the text itself to the truthfulness of what he witnessed: "per le note / di questa comedìa, lettor, ti giuro" (by the notes of this comedy, reader, I swear to you) [*Inf.* 16.128–129]. The situation in *Purgatorio* 30 is even more complex since Dante incorporates the act of swearing—in the form of the authenticating authorial signature— into the narrative itself, into Beatrice's hailing, which he is then "forced" to record, "che di necessità qui si registra" (63), if he wants to be accurate and truthful to what transpired.

While, through the reunion scene with Beatrice, Dante indirectly acknowledges that his poem could be seen as participating in the theatrical mimesis of the *contrasto* and the *tenzone fittizia,* in several important respects he distinguishes his poetic identity from the author figures of these dialogic genres. Most obviously, there is very little actual contrasting going on at the top of Mount Purgatory; while Beatrice assumes the realistic tone and skepticism of the female persona in dialogic poems, Dante's own voice is comically reduced in his exchange with the beloved. Indeed, overwhelmed by shame, the responses of Dante's character are barely articulate amid his sobbing. Furthermore, instead of demonstrating the rhetorical mastery and implicit fraud suggested by Guittone's *ars armandi,* he confesses his deceit, no longer able to hide from his true reflection. If the subjectivity of the male protagonist in dialogic poems is defined by a particular confluence of ego, desire, and linguistic deceit, Dante's self is rendered vulnerable, exposed to the searing, all-seeing gaze of his stern admiral. And while in the *contrasto* and *tenzone fittizia,* rhetorical concealment often belies a confidence in the integrity of the self, a self in control of language instead of possessed by it, in *Purgatorio* 30, confronted by the transformation of his desired object into a speaking subject, Dante accompanies his signature with an emptying out of identity, a kind of kenosis.[14]

Dante's subversion of the poetry of seduction in his encounter with Beatrice is foreshadowed by the encounter with Matelda and the accompanying allusions to Guido Cavalcanti's *ballata,* "In un boschetto trova' pasturella."[15] Dante's first glimpse of the solitary Matelda in the forest of Earthly Paradise, "una donna soletta che si gia" (*Purg.* 28.40), evokes Cavalcanti's description of the shepherdess he found alone in the woods, "che sola sola per lo bosco gia" (12), and canto 29 begins with Matelda "cantando come donna innamorata" just as Cavalcanti's shepherdess "cantava come fosse 'namorata" (7).[16] Just as it is generally acknowledged that Matelda anticipates Beatrice, I would argue that Cavalcanti's *pastorella*, with its playful reversal of gender roles, anticipates Dante's modified *contrasto* in *Purgatorio* 30–31. In fact, "In un boschetto trova' pasturella," the closest any of the *stilnovists* will come to writing a poem *in voce di donna*,[17] already re-interprets the convention from a critical standpoint. The *ballata* begins traditionally enough with the male narrator coming upon a vulnerable peasant girl in a rustic setting. His courtly interaction with her belies his true intent, to possess her sexually: "Fra me stesso diss'i': 'Or è stagione/ di questa pasturella gio' pigliare'" (I was thinking to myself: "Now is the time to take pleasure from this peasant girl") [17–18]. The scheming intentions of Cavalcanti's voyeuristic narrator are soon overridden, however, by the sexual forwardness of the shepherdess who grabs him by the hand, leading him under a tree and showing him the God of Love Himself. The subversive potential of the narrator's sexual passivity was noted by Lapo Farinata degli Uberti, who accuses Cavalcanti, in the parody "Guido, quando dicesti pasturella," of homosexual sodomy.

When Dante's beloved stands above him in judgment, the scene has several features in common with Cavalcanti's *pastorella*, in which the narrator's erotic gaze and intended seduction are suddenly swept aside by the assertiveness of the shepherdess. In a similar fashion, the expectations of Dante's character (and his readers), generated by the elegiac tone of the canto and the various anticipations of Beatrice's arrival in both *Inferno* and *Purgatorio*, are foiled by her immediacy and brashness. Of course, there are also important differences between the Purgatorial scene and the *pastorella*—namely, that Beatrice's superiority over Dante is moral and spiritual, rather than explicitly sexual as in Cavalcanti. Yet the crucial role that the Cavalcantian Matelda plays in the encounter with Beatrice—culminating in Dante's baptism in the River Lethe in *Purgatorio* 31, where the short action verbs detailing Dante's spiritual submission ("tratto m'avea" [94], "abbracciommi," "mi sommerse" [101]) echo Cavalcanti's sexual submission ("per man mi prese" [21], "menòmmi" [23])—suggests that Dante took very seriously the implications of "In un boschetto," in particular its playful dismantling of the male authorial ego.

Dante further tinkers with the conventions of the Italian love lyric by staging his dialogue with the beloved as a confession. He substitutes, in this way, a verbal act of transparency for the rhetorical persuasion and deceit traditionally associated with the male protagonists of dialogic poems. Indeed, compared with the verbal finesse allotted Beatrice (characteristic of the female personae we have looked at), Dante's stuttering, sobbing character is practically silenced. Dante can be seen in this way as inverting the standard hierarchy in the Italian lyric between who speaks and who is spoken about. Furthermore, while in the *contrasto* and the *tenzone fittizia* the relation between author-figure and empirical author is arbitrary, Dante insists that the exchange that takes place with Beatrice in Purgatory is autobiographical truth.[18] In part, as I have suggested, Beatrice's reprimands of Dante participate in the tradition of critical female voices such as those found in the Vatican anthology. Yet the naming of both Dante and Beatrice ("Ben son, ben son Beatrice" [73]) in this canto, along with their shared past, also functions in a similar manner to the poet's reference in *Inferno* 19 to having broken the baptismal font or in *Purgatorio* 27 to having already seen burned bodies ("umani corpi già veduti accesi" [18]); it guarantees a historical existence of the author outside of the narrative. Dante's revision of the tradition of writing in the female voice is thus as radical as it is precarious, since he stakes the success of his project, not on rhetorical mastery, but on its truth claims, on the readers' belief in an extratextual author named Dante and his now disembodied beloved, Beatrice.

And yet, even though Dante clearly distances his dialogue with Beatrice from the more conventional aspects of writing in the female voice, it remains nonetheless significant that the poet returns to this tradition at all, considering his literary career up until this point. In fact, the goal-oriented journey to Beatrice, climaxing in the direct confrontation with her in *Purgatorio* 30 and 31, stands in contrast with the manifesto of disinterested praise of the *Vita Nova* and the decision therein to write about her, not to her. Dante's need to justify this reversal in the poetics of the *poesia della lode* might therefore lie behind his attempts in these cantos to distinguish his new relation to Beatrice from the sort of poetry he had rejected in the *Vita Nova* and the *De vulgari eloquentia*. At the same time, it is also possible that Dante wishes to acknowledge here a certain indebtedness to the dialogic, contrasting poetics preferred by the merchant readers and writers of the Vatican anthology (the same sort of urban readers who would be the first to recognize, circulate, and promote his masterpiece). In this light, while critics have noted the importance of Dante's signature in *Purgatorio* 30 as a way of distinguishing his new theological poetry from its Virgilian and classical influences, the emphasis on poetic individuality in the canto has perhaps been overstated.[19] From a certain perspective, Dante's naming and baptism at this point is a return to a poetic community and a socially recognized identity, an identity constructed around the rites of love. More importantly, in turning away from some of the limits of Virgil's epic worldview, it is striking that Dante would turn toward the socially and semiotically debased *contrasto*. Yet if I am correct in finding traces in *Purgatorio* 30–31 of the theatrical mimesis, heterogeneous voices, and narrative tendencies characterizing the Vatican anthology, perhaps we are meant to recognize the extent to which the poet was influenced by such elements in the creation of his incessantly dialogic "Comedy."

Notes

Notes to Introduction

1. Citations and quotations from the *Vita Nova* (hereafter cited in text as *VN*) are based on Gorni's edition.

2. For an important rethinking of the palinode in Dante, see Ascoli, "Palinode and History."

3. See Hollander, "Dante *Theologus-Poeta*" and Nardi, "Dante profeta," in *Dante e la cultura medievale,* 336–416.

4. Although an issue of *Dante Studies* (1992) collects various important essays on Dante and his audience(s), these are concerned primarily with his implied readership and not with the historical reception of his texts.

5. Contini, *Un'idea di Dante.* For an influential global study in English of the lyric poets in Dante, see Barolini, *Dante's Poets.*

6. Representative of this revisionist trend is Giunta, *La poesia italiana.* See also, among the other contributions by Barolini on this subject, "Guittone's 'Ora parra.'"

7. On the other hand, philosophical and doctrinal examinations of Dante and his circle of poets, at least since the fundamental contributions by Nardi, have elucidated the ideological seriousness and cultural and social import of contemporary poetic debates. See *Dante e la cultura medievale.*

8. Ong, *Orality and Literacy.*

9. Ibid., 115–121.

10. See McGann, *The Textual Condition,* 3–16. McGann is speaking, however, of the specificity of printed texts and bibliographical codes. In fact, it is important not to overemphasize the distinctions between manuscript and print from a purely technical, determinist perspective, but instead to underline the evolving practices of textual

experience and interpretation. In many ways, mechanical reproduction began in late medieval manuscript culture just as the unrepeatability of the autograph continues to this day (see chapter 4).

11. See, for example, Folena, "Überlieferungsgeschichte," 2:319–537, esp. 375.

12. See, for example, Del Sal, "Guittone e i guittoniani."

13. For the New Philology, see the special issue on the subject in *Speculum* 65 (1990) as well as Paden, *The Future of the Middle Ages*. Also of note is Segre's critical review of this volume.

14. See in particular Degenais, "That Bothersome Residue."

15. Joseph Bédier (d. 1938) was one of the first to critique the Lachmannian editing method based on family trees of extant texts. As opposed to this genealogical editing, he promoted editions based primarily on the single most reliable manuscript of a tradition. That the New Philology emerged in the context of medieval French literature is not surprising considering Bédier's continuing influence on the French philological tradition.

16. In the Italian context, the emphasis is often on intellectual history, such as the emergence of the vernacular author-figure, rather than on social or political history. See Borra, *Guittone d'Arezzo*; Holmes, *Assembling the Lyric Self*; and Storey, *Transcription and Visual Poetics*. Storey's work stands out as the first to bring to the attention, at least of an Anglo-American public, the relevance of manuscript culture for medieval Italian studies.

17. The modified Lachmannian methods still practiced, in many ways, by Italian philologists were first formulated by Barbi in *La nuova filologia*.

18. Excellent overviews of the history and current situation of romance philology in Italy can be found in Cerchi, "Filologie del 2000"; Avalle, "Un'idea di filologia romanza," in *La doppia verità*, 705–717; and Segre and Speroni, "Filologia testuale e letteratura italiana."

19. For the private and public readers of the *Vita Nova*, see Ahern, "The New Life of the Book" and "The Reader on the Piazza."

20. Curtius, "The Book as Symbol," in *European Literature*, 302–347; Singleton, *An Essay on the "Vita Nuova*," 22–54. For a rare study comparing Dante's codicological metaphors with contemporary practices, see Ahern, "Binding the Book."

21. Carruthers, *The Book of Memory*.

22. Dionisotti, *Geografia e storia*.

23. On the social and epistolary function of *tenzoni*, see Giunta, *Versi a un destinatario* and *Due saggi*.

24. Slips of the pen, in this light, are as important for the literary historian as slips of the tongue for the psychoanalyst. See Timpanaro, *The Freudian Slip*.

25. For the historiographical importance of clues, see Ginzburg, "Clues: Roots of an Evidential Paradigm," in *Clues*, 96–125.

26. See Antonelli, "Struttura materiale" and Leonardi, "Il canzoniere Laurenziano." For other stimulating studies on the relationship between the early Italian

lyric and manuscript culture, see the works by Giunta cited above and Storey, *Transcription and Visual Poetics*. For the lyric and documentary culture, see especially Brunetti, *Il frammento inedito*.

27. "Un'edizione critica è, come ogni atto scientifico, una mera ipotesi di lavoro, la più soddisfacente (ossia economica) che colleghi in sistema i dati" (A critical edition, like any scientific undertaking, remains a working hypothesis, the one that most satisfactorily [or economically] arranges available data into a system). Contini, "Ricordo di Joseph Bédier," in *Esercizi di lettura*, 358–371 (369).

Notes to Chapter 1

1. The two most important editions of the *rime* also provide the best introductions. See Orlando, *Rime dei Memoriali*, vii–xv and Caboni, *Antiche rime italiane*, 5–21. All quotations of poems from the Memoriali (Mem.) until 1300 are taken from Orlando's edition, subsequently from Caboni. When incipits of some of the better-known poems are used to identify titles of works, they have been normalized according to standard editions. When this book went to press Orlando's edition of the complete corpus of poetry from the Memoriali and other archives in Bologna had not yet been published.

2. Carducci, "Intorno ad alcune rime."

3. Described in Giansante and Marcon, *Giudici e poeti toscani*, 6–7. See also the *Catalogo della mostra dantesca nell'archiginnasio*.

4. Although at times excessive and incautious in its claims, the most comprehensive treatment of Dante's texts in the Archivio di Stato of Bologna remains Livi, *Dante, suoi primi cultori*. For the *Commedia* in particular, see the updated findings in Petrocchi's edition of the *Commedia*, 1:60–61 and 504. Petrocchi appears to confuse passages copied in the Memoriali with passages written simply on the end pages of legal registers, often by visiting notaries (see following note). The differences are crucial for properly dating and placing the early transmission of the poem. For the continuing popularity of Dante for the notaries in Bologna, see Giansante and Marcon, "Frammenti di codici trecenteschi."

5. The first document we have attesting to the early circulation of the *Commedia* is also found in the Bolognese archives. On the cover of a register of juridical acts from 1317, the notary Ser Tieri degli Useppi di San Gimignano transcribed lines 94–96 of *Inferno* 3 and lines 16–17 of *Inferno* 5. The various *rime* and passages from *Inferno* and *Purgatorio* found on the covers and fly leafs of juridical registers in the state archives of Bologna form an important parallel to the Memoriali bolognesi. These transcriptions were left by notaries visiting from outside of Bologna as part of the retinue of the visiting *podestà*.

6. Text of the *Commedia* follows Petrocchi's edition. English translations are based, with slight modifications, on Durling and Martinez for the *Inferno* (*Inf.*) and the *Purgatorio* (*Purg.*) and on Singleton for the *Paradiso* (*Par.*).

7. See Contini's comments in his edition of Dante's *Rime*, 284–285.

8. Important observations about the varied content and makeup of the mini-anthologies of the Memoriali can be found in Orlando's introduction to *Rime dei Memoriali,* xi–xii. See also by the same author, "Un piccolo canzoniere."

9. See Contini, *Poeti del Duecento,* 1:765–766; Orlando, *Rime dei Memoriali,* vii–viii; and Debenedetti, "Osservazioni sulle poesie," 1. Orlando has recently questioned this purely legal hypothesis in "Best sellers e notai."

10. Debenedetti, "Osservazioni sulle poesie," 31.

11. Tamba, *La Società dei Notai,* 33.

12. In his edition of Dante's *Rime,* De Robertis describes Enrichetto's transcription as a "confezione molto accurata" (carefully prepared product) [3:328] and bases his text on it. At least in this case, it seems clear that the notary-copyist was acting intentionally and deliberately.

13. Storey provides original observations about contrasting literary and legal aspects of the transcriptions of the *rime* in *Transcription and Visual Poetics,* 135–156.

14. Petrucci discusses the early parasitical "tracce" of written Italian, in the end pages of Latin books and on the verso side of documents, in "Storia e geografia," 1202–1211. See the expanded discussion in Stussi, *Tracce.*

15. Quoted in Debenedetti, "Osservazioni sulle poesie," 31–32.

16. Ibid., 22–27.

17. Ibid., 25–6.

18. Ibid., 23.

19. Ibid., 33.

20. Ibid., 33. Backtracking in part from his thesis of a strict written transmission of the *rime,* Debenedetti attributes the "lezioni pessime" (very poor readings) in Nicola's transcription to faulty memory.

21. Orlando, *Rime dei Memoriali,* xi–xii, and Avalle, "La tradizione manoscritta," 160–162.

22. The most recent survey of these events is found in Koenig, *Il popolo.* For Bologna in particular, Hessel's *Storia della città* remains essential for this period as does Fasoli's "La legislazione antimagnatizia." My discussion of the Bolognese political struggles relies on these works.

23. Rubinstein first analyzed the anti-magnate laws in terms of a growing legal apparatus and state formation in *La lotta contro i magnati.* Also fundamental in this context are the pages on the anti-magnate laws in Tabacco, *Egemonie sociali,* 330–363.

24. Tamba, *La Società dei Notai,* 29.

25. Ibid., 21–33.

26. The development of the *instrumentum publicum* and the ensuing *fides publica* of the notariate is treated in, among others, Cencetti, "La 'rogatio' "; Costamagna, *Il notaio,* 51–80; and Costamagna and Amelotti, *Alle origini del notariato,* 205–282. Most recently, see Petrucci, "Modello notarile e testualità."

27. "Est autem notarius quedam publica persona publicum officium gerens ad cuius fidem hodie publice decurritur ut . . . in publicam formam reducat ea que ab

hominibus fiunt" (The notary is a public agent, providing a public service; people nowadays have recourse to his attestation so that he may set men's doings into [due] public form). See Salathiel Bononiensis, *Ars notarie,* 2:7.

28. On the social and political implications of the Jovial Friar order, see De Stefano, *Riformatori ed eretici,* 229–256; Koenig, *Il popolo,* 350–368; and Margueron, *Recherches sur Guittone,* 28–29. For crucial documentation on the order, see Federici, *Istoria* and Meersseman, *Dossier de l'ordre,* 295–307.

29. Jacopo della Lana, *Commento dantesco,* 383.

30. "Isti a rusticis truffatorie et derisive appellantur Gaudentes. Quasi dicant: Ideo facti sunt fratres, quia nolunt communicare aliis bona sua, sed volunt tantummodo sibi habere" (Peasants refer to them derisively, tauntingly, as "Jovials." As if to say: They have become friars, and yet they do not want to share their goods with others, but keep everything for themselves). Quoted in De Stefano, *Riformatori ed eretici,* 221.

31. Ibid., 250–251.

32. Hessel, *Storia della città,* 243–258, 266.

33. De Stefano, *Riformatori ed eretici,* 235, and Koenig, *Il popolo,* 366.

34. De Stefano, *Riformatori ed eretici,* 235.

35. Ibid., 232–233 and Koenig, *Il popolo,* 362–363.

36. Tamba, "In margine," 154. Still relevant for their description of the procedure and role of the *Memoriali* are Vittorio, "L'instituto" and Cesarini, "Sull'ufficio."

37. Tamba links the ordinance of the Memoriali and the attempt to limit and regulate the notarial guild in Tamba, "I memoriali del Comune," 258–260.

38. Vittorio, "L'instituto," 100.

39. The ordinance is quoted in Cesarini, "Sull'ufficio," 390.

40. The subscription appears in the second *memoriale* (1266). Cited in Gozzadini, *Cronaca di Ronzano,* 165.

41. These events are described in Koenig, *Il popolo,* 373–406. Tamba discusses their import for the notarial guild in *La Società dei Notai,* 26–31.

42. See Tamba, "I memoriali del Comune," 278.

43. See the description of the physical structure of the Memoriali in Caboni, *Antiche rime italiani,* 10–11, and Continelli, *L'archivio,* xvi.

44. Descriptions of individual registers are found in Continelli, *L'archivio,* 26–40.

45. The term *genre* should only be applied with caution when referring to medieval poetics. Here and throughout this book it is often used simply as a synonym for convention. On the fluidity of poetic categories in the later middle ages see, Barański. "'Tres enim sunt manerie dicendi.'" For a cautious attempt at defining the *tenzone* as a full-fledged genre see, Giunta, *Due saggi.*

46. From the sixteenth article of the Ordinamenti sacrati of 1282, quoted by Fasoli, "La legislazione antimagnatizia," 366.

47. For the meaning of *cantinele* in the Memoriali, see Levi, "Cantilene e ballate," 294–295.

48. Ibid., 296.

49. Text in Contini, *Poeti del Duecento,* 1:230–231.

50. Note also the similarity of "Seguramente" to a truncated *canzone* atributed to Guittone in the Palatine *canzoniere* (Banco Rari 217). For text see Guittone d'Arezzo, *Le rime,* 136:

> Ora vegna a la danza,
> e con baldanza—danzi a tutte l'ore
> chi spera in voi, Amore,
> e di cui lo cor meo disia amanza.
> Oh, quanto è dilettoso esto danzare
> in voi laudare,—beâta Maria!
> E che maggior dolcezza e dilettore
> Ch'aver di voi, Amor.

[Now come to the dance, and dance continuously with boldness, whoever places hope in you, Love, and in that one whom my heart desires to love. O, how delightful it is to dance and praise you, blessed Mary! And the greatest sweetness and delight to hold in you, Love. . . .]

51. Levi, "Cantilene e ballate," 296, and Margueron, *Richerches sur Guittone,* 68, 224–226. Useful documentation of Guittone's relation with Bologna and with the Bolognese order of the Jovial Friars can be found in Gozzadini, *Cronaca di Ronzano,* 46, 103–105, and 184–185.

52. From the sonnet "Bernardo, quell dell'arco del Diamasco" (3), in Onesto da Bologna, *Le Rime.*

53. The anti-*guittonismo* I claim is present in the Memoriali bolognesi needs to be qualified somewhat by the recent discovery by Armando Antonelli (still unpublished when this book went to press) of a poem by Fra Guittone in a contemporary register of the Bolognese archive (although not in the Memoriali).

54. In "Best sellers e notai," Orlando remarks upon the importance of Guittone's absence from the Memoriali, especially given his relationship with contemporary Bolognese poets, but explains it stylistically, pointing to the difficulty involved in copying Guittone's poems: "andrà notata la rarità . . . in particolare, di Guittone; questa mancanza (a dispetto dei rapporti personali fra l'Aretino ed alcuni rimatori bolognesi, si pensi agli stessi Guinizzelli ed Onesto e a Bernardo) è forse attribuibile alla difficoltà del loro dettato, più che a una coscienza letteraria aperta all'innovazione" (the rarity in particular of Guittone should be noted; this absence [despite personal relationships with other Bolognese poets, for instance, Guinizzelli himself and Onesto and Bernardo] is perhaps attributable to the difficulty of their composition, more than to a literary consciousness that is receptive to innovation) [269].

55. For the most recent and comprehensive discussion of the articulation of Guittone's corpus in contemporary manuscripts, see Leonardi, "Il canzoniere Laurenziano."

56. Text in Contini, *Poeti del Duecento,* 2:484. For my translations of Guinizzelli, I consulted Robert Edwards's edition (Guinizzelli, *Works*).

57. See, for example, Bertelli, *Poeti del dolce stil novo,* 60 and Contini, *Poeti del Duecento,* 2:445.

58. See Contini, *Poeti del Duecento,* 2:445, 447, and 484, and Gorni, *Il nodo,* 28–30. Gorni further suggests that the two unrhymed lines per stanza in "Lo fin pregi' avanzato" correspond to the weak bindings, "debel' vimi" (12), mentioned in the sonnet.

59. Wilkins, "Guinizzelli Praised and Corrected," in *The Invention of the Sonnet,* 111–114.

60. See Papahagi, "Guido Guinizelli," 284–286 and Picone, "Guittone, Guinizzelli e Dante," 75–80.

61. See Borra, *Guittone d'Arezzo,* 10; Borsa, "La tenzone"; Rossi (Guinizzelli, *Rime*), 68–74; and Sanguineti (Guinizzelli, *Poesie*), vii–xiii. Giunta reads the *tenzone* as above all rhetorical and conventional in *La poesia italiana,* 180.

62. For Guittone's conversion from *gioia* to *gaudio* and for possible echoes of Guittonian *gaudio* in "O caro padre meo," see also Sanguineti (Guinizzelli, *Poesie*), x.

63. The palinodic aspect of Guittone's later poetry and the intertextual and thematic links to earlier poems are discussed in Picone, "Guittone e i due tempi," and Borra, *Guittone d'Arezzo.*

64. The representation of Guittone as a moralizing *magister* is already present in contemporary lyric anthologies. In the illuminations of the Palatine anthology, for example, he is portrayed as teaching/preaching to various groups of ladies, laymen, or other friars, often with his finger raised in a gesture of argumentation (the *digitus argumentalis*) or admonishment. For the illuminations in the Palatine anthology, see Meneghetti, "Il corredo decorativo."

65. On Matteo Paterino and Guittone, see Giunta, "Letteratura ed eresia nel Duecento: Il caso di Matteo Paterino," in *Codici,* 63–144. This essay has various important parallels with the present discussion.

66. Text in Contini, *Poeti del Duecento,* 2:463–464.

67. See the discussions by Barolini, "Dante and the Lyric Past"; Hartung, "Guinizzelli e la teologia"; and Picone, "Guinizzelli nel Paradiso."

68. Martinez first argued for Guittone's presence at the end of "Al cor gentil" in his lecture "Bolognese Smarts and Dubious Semblances."

69. The rhymes *laude–fraude* are found in "Al cor gentil" (55, 57); *laude–aude–claude–gaude* (1, 3, 5, 7) in "O Caro padre meo" ; and *laude–laude–laude–laude* (1, 3, 5, 7) in "Figlio mio dilettoso." The intertext linking "Al cor gentil" to "O caro padre meo" and "Figlio mio dilettoso" through the *-aude* rhymes was already noted by Martinez in "Bolognese Smarts and Dubious Semblances." The texts of the sonnets are from Contini, *Poeti del Duecento,* 2:484–485.

70. See the entry in Avalle, *Concordanze,* s.v. "aude."

71. For the relation between "O tu, de nome Amor, guerra de fatto" and Guittone's earlier love poetry, especially "Ahi Deo, che dolorosa," see Borra, *Guittone d'Arezzo,* 34–36, and Picone, "Guittone e i due tempi," 77–79.

72. The currency of "O tu, de nome Amor, guerra de fatto" in Guinizzelli's Bologna can also be inferred from the canzone's influence on the Bolognese resident Monte Andrea. In his *canzone* "Ahi misero tapino, ora scoperchio," part of a *tenzone* with the Emilian poet Tomaso da Faenza, Monte continues Guittone's ideological and moralistic battle against erotic lovers or, in Monte's words, "gente di errore" (15). Particularly conspicuous for their derivation from "O tu, de nome Amor" are the militaristic descriptions of Monte's moral attack on lovers and their heterodox philosophy, especially in the first stanza; the critique of the three stages of love (*principio, mezzo, fine*); and the use of the key rhyme words *lauda* and *frauda* (15, 19). See text in Contini, *Poeti del Duecento,* 2:456–459.

73. Borsa, "La tenzone," 50–52; Contini, *Poeti del Duecento,* 1:255; Marti, *Storia,* 1:29–31; Picone, "Guittone, Guinizzelli e Dante," 70–74; Rossi (Guinizzelli, *Rime*), 128–129. For a dissenting view, see Giunta, *La poesia italiana,* 187–196.

74. Moleta, *Guinizzelli in Dante,* 12–16; Papahagi, "Guido Guinizzelli," 277–279; and Picone, "Guittone, Guinizzelli e Dante," 76–78.

75. Despite this social critique of blood nobility, Guinizzelli was himself from an important aristocratic and even magnate family. For Guinizzelli's involvement with the politics of his Ghibelline family, see Antonelli, "Nuovi documenti."

76. This does not mean, of course, that the notaries were irreligious, and it is not uncommon, as already noted, to find Latin prayers instead of vernacular poems filling in the lower margins of registers. Indeed, the recent discovery of a new vernacular *lauda* in the Memoriali (see Kullmann, "Osservazioni") in a register containing fragments of Latin liturgical prayer further demonstrates the marked fluidity of Latin and Italian, sacred and profane, for this community of notaries (and is not unlike the brief citations of Italian poetry and Latin prayers found in Dante's encounters with the poets of *Purgatorio*). Still, the primarily devotional aspects of the register studied by Kullmann (Mem. 78, 1290), when compared, for example, with those of the contemporary Nicola *Johanini Manelli,* seem to be the exception that proves the rule, confirming that the social and ideological background of the notaries does indeed matter, and that it affects the selection of their transcriptions.

77. See Contini, *Poeti del Duecento,* 2:481–482.

78. Raimondi proposes a potential link between the Memoriali bolognesi and Dante's condemnation of Catalano and Loderingo in "I canti bolognesi," 247.

79. For an analysis of the transcription of "Non me poriano zamai far emenda" in another context, see Storey, *Transcription and Visual Poetics,* 143–156.

80. Giansante and Marcon, *Giudici e poeti toscani,* 11. Giansante and Marcon's publication examines the importance of Ugolino in the Memoriali, identifies the preva-

lence of Cino and his circle in the notarial registers, and explores the protohumanist ties of Tuscan poet-judges studying and working in Bologna. This last section of the chapter owes much to their initial research.

81. Livi, *Dante e Bologna,* 22.

82. De Robertis, *Il canzoniere escorialense,* 181–182.

83. Livi, *Dante, suoi primi cultori,* 5–7. See this work for further biographical details about Enrichetto and other notaries working for the Memoriali bolognesi.

84. Surprisingly little has been written about the emergent *signorie* in Bologna. See Vitale, *Il dominio,* 119–194, and Dondarini, *Bologna medievale,* 255–310.

85. Tamba, *La Società dei Notai,* 54.

86. The original social middleness of medieval notaries is best described by Cardini, "Alfabetismo e livelli di cultura," 498. On the changing enrollment practices and closing of the notarial guild, see Tamba, *La Società dei Notai,* 26–28 and 33–56.

87. See the *Enciclopedia dantesca,* s.v. "Cino da Pistoia," and Zaccagnini, *Cino da Pistoia.*

88. Giansante and Marcon, *Giudici e poeti toscani,* 16–17 and Zaccagnini, "Gherardo da Castelfiorentino," 208–209.

89. Zaccagnini, *Cino da Pistoia,* 220, and Zaccagnini, "Gherardo da Castelfiorentino," 208. The document concerns a house in the benefice of S. Procolo that Zaccagnini believes was rented by Cino, Girardo, and five other law students mentioned in the contract.

90. Giansante and Marcon, *Giudici e poeti toscani,* 16, and Zaccagnini, "Gherardo da Castelfiorentino," 208.

91. On the possibility that Girardo and Ugolino knew each other, see Giansante and Marcon, *Giudici e poeti toscani,* 17–18, and Zaccagnini, "Gherardo da Castelfiorentino," 209–210.

92. Biscaro, "Inquisitori ed eretici," 2:349–366, esp. 350, 357.

93. Ibid., 2:357. See also the entry for Cecco in the *Enciclopedia dantesca,* s.v. "Stabili, Francesco."

94. Biscaro, "Inquisitori ed eretici," 2:368.

95. Ibid., 3:268–272.

96. Both Girardo and Francesco also formed part of a Latin epistolary community with the protohumanist Geri d'Arezzo, who also served as a judge *ad maleficia* in Bologna in 1315. See Giansante and Marcon, *Giudici e poeti toscani,* 25–26.

97. See *Enciclopedia dantesca,* s.v. "Francesco da Barberino."

98. For Accursio as a possible lecturer and certain commentator on Dante, see *Enciclopedia dantesca,* s.v.v "Bonfantini, Accursio" and "Stabili, Francesco."

99. This disdain was, according to Quadrio—and in line with Crescimbeni, Mazzuchelli, and others of his time, the cause of Cecco's ruin. See the discussion s.v. "Stabili, Francesco" in the *Enciclopedia dantesca* (5:404) from which this quote is taken.

100. Livi, *Dante e Bologna,* 22.

Notes to Chapter 2

1. Citations from the *Vita Nova* (*VN*) are based on Gorni's edition.

2. For a suggestive reading of the episode of "Donne ch'avete" in the *Vita Nova,* see Gorni, *Il nodo,* 13–21. For the divisions of "Donne ch'avete," see Botterill, "Però che la divisione" and Durling and Martinez, *Time and the Crystal,* 53–70.

3. Compare especially with Psalm 39:4: "et immisit in os meum canticum novum, carmen Deo nostro." Noted by De Robertis in his edition of the *Vita Nova,* 116. Gorni discusses the biblical resonances in the passage in *Il nodo,* 17–18.

4. Durling and Martinez demonstrate that Dante intended at least some of his more qualified readers to continue the dividing process, thus exposing a Neoplatonic pattern of procession and return within the stanza space. See *Time and the Crystal,* 55–57.

5. For the most recent and detailed description of the handwriting of this transcription and others by the same copyist, see Petrucci, "Le mani e le scritture."

6. All quotations from the Vatican anthology (V) are from the text in Avalle, *Concordanze,* unless otherwise noted. The numbering of the poems also follows Avalle, *Concordanze.*

7. Petrucci, "Le mani e le scritture," 41.

8. Barbi, *Problemi di critica dantesca,* 297–304; Contini, *Poeti del Duecento,* 2:693–694; and Petrucci, "Le mani e le scritture," 32 and 41.

9. Recent publications have contributed significantly to our knowledge of and access to the Vatican anthology. For an extremely useful edition of the texts and partial commentary, see Avalle, *Concordanze,* 290–547. See also the recent facsimile edition reproduced in the second volume of Leonardi, *I canzonieri.* Volume 4 (*Studi critici*) of *I canzonieri* contains fundamental essays on Vaticano 3793, several by scholars revising earlier, groundbreaking publications.

10. On the various scholarly accounts of Dante's reliance on a "twin" of the Vatican anthology, see Contini, "Questioni attributive," 386. By the same author, see also "Stilemi siciliani." Giunta (*La poesia italiana,* 37–39) problematizes the exclusiveness and even the primacy of the Vatican anthology in Dante's reception of the early lyric. See the subsequent discussion in Antonelli, "Struttura materiale," 6–7.

11. Antonelli, "Struttura materiale," 9–14.

12. Petrucci, "Le mani e le scritture," 30 and 41.

13. Antonelli, "Struttura materiale," 9–10.

14. The antepenultimate poem of the quire, "Gioiosamente canto" (V 23) by Guido delle Colonne, where the lover assures his beloved that if "tuta Mesina fosse mia, / senza voi, donna, neiente mi saria" (If all Messina was mine, without you, it would be nothing), also seems to be recalled by the jilted speaker of "Oi llassa 'namorata." The hyperbolic language is conventional, of course, but the placement of all three poems together at the end of this quire seems to question this very conventionality.

15. The last two anonymous poems of the eighth quire, "Madonna mia, non chero" (V 169) and "Kompiango mi e laimento e di cor dolglio" (V 170), provide another conspicuous example of the dialogic tendency of the Vatican anthology. In "Madonna mia, non chero," the male speaker announces his imminent separation from his beloved because of her harshness and pride. As if responding, the lady in "Kompiango mi e laimento e di cor dolglio" realizes that she has lost her lover through pride and disdain: "fui credera / salvagia e dura e fera" (I was cruel, savage, harsh, and proud) [8–9]. By placing the two compositions in this order, the compiler of the Vatican anthology turns a monologue into a dialogue and inserts the missing female voice into the end of the quire.

16. The following poems are written wholly or partially in the female voice: quire 2, "Oi llassa 'namorata" (V 26); quire 3, "Di dolore mi comviene cantare" (V 52); quire 4, "Nonn avene d'allegranza" (V 65), "Morte fera e dispietata" (V 74), "Dispietata morte e fera" (V 75), "L'altrieri fui im parlamento" (V 76); quire 8, "Kompiango mi e laimento e di cor dolglio" (V 170); quire 12, "Part'io mi chavalcava" (V 266). Quires 5, 6, and 13 do not contain anonymous poems in the female voice. Quires 7, 9, 10, 11, and 14 do not contain anonymous "filler" poems. Interestingly, V 26, V 52, V 76, and V 170 are all in the final or penultimate position of their respective quires. Several of the poems are discussed in Kleinhenz, "Pulzelle e maritate."

17. For an account of the role of the *contrasto* in early Italian literature, see the introduction in Arveda, *Contrasti,* i–cxxviii. For an important new account of the social uses of dialogic genres in Italian poetic culture, see Giunta, *Versi a un destinatario,* 255–266.

18. In fact, the nameless jongleur of "Rosa fresca aulentissima," the first poem of quire 4, echoes the same metaphoric language and floral imagery used in the anonymous poem "Dela primavera" (V 53), the last poem of quire 3. The lyric speaker of "Dela primavera" attempts to court his unheard and unseen beloved by calling her "rosa di magio colorita e fresca" (15) and "rosa tenerella" (56), recalling the similar apostrophes "rosa fresca aulentissima" (1) and "rosa fresca del' ortto" (13) of the *contrasto*. Because of the contiguous placement of the two poems, the female speaker in "Rosa fresca aulentissima" appears to critique the male protagonist of the *contrasto* as well as the lyric voice of "Dela primavera."

19. See Contini, *Poeti del Duecento,* 1:173–185 and 2:819, with relevant bibliography. Of particular note is Monteverdi, "'Rosa fresca aulentissima.'"

20. See Leonardi's analysis of Guittone's comic distancing from the language of courtly love in the introduction and commentary to his edition of the sonnets: Guittone d'Arezzo, *Canzoniere.*

21. Avalle discusses this *ars armandi* in "Il manuale del libertino," in *Ai luoghi di delizia pieni,* 56–86.

22. The social and epistolary nature of vernacular poetry of this period is emphasized in Giunta's *Versi a un destinatario.* For the early history of the Italian sonnet, see Kleinhenz, *The Early Italian Sonnet.*

23. Antonelli, "Struttura materiale," 15, and Giunta, "Un'ipotesi."

24. For a recent comprehensive analysis of the social makeup of the Florentine ruling classes, see Najemy, *Corporation and Consensus.*

25. Antonelli, "Struttura materiale," 15 and 23; Antonelli and Bianchini, "Dal 'clericus' al Poeta," 186–189; Monte Andrea, *Le rime,* 246–266; and Chiaro Davanzati, *Rime,* 368–371.

26. Antonelli, "Struttura materiale," 23.

27. Brunetto Latini, *La Rettorica,* 147–48. For illuminating discussions of Brunetto's adaptation of Ciceronian adversarial rhetoric for the Florentine city-state republic, including analyses of the passage quoted above in the text, see, among others, Cox, "Ciceronian Rhetoric"; Milner, "Exile, Rhetoric"; and Ward, "Rhetorical Theory."

28. See discussions of the *tenzone* in Avalle, *Ai luoghi di delizia pieni,* 105–106, and Giunta, *Due saggi,* 57–58.

29. Giunta, "Corrispondenze in canzoni," 59.

30. Contini aptly describes the Amico as "un settatore del vecchio modo" (adherent of the old style) in *Poeti del Duecento,* 2:696.

31. Scariati, *La corona,* xxxv. Contini is typically more elusive. His note reads simply: "Parla la canzone, a cui si rivolgeva il congedo di Dante" (The *canzone* is speaking, to which Dante's *congedo* was addressed), *Poeti del Duecento,* 2:700.

32. For the translation of "Donne ch'avete" and its prose *ragione,* I have consulted Durling and Martinez, *Time and the Crystal,* 292–297.

33. Durling and Martinez, *Time and the Crystal,* 53–70.

34. Scariati (*La corona,* xxxvi) speaks of a possible "parodia programmatica."

35. Gorni (*Il nodo,* 97) suggests a more positive correspondence between Dante and the Amico (to be identified, in his still provocative reading, as Lippo Pasci de' Bardi). Although my conclusions differ in many aspects from those of Gorni, I am indebted to his treatment of the relationship between the Amico di Dante (or Lippo) and Dante in his chapter "Lippo amico," 71–98.

36. Noted in Gorni's edition, 107.

37. The most comprehensive and useful account of this questionably productive debate is found in Fenzi, *La canzone d'amore,* 9–70.

38. Gorni (*Il nodo,* 156–57) suggests that the emphasis on "chominçato" in "Ben aggia" echoes the discussion of the "cominciamento" in the prose introduction to "Donne ch'avete," and he points in particular to how "che ben à cchominçato e meglio prende!" (18) of the Amico's *canzone* echoes "pensando di prenderle per mio cominciamento" (*VN* 10.14) of the *Vita Nova.* Yet, as Contini correctly notes (*Poeti del Duecento,* 2:698), the idea of *cominciare* is implicit in Dante's claim that he will not finish his praise for Beatrice ("non perch'io creda sua laude finire" [31]), and the connection is made explicit in lines 31–32 of "Ben aggia": "ché 'n tutto vole quella laude chonpiére / ch'à cchomincata per sua chortesia." As we shall see shortly, Dante's theory of the *cominciamento* is, in fact, an important thematic re-

sponse to the forward-moving emphasis of "Ben aggia," the quick succession from *cominciare* to *compiere*—and not, in my opinion, the other way around.

39. De Robertis considers the version of "Donne ch'avete" found in the Vatican anthology, as well as the response of "Ben aggia," evidence of the circulation of Dante's *canzone* before the *Vita Nova,* part of the so-called *tradizione estravagante.* See De Robertis, "La tradizione estravagante," 68–70, and his edition of the *Rime,* 2:962.

40. See also the discussion in Scariati, *La corona,* xxxv–xxxvi.

41. For the importance of *cominciare* in the *Vita Nova,* see Barolini, "'Cominciandomi dal principio'"; De Robertis, "Incipit Vita Nova"; and Gorni, *Il nodo,* 143–186.

42. These occurences of *cominciare* in "Ben aggia" are always linked with progressing and finishing: "che ben à cchomínçato e meglio prende!" (18) and "ché 'n tutto vole quella laude chonpiére / ch'à cchomínçata per sua chortesia" (31–32).

43. On the potential connection between "Voi che portate" / "Se' tu colui" and "Donne ch'avete" / "Ben aggia," see Contini, *Poeti del Duecento,* 2:697; Gorni, *Il nodo,* 72; and Scariati, *La corona,* xxxvi–xxxvii.

44. See the discussion and notes in Strocchia, *Death and Ritual,* 10–11.

45. No doubt such loaded terms as *private* and *public* always carry with them some risk of anachronism when used in a premodern context, and I am not arguing for the existence of private and public spheres in the sense given them by Jürgen Habermas. At the same time, it is important not to underestimate the sophisticated legal understanding of *public* developed in the late medieval Italian city-states. And Dante seems aware in the *Vita Nova* of the changing private lives of individuals in this period, just as he contributes to the construction of a private sphere through his text. For the important phenomenon of female readership in this period, see Bruni, "Figure della committenza," 108–111; Giunta, *Versi a un destinatario,* 397–402; and McCash, *The Cultural Patronage,* 1–49.

46. Texts of Dante's *rime* are based on the De Robertis edition, but see also the commentaries in Contini's edition, 74–77, and Foster and Boyde, *Dante's Lyric Poetry,* 2:111–114.

47. Contini (Dante, *Rime*), 74.

48. "Ch' al mio parere ella non rappresenta / quella che fa parer l'altre beate" (7–8). See discussion in Contini (Dante, *Rime*), 76.

49. Ibid., 74.

50. Further evidence that these are deliberate, conceptually driven revisions is provided by another, related change: "mia donna" to "madonna" (13) in "Lasso, per forza di molti sospiri." However, it is difficult to claim with certainty that this is an authorial variant and not a scribal error, since in contemporary scripts the stems of *m*'s could easily be confused with *i*'s and vice versa. That said, it is suggestive that the transcription of "Donne ch'avete" in the Vatican anthology, for the most part exceptionally correct, does contain at least one notable alternative reading from the accepted text: "di mia donna intende" for "di madonna intende" (23).

51. On the other hand, in the poem "Venite a 'ntender li sospiri miei," Dante changes "nostra donna" (10) from an earlier version to "donna mia" in the text of the *Vita Nova*. Since, according to the narrative of the *Vita Nova*, the sonnet was written for a close relative of Beatrice, he may have wanted to reserve his collective mourning of "our lady" for "Donna pietosa," where Beatrice assumes iconic status for himself and the ladies. Dante's careful and deliberate uses of "donna mia" and "nostra donna" also raise the stakes for Cavalcanti's sonnet "Una figura della Donna mia," where the *Donna* in question refers ambiguously to either the poet's lady or an iconic image of the Virgin. For the earlier version of "Venite a 'ntender," see De Robertis's edition of the *Rime*, 3:403–405. For the idolatrous connotations of the sonnet and its potential parody of the *Vita Nova*, see Martinez, "Guido Cavalcanti's 'Una figura.'"

52. In the introduction to the *Decameron*, Boccaccio emphasizes the role of women both in rites of mourning for the deceased ("era usanza, sí come ancora oggi veggiamo usare, che le donne parenti e vicine nella casa del morto si ragunavano e quivi con quelle che piú gli appartenevano piagnevano" [it was customary, just as we still see today, that female relatives and neighbors gather in the house of the deceased and weep alongside those that were closest to him][1, intr. 32]) and in caring for the dying in their last moments ("senza aver molte donne da torno morivan le genti" [people were dying without the company of groups of women][1, intr. 34]). He views the breakdown of these gendered rituals as symptomatic of the breakdown of society caused by the Plague. Text in Boccaccio, *Decameron*. See also Migiel, *A Rhetoric*, 17–28.

53. Martinez discusses the subjective and objective aspects of the episode with respect to the mixture of prose and verse in "*Versus* and *Prorsus*."

54. Considering contemporary poetic practices, the choice of the stilnovist poets *not* to construct a fictional female voice for the beloved must have appeared to contemporaries as deliberate.

55. See the discussion of the various implied audiences of the *Vita Nova* in Ahern, "The New Life of the Book." For important contrasts in the *Vita Nova* between the performative audience and a textual readership, see also Ahern's "The Reader on the Piazza."

56. The scholarship on this canto is vast. For the questions of Dante's historiography and theological poetics, see especially Barolini, *Dante's Poets*, 40–57, 85–90; De Robertis, "Definizione dello stil novo"; Gorni, *Il nodo*, 13–21; Hollander, "*Dante's 'dolce stil novo'*"; Marti, *Storia dello stil novo*, 1:47–62; Martinez, "The Pilgrim's Answer"; and Mazzotta, *Dante, Poet of the Desert*, 192–208.

57. See also Gorni, *Il nodo*, 15.

Notes to Chapter 3

1. *De vulgari eloquentia* (hereafter cited in text at *DV*) 2.3.7. All citations from the treatise are from Mengaldo's edition in *Opere minori*. English translations are based

on Botterill, *Dante's "De vulgari eloquentia,"* slightly adapted. Henceforth when notes refer to the commentary rather than the text of the *De vulgari*, it will be cited by editor. Unless otherwise noted, references to Mengaldo's edition always refers to the volume published by Ricciardi in 1979.

2. The philosophical and linguistic studies of the *De vulgari* are numerous and often excellent. I have benefited in particular from Corti, *Dante a un nuovo crocevia*; Grayson, "'Nobilior est vulgaris'"; Marigo (Dante, *De vulgari*), xv–clvi; Nardi, "Il linguaggio," in *Dante e la cultura medievale*, 173–195; Pagani, *La teoria linguistica*; Scaglione, "Dante and the Ars Grammatica"; and Vinay, "La teoria linguistica."

3. In addition to Mengaldo's introduction and notes to the Ricciardi edition, see also his introduction to an earlier edition of the *De vulgari* (1968)—now reprinted as "Introduzione al *De vulgari eloquentia*," in *Linguistica e retorica di Dante*, 1–123—as well as his crucial entry in the *Enciclopedia dantesca*, s.v. "*De vulgari eloquentia*."

4. Dante's reliance on a "gemello" of the Vatican anthology is laid out by Contini in "Questioni attributive," 386, and "Stilemi siciliani," 83–88. Giunta (*La poesia italiana*, 37–39) has recently called into question the primacy of the Vatican anthology in Dante's reception of the early lyric. See the subsequent discussion in Antonelli, "Struttura materiale," 6–7.

5. I do, however, owe a noticeable debt to Antonelli for his several brief but suggestive comments on the relationship between the *De vulgari* and the Vatican anthology in Antonelli, "Struttura materiale."

6. For Dante's desire to return to a preexilic, linguistic Eden, see Cestaro, *Dante and the Grammar of the Nursing Body*, 58–70.

7. Mengaldo, *Linguistica e retorica di Dante*, 108.

8. Guittone d'Arezzo, *Canzoniere*; Monte Andrea, *Le rime*; Panuccio del Bagno, *Le rime di Panuccio del Bagno*.

9. For an in-depth and influential study of Dante's agonistic relationship to other vernacular authors, see Barolini, *Dante's Poets*.

10. For Angelo Colucci's use of the Vatican anthology, see Bologna, "La copia colocciana," 105–152.

11. Mengaldo, *Linguistica e retorica di Dante*, 96.

12. See the discussion in Antonelli, "Struttura materiale."

13. One of Mengaldo's most important contributions is to have demonstrated Dante's reliance on a pre-existing literary tradition of dialect parody for his citations in book 1. In addition to the studies cited above, see the useful summary of his ideas about Dante and contemporary poets and poetry in Mengaldo, "Dante come critico."

14. The so-called Canzone del Castra, "Una fermana scopai da Cascioli," is discussed in *DV* 1.11.4, while the heterogeneous "Rosa fresca aulentis[s]ima / ch'apari inver' la state," referred to by its third verse, "Tragemi d'este focora / se t'este a bolontate," is found in *DV* 1.12.6.

15. See the discussion of Brunetto and bibliographical references in chapter 2.

16. Appearing as "Lupum" in the manuscripts, editors have traditionally substituted "Lapum" for Lapo Gianni. Gorni has proposed substituting "Lippum" for Lippo dei Pasci dei Bardi. See "Lippo contro Lapo" in *Il nodo,* 99–124, and "Paralipomeni a Lippo," 11–29.

17. Durling and Martinez argue that in the *De vulgari* Dante views the *petrose* as an important turning point in his poetic career. See *Time and the Crystal,* esp. 261–267.

18. Mengaldo, (Dante, *De vulgari*), 16.

19. For the influence of institutional and sociopolitical factors in Dante's thinking about an illustrious vernacular, see Vinay, "Ricerche" and "La teoria linguistica."

20. See *DV* 1.12.6; 1.12.9; 1.13.5; 1.14.3; 1.14.7; and 1.15.6.

21. See Cestaro, *Dante and the Grammar of the Nursing Body,* 59–70.

22. For the central role of authority in the *De vulgari,* see Ascoli, "'Neminem ante nos,'" 186–231.

23. Mengaldo, *Linguistica e retorica di Dante,* 93–95.

24. Dante applies the Latin term for scorn or reproach, *improperium,* in the sense of a literary parody or satire in two passages. Before citing the example of the Canzone del Castra, he cites a tradition of poetic parodies of the peoples of Rome, the Marches, and Spoleto: "Nec pretereundum est quod in improperium istarum trium gentium cantiones quamplures invente sunt" (Nor should I fail to mention that a number of poems have been composed in derision of these three peoples) [*DV* 1.11.4]. In the next paragraph, he similarly uses the term to describe a parody of the Lombard dialect, "Enter l'ora del vesper": "Post quos Mediolanenses atque Pergameos eorumque finitimos eruncemus, in quorum etiam improperium quendam cecinisse recolimus" (After these let us root out the Milanese, the people of Bergamo, and their neighbors; I recall that somebody has written a derisive song about them too) [DV 1.11.5].

25. See Mengaldo, *Linguistica e retorica di Dante,* 94–95.

26. Contini, "La poesia rusticale come caso di bilinguismo," in *Ultimi esercizi,* 16–17, and Segre, "Polemica linguistica ed espressionismo dialettale nella letteratura italiana," in *Lingua, stile, e società,* 398–399. See also, among others, Brugnolo, "Parodia linguistica e parodia letteraria nel contrasto bilingue 'Domna, tanto vos ai preiada' di Raimbaut de Vaqueiras," in *Plurilinguismo,* 9–65.

27. See Brugnolo, *Plurilinguismo,* 9–65, and, for a comparison with the Italian tradition, Segre, *Lingua, stile, e società,* 398–400. The tradition of the Italian *contrasto* is discussed at length in the introduction to Arveda, *Contrasti,* xi–cxx. For the influence of the *pastorela* genre on the *contrasto,* see il–lviii.

28. The formulation "poesia dialettale riflessa" was first proposed for these poems by Contini, "*Ultimi esercizi,*" 13.

29. Ibid., 13.

30. For Dionisotti, *Geografia e storia,* 36: "Parlar di lingua italiana prima di Dante è come parlar di cristianesimo prima di Cristo" (Speaking about an Italian language

before Dante is like speaking about Christianity before Christ). For an important elaboration on this view, see Barański, "I trionfi del volgare: Dante e il plurilinguismo," in *"Sole nuovo, luce nuova,"* 41–77.

31. For the gradual shift from a spontaneous feminine vernacular to a masculine, rule-bound vernacular, see Cestaro, *Dante and the Grammar of the Nursing Body,* 49–76. For a more general treatment on the relationship between Latin and the vernacular, see Grayson, "'Nobilior est vulgaris.'" Grayson (esp. p. 61) makes an important distinction, however, between Dante's search for greater stability in Italian and the full-fledged grammatical regularization of Latin.

32. Still useful is Monteverdi's groundbreaking study, "'Rosa fresca aulentissima.'"

33. See the linguistic discussions of these terms in Contini, *Poeti del Duecento,* 1:174–175; Mengaldo, (Dante, *De vulgari*), 103–104; and Segre, *Lingua, stile, e società,* 398–399.

34. On "terrigenis," see Marigo (Dante, *De vulgari*), 102; Mengaldo, (Dante, *De vulgari*), 102–103; and Pagliaro, *Poesia giullaresca,* 307.

35. For Castra vs. Osmano see *Letteratura italiana,* s.v. "Castra."

36. On Dante's interiorization of *convenientia* see Mengaldo's entry, s.v. *"De vulgari eloquentia"* in the *Enciclopedia dantesca,* 2:409–410, and Mengaldo, *Linguistica e retorica di Dante,* 56–58.

37. "Et cum loquela non aliter sit necessarium instrumentum nostre conceptionis quam equus militis, et optimis militibus optimi conveniant equi, ut dictum est, optimis conceptionibus optima loquela conveniet" (And since language is nothing other than the vehicle indispensable to our concepts, as a horse is to a knight, and since the best horses are suited to the best knights, as I said, the best language is suited to the best concepts) [*DV* 2.1.8].

38. In the previous chapter, we examined how "Ben aggia," the anonymous response to "Donne ch'avete," was influenced by the dialogic culture exemplified in the Vatican anthology and how in the *Vita Nuova* Dante confronts this skewed rereading of his text.

39. Barański, "Dante's Biblical Linguistics."

40. See, for example, Barański, "Dante's Biblical Linguistics," 109, and Ascoli, "'Neminem ante nos,'" 201–202.

41. For further bibliography and concise summary of critical interpretations, see Mengaldo (Dante, *De vulgari*), 42.

42. Barański, "Dante's Biblical Linguistics," 118.

43. Although he does not link Dante's discussion with contemporary vernacular poetics and politics, Barański already recognizes the rhetorical element of Dante's biblical narrative.

44. "'De fructu lignorum que sunt in paradiso vescimur; de fructu vero ligni quod est in medio paradisi precepit nobis Deus ne comederemus nec tangeremus,

ne forte moriamur'" ("We may eat of the fruit of the trees that are in Paradise: but God has forbidden us to eat or to touch the fruit of the tree that is in the middle of Paradise, lest we die") [*DV* 1.4.2].

45. Gorni, "La teoria del 'cominciamento,'" in *Il nodo*, 143–186.

46. For the medieval background relating to the Tower of Babel story, see Borst, *Der Turmbau von Babel*, 2.2; Copeland, *Rhetoric, Hermeneutics and Translation*, 212–216; and Lusignan, *Parler vulgairement*, 51–53. Building on the work of Borst, Lusignan finds in Dante the culmination of a shift in exegetical accounts of Babel in which the confusion of languages is gradually replaced with the division of languages, and hence an opportunity for medieval classification and *divisio*. This seems only in part accurate, however, given the distinct moralizing by Dante of the Babel myth, as recently emphasized by Barański in "Dante's Biblical Linguistics."

47. Marigo (Dante, *De vulgari*), 42; Mengaldo, (Dante, *De vulgari*), 60–61.

48. Corti, "Dante e la torre," in *Il viaggio testuale*, 245–256.

49. See Corti, in *Il viaggio testuale*, 255, and Ascoli, "'Neminem ante nos,'" 224–225.

50. For the most recent and compelling account of the social makeup of Dante's Florence, see Najemy, *Corporation and Consensus*.

51. On the anti-magnate legislation, see Fasoli, "Ricerche sulla legislazione antimagnatizia," 122; Rubinstein, *La lotta contro i magnati*; and Tabacco, *Egemonie sociali*, 330–363.

52. For the legal revolution of the *popolo* government, see Najemy, *Corporation and Consensus*; Rubinstein, *La lotta contro i magnati*; and Tabacco, *Egemonie sociali*. On the question of *universitas*, see additionally Najemy, "Dante and Florence" and Wallace, *Chaucerian Polity*.

53. Cited in Najemy, "Dante and Florence," 80.

54. "Subsistant igitur ignorantie sectatores Guictonem Aretinum et quosdam alios extollentes, nunquam in vocabulis atque constructione plebescere desuetos" (So let the devotees of ignorance cease to extol Guittone d'Arezzo and others like him, for never, in either vocabulary or construction, have they been anything but plebeians) [*DV* 2.6.8]. ˙

55. Durling and Martinez, *Time and the Crystal*, 1–32.

56. Dante relies on a similarly deterritorialized and non-horizontal perspective when he defines his illustrious vernacular as dependent upon a utopian imperial court. See Marchesi, "Dante's Vertical Utopia."

57. The tensions between poetic authority and historicity are discussed at length in Ascoli, "'Neminem ante nos.'"

58. "Hoc vocabulum per solius artis respectum inventum est, videlicet ut in quo tota cantionis ars esset contenta, illud diceretur stantia, hoc est mansio capax sive receptaculum totius artis" (This word was coined soley for the purpose of discussing poetic technique, so that the object in which the whole art of the *canzone* was enshrined should be called a *stanza*, that is a capacious dwelling or receptacle for the art in its entirety)]*DV* 2.9.2]. The architectural notions of Dante's pseudo-etymology

are already noted by Marigo (Dante, *De vulgari*), 241: "La *stanza* sta alla canzone quasi come la camera all'intera casa" (The *stanza* is to the *canzone* what the room is to the entire house). We have also seen in chapter 2 how the architectural metaphor of the room, the *camera,* also characterized the interior poetics of the *Vita Nova.*

59. See the examination of Dante's linguistic theories in the *De vulgari* and the female body in Cestaro, *Dante and the Grammar of the Nursing Body,* 49–76.

Notes to Chapter 4

1. Although I have examined a variety of typologies of account books, the observations in this chapter are based, above all, on the major ledgers of the merchant supercompanies. The accounting books of the smaller and middling companies, and the less important books of the larger companies, are less innovative and more dependent on notarial documentary models. In particular, I examined the books of account discussed by Melis (*Storia della ragioneria,* 480–518) for their precocious developments in accounting techniques, especially regarding double-entry bookkeeping. The account books from the following companies share characteristics essential for the present study: Alberti del Giudice (Biblioteca Nazionale, NA 239); Del Bene (Archivio di Stato di Firenze, Archivio del Bene, 3); Farolfi (Archivio di Stato di Firenze, Strozziane seconda serie, n. 84bis); Fini (Archivio di Stato di Firenze, Archivio dei Capitani di Or San Michele, n. 220); and Peruzzi (Biblioteca Riccardiana, 2414–2417). Sapori provides excellent editions of the Alberti del Giudice and Peruzzi accounting books—complete with introductions, descriptions of the manuscripts, and reproductions, in *I libri degli Alberti del Giudice* and *I libri di commercio dei Peruzzi.* For codicological descriptions and philological analysis of the account books of the Fini and Farolfi companies, see Castellani, *Nuovi testi,* 2:674–696 and 2:708–803.

2. Petrucci published his initial identification of the primary hand of Vaticano 3793 as *mercantesca* in "Scrivere il testo," 223–224. See his more recent and detailed analyses in "Le mani e le scritture" and "Fatti protomercanteschi."

3. For the mercantile aspects of the handwriting and layout of the Vatican anthology, see (in addition to the above-cited articles by Petrucci) Antonelli, "Struttura materiale"; Bologna, *Tradizione e fortuna,* 120–124; Giunta, "Un'ipotesi," 25; and Miglio, "Criteri di datazione," 151–153. For similarities in language and orthography with contemporary texts written by merchants, see Larson, "Appunti sulla lingua," 91. For the irregular codicological elements of the manuscript, specifically regarding the quality of its parchment, see Palma, "Osservazioni," 54–55.

4. For a brief outline of the *mercantesca* script, see Cencetti, *Lineamenti,* 232–233, 248–249. Orlandelli discusses the fundamental characteristics of *mercantesca,* as well as its historical origins and context, in "Osservazioni." For a discussion of the emergence of this mercantile script, and its origins in the so-called proto-*mercantesca,* see Miglio, "L'altra metà" and "Criteri di datazione." In "L'altra metà," Miglio analyzes

the invaluable reproductions of early Italian documents found in Castellani, *La prosa italiana*. Another important collection of reproductions of documents in *mercantesca* is Melis, *Documenti*. Most recently, see Petrucci, "Fatti protomercanteschi."

5. See the description of the various hands in Petrucci, "Le mani e le scritture."

6. For the definitions of "register-book" and "courtly-reading" book, see Petrucci, *Writers and Readers,* 180–181, and "Storia e geografia," 1219–1222.

7. Antonelli, "Struttura materiale," 13–14.

8. Giunta points out an additional intersection between the rubrics in Vaticano 3793 and contemporary books of account. The anonymous compiler of the Vatican anthology refers to previously cited poets with the abbreviation of "medesimo" as in "Chiaro medesimo" and "Guitone medesimo" instead of "Chiaro Davanzati di Firenze" and "Guitone del Viva d'Arezo." The accountants of merchants' books use a similar abbreviation when referring to debtors and creditors already registered by their full titles in the text; thus, for example, "Lipo f. Rinieri del popolo San Brocholo" becomes "Lipo medesimo." See "Un'ipotesi," 25.

9. For a different perspective on the singular methods of transcribing Monte's poetry in the Vaticano, see Storey, *Transcription and Visual Poetics,* 71–109.

10. See Orlandelli, "Osservazioni," 447–448.

11. Storey (*Transcription and Visual Poetics,* 31–41) discusses the visual layout of Panuccio's poems in the Vatican anthology and other manuscripts.

12. Melis, *Documenti,* 480–518.

13. For the relation of double-entry bookkeeping and the rise of capitalism, see, with relevant bibliography, Yamey, "Scientific Bookkeeping" and Edwards, *A History of Financial Accounting,* 59–63. For the relation between new bookkeeping techniques and resident mercantilism, see the balanced and convincing account given in Lane, "Double Entry Bookkeeping."

14. The conception of the Vatican anthology as an already bound book does not pertain to the original compiler and primary copyist of the anthology, for whom the traditional division of quires remains essential.

15. For consideration of blank space in the Laurentian anthology, including its own status as a "canzoniere aperto," see Leonardi, "Il canzoniere Laurenziano." For the troubadour anthologies, see Lachin, "Partizioni e struttura."

16. This section revises my previous ideas in "Merchant Bookkeeping" about blank space in the Vatican anthology, which were critiqued in Antonelli, "Struttura materiale," 10.

17. A history of the Florentine notarial archive and of the archival practices of the Florentine and Tuscan notaries is provided by Biscione, "La conservazione." My results are based on a necessarily cursory, yet quantitatively exhaustive, analysis of the protocols in the Fondo Notarile Antecosimiano of the Archivio di Stato of Florence. I examined numerous protocols before 1325 and all registers between 1290 and 1310.

18. Destrez, *La pecia* and Fink-Errera, "La produzione."

19. The existence of the merchants' bound blank book also contrasts sharply with the medieval conception of the independent booklet, so essential in forming the various miscellanies of the period. See Robinson, "The 'Booklet'" and Hanna, "Booklets in Medieval Manuscripts: Further Considerations" in *Pursuing History,* 21–34 and 284–287.

20. Besides the Peruzzi account books, the page references in the account books of the Farolfi and of the Gentile Sassetti companies (see Castellani, *Nuovi testi,* 286) are also organized "a libro aperto."

21. This new method of page numbering may not be exclusive to merchants' writing methods and, in fact, even Petrarch appears to perceive the book in a similar fashion as evident from references in his marginal notes. Nonetheless the emergence of the open-page face in the most important merchant and merchant-banking ledgers of the period is conspicuous.

22. This new spatial paradigm applied to the microcosm of the book has repercussions that, to my knowledge, have yet to be explored. Suggestively, the merchants of the period were also reducing the external world into measurable, homogenous units in their maps and merchant handbooks. For the shift in merchants' consciousness from the traditional hierarchical model of space to a rationalized, homogenous one, see Le Goff, *Time, Work, and Culture,* 34–37, and Harvey, *The Condition of Postmodernity,* 240–259.

23. For the development of the blank, bound book— the writing book, the book "per scrivere"—and the private diaries of Florentine merchants, the famous *libri di ricordanze* or *di famiglia,* see Allegrezza, "La diffusione," 253–255. Allegrezza also points out the diminishing importance of regular quires in these books.

24. For the ways in which High Scholastic thought both influenced and was influenced by the divisions in books, see Parkes, "The Influence of the Concepts of *Ordinatio* and *Compilatio.*"

25. Curtius, "The Book as Symbol," in *European Literature,* 302–347.

26. See Sapori's description (*I libri di commercio dei Peruzzi,* li–lxi) of the quires in the Peruzzi account books—both extant and original.

27. For the diverse sets of page numbering in Vaticano 3793, and what they reveal about the various stages of the anthology's history as a book, see Egidi's introduction in his diplomatic edition, *Il libro,* and Petrucci, "Le mani e le scritture," 40–41.

28. Petrucci, "Le mani e le scritture," 41.

29. For a transcription of the fragment, see Rostagno, "Frammenti." Important, albeit incomplete, codicological descriptions are found in *Mostra di codici romanzi,* 83; Panvini, "Studio sui manoscritti," 26–28; and Rostagno, "Frammenti," 141–147.

30. On the relation between the fragment and the Vatican anthology, see Antonelli, "Struttura materiale," 22; Bologna, "Sull'utilità," 2:560–563; Brunetti, *Il frammento inedito,* 271–278; Larson, "Appunti sulla lingua," 101–103; Monte Andrea, *Le rime,* 15; Panvini, "Studio sui manoscritti," 27–28; and Rostagno, "Frammenti,"

141–142. Panvini argues that the Nazionale fragment derives from the Vatican anthology, while Rostagno proposes a shared exemplar for both anthologies. Since I first published my own findings on the problem in "Merchant Bookkeeping" both Antonelli and Larson, working independently, have confirmed that the fragment is most likely a *descriptus* of the Vaticano. For differing views and evidence, see Bologna and Brunetti, cited above.

31. Minetti (Monte Andrea, *Le rime*, 15) intelligently and cautiously warns against the "impossibilità" of determining if the Nazionale fragment derives from the Vatican anthology or if they both derive from a common tradition. In particular, Minetti cites Avalle (*Principi,* 98–99), who also cautions that sure tests ("prove sicure") are rare for thirteenth-century manuscripts, especially vernacular manuscripts. Nevertheless, I believe we now have convincing evidence demonstrating the fragment's direct reliance on the Vatican anthology.

32. This sonnet is attributed to Misser Francesco in the fragment but to Tomaso da Faenza in other manuscripts, including the Vatican anthology. See Panvini, "Studio sui manoscritti," 26–28.

33. See Bologna, "Sull'utilità," 561–562.

34. Perhaps the largest discrepancy in the texts is in verse 152 of Monte Andrea's "Tanto m'abonda matera, di soperchio" (V 287). In the Vatican anthology, we have "solo alsuo paragone tisagi il prega," while the Nazionale fragment reports "solo alei fue paragone ti sagi ilprega." However, if we go back to the Vatican manuscript itself, we notice that the *s* of "suo" is superimposed over an earlier *t*. The bar of the *t* crossing the elongated cursive *s* resembles, in fact, the elongated cursive *f*. Thus we have the nonsensical "alfuo," perhaps corrected by the scribe of the fragment into "alfue" with additional interpolations to make sense of the line. In Monte Andrea's "Ancor di dire non fino, perché" (V 288), we have an even more revealing discordance between "vede" (69) in the Vatican anthology and "verde" in the fragment. However, in the Vatican "original," the *d* of "vede" is superimposed on a previous *r*. Both letters remain visible and it appears that the scribe of the fragment copied both. More clear-cut still is the case of "antico" > "amico" (65). In the Vatican anthology, the initial stroke of the *t*, the head, overlaps with the *n* and the bar of the same *t* instead blends in with the following *i* in such a way that the text appears to read "amico" to all but the most careful copyists—copyists already accustomed to the *mercantesca* script. In a similar vein, "cope" ("c'op'è) of Guittone's "Me pare avere bene dimostrata via" (V 425.14) corresponds to the variant "core" in the fragment. Yet the *p*'s and *r*'s in hand 1 of the Vatican anthology are at times quite similar, especially in this case where the bow of the *p* is not completely formed or closed. Out of the context of the poem, one might easily read "core" in the Vatican anthology instead of "cope". In addition, the ambiguity between *r* and *p* is possible above all in cursive scripts of this period, with the distinctive feature of the *r*'s stem descending beneath the line and then swinging back up.

Although these examples are consistent and highly suggestive, variants such as "como" from "channo" (V 282.5) and "cura" from "oura" (V 420.11) instead suggest scribal misreadings stemming from a manuscript transcribed in Gothic *textura*. One might thus hypothesize a *textualis* intermediary between the Vatican anthology in *mercantesca* and the Nazionale fragment in *textualis*. The suggestive philological and material relationship between the two manuscripts still requires further study.

35. First of all, one notices the occasional absence of the normal closure of e > i in the prototonic position normally found in medieval Tuscan. For example, the copyist of the fragment transcribes "retegno" for "ritegno" (V 287.140); "desciese" for "disciese" (V 288.53); and "ensegna" for "imsegna" (V 428.8) This is particularly noticeable in the atonic monosyllables. Hence, instead of *mi, ti, di, si,* we consistently find in the Nazionale fragment *me, te, de,* and *se.*

Second, even more conspicuous is the closing of *é* to *i* and, above all, of *ó* to *u.* The occurrences of the first phenomenon are less frequent ("seguire" > "siguire" [V 281.50], but transcriptional "errors" in *u* are prominent enough to suggest a non-Tuscan copyist. Especially frequent are the cases of *cun* or *cum* for *con.* But one also notes "dolorusi," "lu," "luro," "vurebe," "multo," "cundurà," and others.

Finally, in Monte Andrea's "Ancor di dire nom fino, perché" (V 288), we find the even more characteristic palatalization of *s* before *i:* "siamo" > "sciamo" (58) and "sia" > "scia" (93).

These scribal variants are difficult to interpret for several reasons. First of all, the language of the Nazionale fragment remains clearly Florentine, with all of the defining Florentine attributes. Second, the scribe of the fragment does little interpretation and generally sticks to the base text, even where it is obviously corrupt and nonsensical. Finally, the growing literary prestige of the Florentine koiné no doubt influenced the transcription. Larson ("Appunti sulla lingua," 101–103), confirming Castellani's analysis, suggests that the fragment was copied by an Emilian or Romagnol hand from a Florentine exemplar. In this context, he also incorrectly claims that I attributed the manuscript to a copyist from the Marches in "Merchant Bookkeeping."

36. Rostagno, "Frammenti," 145.

37. See Lenzi, *Il libro del Biadaiolo.* For important codicological, paleographic, and historical considerations, see Miglio, "Considerazioni" and "Per una datazione." See also Branca, "Un biadaiolo lettore."

38. Miglio, "Considerazioni," 311.

39. The work of the Maestro del Biadaiolo is a standard reference point in the major treatments of art in the fourteenth century, especially regarding manuscript illumination. See, for example, D'Ancona, *La miniatura fiorentina,* 1:17–19; Salmi, *La miniatura fiorentina,* 11–12; and Toesca, *Il Trecento,* 806–807.

40. Miglio, "Considerazioni," 318.

41. Ibid., 319–320.

42. The emergence of the book as a private diary and the related emergence of the author's book or the authentic autograph manuscript come at a surprising moment in the history of the book in late medieval Italy. Even before the advent of the printing press, the reproduction of the book was reaching new heights due to the rise of the universities and the expansion of a lay, urban readership. Lay scribes worked for professional scriptoria in order to accommodate this growth of lay literacy and the ensuing explosion in book production. The contemporaneous increase in autograph manuscripts and the subsequent renewed emphasis on the book as a physical object are not only the result of this spread of reading and writing among the general public, but might also be a reaction to it. In this sense, the manuscript as private book contradicts Benjamin's thesis about the mechanical reproduction of art. At least in the case of the manuscript book, the reproduction of the work of art does not usurp or surpass the contextualized, authentic art object—localized in time and space—but rather appears to cause it. Reproduction and the concept of authenticity are two sides of the same coin. See Benjamin, "The Work of Art in the Age of Mechanical Reproduction," in *Illuminations,* 217–251. See especially 221, where Benjamin evokes the medieval manuscript as an example of the contextualized, precapitalist work of art. Petrucci offers a synthetic history of literacy and the book in Italy in *Writers and Readers,* 169–235. For a highly suggestive study of Petrarch's relation to the notarial culture of the draft, see also his "Minute, Autograph, Author's Book," in *Writers and Readers,* 145–168.

43. Ong, *Orality and Literacy,* 129.

Notes to Chapter 5

1. Notable exceptions are the contributions of Storey, *Transcription and Visual Poetics,* 40–45 and 71–109; "Lo 'stoscio' montiano-dantesco"; and "The Poetry and Literary Culture." See also the various discussions of Monte in Giunta, *La poesia italiana* and, for the Vatican anthology in particular, Holmes, *Assembling the Lyric Self,* 82–87. Leonardi outlines a potential debate about poverty between Monte, on one side, and Dante and Jacopone da Todi on the other, in "Jacopone poeta francescano." For Monte and poverty, see also Alfie, *Comedy and Culture,* 83–86.

2. In "Jacopone poeta francescano," Leonardi finds thematic as well as stylistic parallels between Monte and Dante that complement the discussion in this essay. Del Sal's article "Guittone e i guittoniani" concludes, on the other hand, that Monte's poetry is of purely formal interest for Dante, serving as a "vademecum of rimas caras" (135–136).

3. Of course, Dante's treatment of Fortune extends beyond the cantos touched upon in this chapter (for example, the important discussion of Fortune and her

wheel in *Inferno* 15). My examination is limited to the points in which Monte's perspective on Fortune and history come up against Dante's.

4. Quire 14 repeats poets from earlier sections and seems compiled with extra poems at a later stage.

5. The banker "Monteandreas de Florentia," living in Bologna, can be found in the records of the Memoriali bolognesi from 1267 to 1274. See the short biography for Monte in *Letteratura italiana,* s.v. "Monte Andrea."

6. For the bourgeois and mercantile producers, readers, and possessors of the manuscript, see the discussion in Petrucci, "Le mani e le scritture."

7. Antonelli, "Struttura materiale," 33, and Contini, *Poeti del Duecento,* 1:447.

8. For the debate on poverty in medieval Italian literature, and its possible sources in goliardic poetry, see Alfie, *Comedy and Culture,* 83–113; Marti, *Cultura e stile,* 1–40; and Suitner, *La poesia satirica,* 148–160.

9. Drawing on the treatment of Fortune, poverty, and money in the Latin and romance traditions, and adapting them for an urban Italian public, Monte can be seen as anticipating the comic-realist works of Nicolò de' Rossi, Cecco Angiolieri, and Pietro dei Faitinelli. For Monte as prototype, see Alfie, *Comedy and Culture,* 83–86.

10. "Tanto m'abonda matera, di soperchio" (104–108). See also, among numerous passages, lines 100–103 of "Più soferir no.m posso ch'io non dica":

> Sia 'n ommo cortesïa ë larghez[z]a,
> tuta bontà, senno ë gentilez[z]a:
> dico ch'è spenta, s'elgli è d'aver netto.

> [Let a man have courtesy, generosity, goodness, knowledge, and nobility, all is extinguished if he has no assets.]

All quotations from Monte are taken from Monte Andrea, *Le rime,* which follows closely the text of the Vatican anthology.

11. In Guittone's letter to Monte, he similarly puns on Monte's name, "nel gran monte de vertù montando" (Guittone, *Lettere,* 3.63), and the compiler of the Vatican anthology may have been familiar with such name games, which were not infrequent among Guittone and his contemporaries. For word play in Guittone, see Margueron, *Recherches sur Guittone,* 13–16 (14n. for Monte's name in particular).

12. The critique I propose Dante is lodging against Monte and his merchant-banker milieu should not, however, be taken as an attack on the urban classes *tout court.* On the contrary, as suggested in chapter 3 on the *De vulgari,* Dante's antagonism toward the alliance of merchant-bankers and magnates that had taken over the Florentine government and instigated his exile has much in common with the rhetoric and ideology of the guild-based *popolo* government. I would further argue that the protocapitalism and international finance emerging in Florence in this period was viewed by Dante as corrupting the original ideals of the popular movement and the

intellectual meritocracy based on the noble heart. In this respect, the critique in *Convivio* 4.1 of Frederick II's assertion that nobility is based on "old money" ("antica richezza") can be seen as an important precedent for his implicit attack on Monte's similar beliefs. Dante's defense of nobility as based on a noble heart is thus hardly a defense of the Florentine magnates. On the contrary, he seeks to undermine the basis of their authority.

13. For the "ontoso metro," see Suitner, *La poesia satirica,* 19–22. Suitner suggests a passage from the *Carmina Burana* as the ultimate source for the sinner's mini-debate.

14. Mazzotta notes the significance of the incomplete circles of the avaricious and prodigal in his important discussion of Fortune in *Inferno* 7. See his *Dante, Poet of the Desert,* 319–328. See also the commentary in Durling and Martinez (Dante, *The Divine Comedy*), 1:123–124.

15. For the episode of Cacciaguida and Dante's transformation of history, see the important discussions in Freccero, "The Prologue Scene," in *Dante,* 24–28; Mazzotta, *Dante, Poet of the Desert,* 136–146; and Schnapp, *The Transfiguration of History.*

16. In Ascoli's recent articles on Dante and authority, he examines the rhetorical strategies Dante employs to transform his problematic historicity, his historical "stain": "The Vowels of Authority"; "'Neminem ante nos'"; and "Access to Authority." In the specific context of sacred history, see also Schnapp, *The Transfiguration of History.*

17. See also the *rime derivative, abbia–labbia–rabbia* (5, 7, 9) and *stanche–anche–branche* (65, 67, 69), and the *rima equivoca, langue–l'angue* (82–84). For the correspondence of these and other rhymes in Monte's corpus and in other thirteenth-century poets, see the respective entries in Avalle, *Concordanze.*

18. See Storey, *Transcription and Visual Poetics,* 37–43, and "Poetry and Literary Culture," 67–145.

19. The line is ambiguous. It could mean simply that Dante was unfortunate or that he was Beatrice's true friend (not only when good fortune made it convenient). The two senses are related, however, and both important in the context of my discussion.

20. The anonymous early fourteenth-century *canzone* "Molti sono que' che lodan povertate," sometimes attributed to Giotto, is particularly interesting for its hostility toward ideals of poverty promoted by the Spiritual Franciscans. For the contemporary debates about poverty found in thirteenth-century poetry (most notably, the anonymous "Canzone del Fi' Aldobrandino" and various sonnets by Cecco Angiolieri), see Alfie, *Comedy and Culture,* 83–113; Havely, *Dante and the Franciscans,* 8–24; and Suitner, *La poesia satirica,* 148–160. Alfie includes Monte Andrea as an important early participant in this debate. For changes in social attitudes toward poverty, in addition to the pages cited from Havely, see Manselli, "De Dante."

21. See Havely, *Dante and the Franciscans.*

22. For tensions and alliances between the mendicants and an increasingly protocapitalist society, see Little, *Religious Poverty.*

23. Insisting on the dialogue between Dante's representation of history and the contemporary social and cultural discourses that condition his representation, Ascoli critiques an examination of history in Dante solely "from the inside." See especially the discussions in "'Neminem ante nos,'" 186–193, and "Palinode and History," 155–160.

24. See Pasquini's discussion in the *Enciclopedia dantesca,* s.v. "stoscio."

25. Storey gives an account of the parallels between Dante's and Monte's use of *stoscio* and *scroscio* in "Lo 'stoscio' montiano-dantesco."

26. In some early manuscripts, we find *stroscio* for *scroscio.* More conspicuously, *scroscio* instead of *stroscio* appears in various early manuscripts and in the early commentators. See the most recent discussion and further bibliography in Storey, "Lo 'stoscio' montiano-dantesco," 385–386. See also *Enciclopedia dantesca,* s.v..v. "stoscio" and "scroscio."

27. Leonardi briefly notes the use of Monte's rhymes and their relation to the usurers in "Il *Fiore,*" 254 and 264.

28. See also Cacciaguida's disgust at the corrupting influence of the new money brought in by the banking classes in Florence : "tal fatto è fiorentino e cambia e merca, / che si sarebbe vòlto a Simifonti / là dove andava l'avolo a la cerca" (there is one who has become a money changer and trader, who would have lived on at Simifonti where his own grandfather went a-begging) [*Par.* 16.61–63]. Dante's contempt for money lending and changing is especially curious considering that his own father may have been a money changer, as revealed in his *tenzone* with Forese.

29. In the *Ovide moralisé,* Phaeton's mad flight is also compared to Lucifer's climb and fall. See the passage regarding Phaeton in book 2, especially:

> A grant honte et a grant meschief
> Trebuscha Lucifer jadis,
> Par son orgueil, de Paradis.
> Monter volt plus qu'il ne devoit.
>
> (706–709)

[To his great dishonor and misfortune, Lucifer fell, on account of his pride, from Paradise. He wanted to ascend more than he should have.]

We have already seen how Lucifer's fate is identified with the theme of Fortune in canto 7. Text follows the edition by de Boer, *Ovide moralisé.*

30. For the solar motion of Geryon's spiral, see Freccero, "Dante's Pilgrim in a Gyre," in *Dante,* 70–92, and Martinez, "Geryon's Spiral Flight," in Durling and Martinez (Dante, *The Divine Comedy*), 1:560–563.

31. Durling, "Deceit and Digestion"; Durling, "The Body Analogy," in Durling and Martinez (Dante, *The Divine Comedy*), 1:576–577, as well as the commentary by Durling and Martinez on pages 472–481; and Shoaf, *Dante, Chaucer,* 39–48.

32. Durling, "The Body Analogy," in Durling and Martinez (Dante, *The Divine Comedy*), 1:576–577.

33. See Shoaf, *Dante, Chaucer,* 40.

34. For important stylistic observations regarding this canto, see Contini, "Sul XXX dell'Inferno," in *Un'idea di Dante,* 159–170.

35. Contini, *Un'idea di Dante,* 167, 170. See also the commentaries in the editions of the *Commedia* by Sapegno, 345, 350; Barbi and Casini, 1:289; Chiavacci Leonardi, 1:884, 903; and Bosco and Reggio, 1:426–427. The closest verbal parallel is with lines 3–4 of Cecco Angiolieri's "Dante Alleghier, s'i' so' buon begolardo": "S'eo desno con altrui, e tu vi ceni; /s'eo mordo 'l grasso, e tu vi suggi 'l lardo" (If I lunch with others, you dine; if I bite the fat, you suck on the lard). Cecco's sonnet, a response to a lost sonnet of Dante, echoes the back-and-forth syntactic structure of Adamo and Sinone, especially line 115: "S'io dissi falso, e tu falsasti il conio" (If I spoke falsely, you falsified coins). Cecco's poem can be found in *Poeti del Duecento,* 2:386. It should be noted, however, that not all Angiolieri scholars believe this was an actual exchange (*tenzone*) since Dante's replies do not exist. See the discussions in Alfie, *Comedy and Culture,* 151–152, and Angiolieri, *Le rime,* 219–220. In addition, not all scholars accept the authenticity of the debate between Forese and Dante. See Durling's discussion in Durling and Martinez (Dante, *The Divine Comedy*), 1:612–614.

36. Contini, *Un'idea di Dante,* 163–164, 166. See also the commentaries of Sapegno, 348–349; Chiavacci Leonardi, 1:883, 895; and Pasquini and Quaglio, 377–379.

37. See especially the concordance of rhymes in Avalle, *Concordanze,* s.v.v., "erte," "arco," "oncio/a," "arno," and "onio."

38. See the sonnets numbered 778–780, 863–864, and 882–898, in Avalle, *Concordanze,* and in Leonardi, *I canzonieri.*

39. For the importance of the political *tenzone* in the culture of Florence's ruling urban class and in the Vatican anthology, see Antonelli, "Struttura materiale," 15 and 23, and Antonelli and Bianchini, "Dal 'clericus' al Poeta," 188–189.

40. In the *Ovide moralisé,* Hecuba also serves as an exemplary figure for the effects of Fortune's sudden blow. See 13:2057 -2067.

41. Noted in the commentaries. See, for example, Chiavacci Leonardi (896) and Durling and Martinez (1:476).

42. Dante's borrowing of the rhymes *isquatra–latra* from "Tanto m'abonda matera" in *Inf.* 6, the first canto to deal directly with Florentine politics and the problem of the magnates, provides further evidence that he associates Monte's poetry and vision of Fortune with a specific social class.

43. In Monte Andrea, *Le rime,* 57–61 and 75–81.

44. Heilbronn, "Master Adam" and Musseter, "*Inferno* XXX."

45. See Martinez, "Cavalcanti's 'Man of Sorrows.'"

46. On the allegorical and typological senses of Lamentations, see Martinez, "Mourning Beatrice."

47. See the commentaries of Bosco and Reggio, 1:426–427; Durling and Martinez, 1:480; Chiavacci Leonardi, 1:884; and Pasquini and Quaglio, 378–379.

48. See chapter 2.

Notes to Epilogue

1. Levinas, *Proper Names,* 4.

2. The bibliography for philosophical and linguistic approaches to proper names is vast. Especially important for the present discussion are Barthes, *S/Z,* 94–97; Derrida, "Signature Event Context"; Kripke, *Naming and Necessity*; Russell, "On Denoting," in *Logic and Knowledge,* 41–56; and Searle, "Proper Names."

3. On the naming of Dante in the canto, see Cervigni, "Beatrice's Act of Naming"; Curtius, *European Literature,* 515–518; and Spitzer, "Note," 416–418.

4. The standard discussion of the signatures of medieval authors is Curtius, *European Literature,* 515–518; but see also Kirkham, *Fabulous Vernacular,* 76–134.

5. Similar ambiguity and deixis occur in *Inferno* 29.57, where Justice punishes "i falsador che qui registra" (the falsifiers that it registers here).

6. The continuity of this tradition is demonstrated by Sarolli's important interpretation of Dante's name in *Prolegomena,* 233–246.

7. Kirkham, *Fabulous Vernacular,* 117–119.

8. See Pertile's discussion of the *interpretatio nominis* of "Durante" in the *Fiore*: "Lettura dei sonetti CLXXI–CCX," 149–153.

9. On Beatrice's naming of Dante as a type of baptism and social rite, see Cervigni, "Beatrice's Act of Naming," 92. Cervigni's study also seeks to frame the "naming event" in *Purgatorio* 30 in the context of contemporary philosophical discussions about proper names.

10. Hawkins, "Dido, Beatrice, and the Signs"; Hollander, *Il Virgilio dantesco,* 132–134; and Jacoff, "Intertextualities in Arcadia."

11. Freccero, "Manfred's Wounds," in *Dante,* 195–208. See also Freccero's letter to Harold Bloom quoted in Bloom, *The Anxiety of Influence,* 122–123.

12. See the stylistic analysis in Marti, *Realismo dantesco,* 30–32. For the potential significance of the "comic" aspects of Beatrice's speech, see Auerbach, "Sacrae Scripturae sermo humilis," in *Studi su Dante,* 165–173.

13. In many ways this critique is anticipated by the ladies' critique of Dante's poetry in the *Vita Nova,* a critique that led to the advent of Dante's *stile della lode.*

14. For an analysis of the question of subjectivity in Beatrice's naming of Dante, see Cestaro, *Dante and the Grammar of the Nursing Body,* 146–148.

15. All citations are from De Robertis's edition.

16. Barolini, *Dante's Poets,* 148–153; Contini, *Un'idea di Dante,* 143–158; Hawkins, "Watching Matelda."

17. The speech of the shepherdess is presented indirectly by the male narrator in Cavalcanti's poem, who is remembering a past event. In this light it is suggestive that the passage in *Inferno* 2 in which we first encounter, indirectly, Beatrice's voice, in Virgil's account, contains a reminiscence of "In un boschetto." If the shepherdess is "più che la stella—bella" (2), Beatrice, when she speaks "in sua favella" (57) is " beata e bella" (53) and her eyes light up "più che la stella" (55).

18. On Dante's use of both a poetic *I* and an empirical *I* in the *Commedia,* see Spitzer, "Note," 416–417.

19. Bloom himself suggests that Dante's relationship to other poets should be distinguished from romanticist individuality. After his citation of Freccero's letter, he contrasts the agonism of modern, post-enlightenment poets with the "sharing-with-others" in Dante (*Anxiety of Influence,* 123).

Bibliography

Ahern, John. "Binding the Book: Hermeneutics and Manuscript Production in *Paradiso 33*." *PMLA* 97.5. (Oct., 1982): 800–809.

———. "The New Life of the Book: The Implied Reader of the *Vita Nuova*." *Dante Studies* 110 (1992): 1–16.

———. "The Reader on the Piazza: Verbal Dual in Dante's *Vita Nuova*." *Texas Studies in Literature and Language* 32 (1990): 18–39.

Alfie, Fabian. *Comedy and Culture: Cecco Angiolieri's Poetry and Late Medieval Society.* Leeds: Northern Universities Press, 2001.

Allegrezza, Franca. "La diffusione di un nuovo prodotto di bottega: Ipotesi sulla confezione dei libri di famiglia a Firenze nel Quattrocento." *Scrittura e civiltà* 15 (1991): 247–265.

Angiolieri, Cecco. *Le rime.* Rome: Archivio Guido Izzi, 1990.

Antonelli, Armando. "Nuovi documenti sulla famiglia Guinizzelli." In *Da Guido Guinizzelli a Dante: Nuove prospettive sulla lirica del Duecento,* edited by Furio Brugnolo and Gianfelice Peron, 59–106. Padua: Il Poligrafo, 2004.

Antonelli, Roberto. "Struttura materiale e disegno storiografico del canzoniere Vaticano." In *I canzonieri della lirica italiana delle origini,* edited by Lino Leonardi, 4:3–23. Florence: SISMEL-Edizioni del Galluzzo, 2001.

Antonelli, Roberto, and Simonetta Bianchini. "Dal 'clericus' al Poeta." In *Letteratura Italiana,* edited by Alberto Asor Rosa, 2:171–227. Turin: Einaudi, 1983.

Arveda, Antonia. *Contrasti amorosi nella poesia italiana antica.* Rome: Salerno, 1992.

Ascoli, Albert. "Access to Authority: Dante in the *Epistle to Cangrande*." In *Seminario dantesco internazionale / International Dante Seminar 1,* edited by Zygmunt G. Barański, 309–352. Florence: Le Lettere, 1997.

————. "'Neminem ante nos': Historicity and Authority in the *De vulgari eloquentia*." *Annali d'Italianistica,* 8 (1990): 186–231.

————. "Palinode and History in the Oeuvre of Dante." In *Dante Now: Current Trends in Dante Studies,* edited by Theodore Cachey, Jr., 155–160. Notre Dame, IN: University of Notre Dame Press, 1995.

————. "The Vowels of Authority (Dante's *Convivio* IV.vi.3–4)." In *Discourses of Authority in Medieval and Renaissance Literature,* edited by Kevin Brownlee and Walter Stephens, 23–46. Hanover, NH: University Press of New England, 1989.

Auerbach, Erich. *Studi su Dante.* Milan: Feltrinelli, 1978.

Avalle, d'Arco Silvio. *Concordanze della lingua poetica italiana delle origini.* Milan-Naples: Ricciardi, 1992.

————. *La doppia verità: Fenomenologia ecdotica e lingua letteraria nel Medioevo romanzo.* Florence: SISMEL-Edizioni del Galluzzo, 2002.

————. *Ai luoghi di delizia pieni: Saggio sulla lirica italiana del 13° secolo.* Milan-Naples: Ricciardi, 1977.

————. *Principi di critica testuale.* Padua: Antenore, 1978.

————. "La tradizione manoscritta di Guido Guinizzelli." *Studi di filologia italiana* 11 (1953): 160–162.

Barański, Zygmunt. "Dante's Biblical Linguistics." *Lectura Dantis* 5 (1989): 105–143.

————. *"Sole nuovo, luce nuova": Saggi sul rinnovamento culturale in Dante.* Turin: Scriptorium, 1996.

————. "'Tres enim sunt manerie dicendi . . . ': Some Observations on Medieval Literature, 'Genre,' and Dante." In *"Libri poetarum in quattuor species dividuntur": Essays on Dante and "Genre,"* edited by Zygmunt G. Barański, 9–60. Supplement to *The Italianist* 15. Reading: University of Reading, Department of Italian Studies, 1995.

Barbi, Michele. *La nuova filologia e l'edizione dei nostri scrittori da Dante al Manzoni.* Florence: Sansoni Editore, 1938.

————. *Problemi di critica dantesca.* Florence: Sansoni, 1964.

Barolini, Teodolinda. "'Cominciandomi dal principio infino a la fine' (V.N., XXIII, 15): Forging Anti-narrative in the 'Vita Nuova.'" In *"La gloriosa donna de la mente": A commentary on the "Vita Nuova,"* edited by Vincent Moleta, 119–140. Florence: Olschki, 1994.

————. "Dante and the Lyric Past." In *The Cambridge Companion to Dante,* edited by Rachel Jacoff, 14–33. Cambridge: Cambridge University Press, 1993.

————. *Dante's Poets: Textuality and Truth in the "Comedy."* Princeton: Princeton University Press, 1984.

————. "Guittone's 'Ora parrà,' Dante's 'Doglia mi reca,' and the *Commedia*'s Anatomy of Desire." In *Seminario dantesco internazionale / International Dante Seminar 1,* edited by Zygmunt Barański, 3–23. Florence: Le Lettere, 1997.

————. *The Undivine Comedy: Detheologizing Dante.* Princeton: Princeton University Press, 1992.

Barthes, Roland. *S/Z.* Translated by Richard Miller. New York: Hill and Wang, 1991.

Benjamin, Walter. *Illuminations: Essays and Reflections.* Edited by Hannah Arendt. New York: Random House, 1988.

Bertelli, Italo. *Poeti del dolce stil novo: Guido Guinizzelli e Lapo Gianni.* Pisa: Nistri-Lischi, 1963.

Biscaro, Gerolamo. "Inquisitori ed eretici a Firenze (1319–1334)," *Studi medievali* 2/3 (1929–1930): 347–375 and 266–287.

Biscione, Giuseppe. "La conservazione delle scritture notarili a Firenze dal XII secolo all'istituzione del pubblico generale archivio dei contratti." In *Dagli archivi all'Archivio: Appunti di storia degli archivi fiorentini,* edited by Carlo Vivoli, 27–52. Pisa: Edifir, 1991.

Bloom, Harold. *The Anxiety of Influence.* New York: Oxford University Press, 1973.

Boccaccio, Giovanni. *Decameron.* Edited by Vittore Branca. 2 vols. Turin: Einaudi, 1992.

Bologna, Corrado. "La copia colocciana del canzoniere Vaticano (Vat. Lat. 4823)." In *I canzonieri della lirica italiana delle origini,* edited by Lino Leonardi, 4:105–152. Florence: SISMEL-Edizioni del Galluzzo, 2001.

———. "Sull'utilità di alcuni *descripti* umanistici di lirica volgare antica." In *La filologia romanza e i codici: Atti del convegno; Messina, Università degli studi, Facoltà di lettere e filosofia, 19–22 dicembre 1991,* edited by Saverio Guida and Fortunata Latella, 2:531–587. Messina: Sicania, 1993.

———. *Tradizione e fortuna dei classici italiani.* 2 vols. Turin: Einaudi, 1993.

Borra, Antonello. *Guittone d'Arezzo e le maschere del poeta: La lirica cortese tra ironia e palinodia.* Ravenna: Longo, 2000.

Borsa, Paolo. "La tenzone tra Guido Guinizzelli e frate Guittone d'Arezzo." *Studi e problemi di critica testuale* 65 (2002): 47–88.

Borst, Arno. *Der Turmbau von Babel: Geschichte der Meinungen über Ursprung und Vielfalt der Sprachen und Völker.* 4 vols. Stuttgart: Anton Hiersemann, 1957–1963.

Botterill, Steven. "'Però che la divisione non si fa se non per aprire la sentenzia de la cosa divisa' (*V.N. XIV,* 13): The *Vita Nuova* as Commentary." In *La gloriosa donna de la mente": A Commentary on the "Vita Nuova,"* edited by Vincent Moleta, 61–76. Florence: Olschki, 1994.

Branca, Vittore. "Un biadaiolo lettore di Dante nei primi decenni del '300." *Rivista di cultura classica e medievale* 8 (1965): 200–215.

Brugnolo, Furio. *Plurilinguismo e lirica medievale.* Rome: Bulzoni Editore, 1983.

Brunetti, Giuseppina. *Il frammento inedito "Resplendiente stella de albur" di Giacomino Pugliese e la poesia italiana delle origini.* Tübingen: Niemeyer, 2000.

Brunetto Latini. *La Rettorica.* Edited by Francesco Maggini. Florence: Le Monnier, 1968.

Bruni, Francesco. "Figure della committenza e del rapporto autori-pubblico: Aspetti della comunicazione nel Basso Medioevo." In *Patronage and Public in the Trecento,* edited by Vincent Moleta, 108–111. Florence: Olschki, 1986.

Caboni, Adriana, ed., *Antiche rime italiane tratte dai Memoriali bolognesi.* Modena: Società Tipografica Modenese, 1941.

Cardini, Franco. "Alfabetismo e livelli di cultura nell'età comunale." *Quaderni storici* 13.38 (1978): 488–522.

Carducci, Giosuè. "Intorno ad alcune rime dei secoli XII e XIV ritrovate nei Memoriali dell'Archivio Notarile di Bologna." *Atti e Memorie della R. Deputazione di storia patria per le province di Romagna* 2.2 (1876): 105–220.

Carruthers, Mary J. *The Book of Memory: A Study of Memory in Medieval Culture.* Cambridge: Cambridge University Press, 1990.

Castellani, Arrigo. *Nuovi testi fiorentini del Dugento.* 2 vols. Florence: Sansoni, 1952.

———. *La prosa italiana delle origini.* 2 vols. Bologna: Pàtron, 1982.

Catalogo della mostra dantesca nell'archiginnasio. Bologna: Zanichelli, 1921.

Cavalcanti, Guido. *Rime.* Edited by Domenico De Robertis. Turin: Einaudi, 1986.

Cencetti, Giorgio. *Lineamenti di storia della scrittura latina.* Bologna: Pàtron, 1954.

———. "La 'rogatio' nelle carte bolognesi: Contributo allo studio del documento notarile italiano nei secoli XI–XII." In *Notariato medievale bolognese,* 1:219–352. Rome: Consiglio Nazionale del Notariato, 1985.

Cerchi, Paolo. "Filologie del 2000." *Rassegna europea di letteratura italiana* 17 (2001): 135–153.

Cervigni, Dino. "Beatrice's Act of Naming." *Lectura Dantis* 8 (1991): 85–93.

Cesarini, Wildar Sforza. "Sull'ufficio bolognese dei Memoriali (secoli *XIII–XV*)." *L'Archiginnasio* 9 (1914): 379–392.

Cestaro, Gary P. *Dante and the Grammar of the Nursing Body.* Notre Dame, IN: University of Notre Dame Press, 2003.

Continelli, Luisa. *L'archivio dell'Ufficio dei memoriali/inventario.* Bologna: Istituto per la storia dell'Università, 1988.

Contini, Gianfranco. *Esercizî di lettura sopra autori contemporanei.* Turin: Einaudi, 1974.

———. *Un'idea di Dante: Saggi danteschi.* Turin: Einaudi, 1976.

———. "Questioni attributive nell'ambito della lirica siciliana. " In *Convegno internazionale di studi federiciani,* 367–395. Palermo: Renna, 1952.

———, ed. *Poeti del Duecento.* 2 vols. Milan-Naples: Ricciardi, 1960.

———. "Stilemi siciliani nel *Detto d'Amore.*" In *Atti del Convegno di studi su Dante e la Magna Curia,* 83–88. Palermo: Centro di studi filologici e linguistici siciliani, 1967.

———. *Ultimi esercizî ed elzeviri.* Turin: Einaudi, 1989.

Copeland, Rita. *Rhetoric, Hermeneutics and Translation in the Middle Ages: Academic Traditions and Vernacular Texts.* Cambridge: Cambridge University Press, 1991.

Corti, Maria. *Dante a un nuovo crocevia.* Florence: Libreria Commissionaria Sansoni: 1981.

———. *Il viaggio testuale.* Turin: Einaudi, 1978.

Costamagna, Giorgio. *Il notaio a Genova fra prestigio e potere.* Rome: Consiglio Nazionale del Notariato, 1970.

Costamagna, Giorgio, and Mario Amelotti. *Alle origini del notariato italiano.* Rome: Consiglio Nazionale del Notariato, 1975.

Cox, Virginia. "Ciceronian Rhetoric in Italy, 1260–1350." *Rhetorica* 17 (1999): 239–288.

Curtius, Ernst Robert. *European Literature and the Latin Middle Ages.* Translated by Willard R. Trask. Princeton: Princeton University Press, 1990.

D'Ancona, Paolo. *La miniatura fiorentina (secoli XI–XVI).* 2 vols. Florence: Olschki, 1914.

Dante Alighieri. *Commedia.* Edited by Anna Chiavacci Leonardi. 3 vols. (Milan: Mondadori, 1997).

———. *Commedia: Inferno.* Edited by Emilio Pasquini and Antonio Quaglio. Milan: Garzanti, 1982.

———. *La Commedia secondo l'antica vulgata.* Edited by Giorgio Petrocchi. 4 vols. Milan: Mondadori, 1966–1967; rev. ed., Florence: Le Lettere, 1994.

———. *Dante's "De vulgari eloquentia."* Edited and Translated by Steven Botterill. Cambridge: Cambridge University Press, 1996.

———. *Dante's Lyric Poetry.* Edited by Kenelm Foster and Patrick Boyde. 2 vols. Oxford: Oxford University Press, 1967.

———. *De vulgari eloquentia: Introduzione e Testo.* Edited by Pier Vincenzo Mengaldo. Padua: Editrice Antenore, 1968.

———. *De vulgari eloquentia.* In *Opere minori,* edited and translated by Pier Vincenzo Mengaldo, 2:3–237. Milan-Naples: Ricciardi, 1979.

———. *De vulgari eloquentia: Ridotto a miglior lezione e commentato e tradotto.* Edited and translated by Aristide Marigo. Florence: Le Monnier, 1968.

———. *La divina commedia.* Edited by Silvio Adrasto Barbi and Tommaso Casini. 3 vols. Florence: Sansoni, 1965.

———. *La divina commedia.* Edited by Umberto Bosco and Giovanni Reggio. 3 vols. Florence: Le Monnier, 1988.

———. *La divina commedia.* Edited by Natalino Sapegno. Milan: Ricciardi, 1957.

———. *The Divine Comedy.* Translated by Charles S. Singleton. 3 vols. Princeton: Princeton University Press, 1970.

———. *The Divine Comedy of Dante Alighieri.* Edited by Robert M. Durling and Ronald Martinez. New York: Oxford University Press, 1996.

———. *Rime.* Edited by Gianfranco Contini. Turin: Einaudi, 1995.

———. *Rime.* Edited by Domenico De Robertis. 3 vols. Florence: Le Lettere, 2002.

———. *Vita Nova.* Edited by Guglielmo Gorni. Turin: Einaudi, 1996.

———. *Vita Nuova.* In *Opere minori,* edited by Domenico De Robertis. Vol 1, pt. 1. Milan-Naples: Ricciardi, 1984.

Davanzati, Chiaro. *Rime.* Edited by Aldo Menichetti. Bologna: Commissione per i Testi di Lingua, 1964.

Debenedetti, Santorre. "Osservazioni sulle poesie dei Memoriali bolognesi." *Giornale storico della letteratura italiana* 125 (1948): 1–41.

de Boer, Cornelis. *Ovide moralisé: Poème du commencement du quatorzième siècle, publié d'après tous les manuscrits connus.* Amsterdam: J. Muller, 1915.

Degenais, John. "That Bothersome Residue: Toward a Theory of the Physical Text." In *Vox Intexta: Orality and Textuality in the Middle Ages*, edited by Alger N. Doane and Carol B. Pasternack, 246–259. Madison: University of Wisconsin Press, 1991.

Del Sal, Nievo. "Guittone e i guittoniani nella *Commedia*." *Studi danteschi* 61 (1989): 109–152.

De Robertis, Domenico. *Il canzoniere escorialense e la tradizione "veneziana" delle rime dello stil novo*. Giornale storico della letteratura italiana: Supplemento n. 27. Turin: Casa Editrice Loescher-Chiantore, 1954.

———. "Definizione dello stil novo." *L'approdo* 3 (1954): 59–64.

———. "'Incipit Vita Nova' (V.N., I): Poetica del (ri)cominciamento." In *"La gloriosa donna de la mente": A Commentary on the "Vita Nuova,"* edited by Vincent Moleta, 11–19. Florence: Olschki, 1994.

———. "Sulla tradizione estravagante delle rime della 'Vita Nova.'" *Studi danteschi* 44 (1967): 5–84.

Derrida, Jacques. "Signature Event Context." *Glyph* 1 (1977): 172–197.

De Stefano, Antonino. *Riformatori ed eretici del Medioevo*. Palermo: Società siciliana per la storia patria, 1990.

Destrez, Jean. *La pecia dans les manuscrits universitaires du XIIIe et du XIVe siècle*. Paris: Vautrain, 1935.

Dionisotti, Carlo. *Geografia e storia della letteratura italiana*. Turin: Einaudi, 1999.

Dondarini, Rolandini. *Bologna medievale nella storia della città*. Bologna: Pàtron, 2000.

Durling, Robert M. "Deceit and Digestion in the Belly of Hell." In *Allegory and Representation: Selected Papers from the English Institute, 1979–90*, edited by Stephen J. Greenblatt, 61–93. Baltimore: Johns Hopkins University Press, 1981.

Durling, Robert M., and Ronald Martinez. *Time and the Crystal: Studies in Dante's Rime petrose*. Berkeley and Los Angeles: University of California Press, 1990.

Edwards, J. R. *A History of Financial Accounting*. London and New York: Routledge, 1989.

Egidi, Francesco. *Il libro de varie romanze volgare, cod. vat. 3793*. Rome: Società Filologica Romana, 1908.

Enciclopedia dantesca. 6 vols. Rome: Istituto della Enciclopedia Italiana, 1970–1983.

Fasoli, Gina. "La legislazione antimagnatizia a Bologna fino al 1292." *Rivista di storia del diritto italiano* 6 (1933): 351–392.

———. "Ricerche sulla legislazione antimagnatizia nei comuni dell'alta e media Italia." *Rivista di storia del diritto italiano* 12 (1939): 86–133 and 240–309.

Federici, Domenico Maria. *Istoria de' Cavalieri gaudenti*. 2 vols. Venice: Coleti, 1787.

Fenzi, Enrico. ed. *La canzone d'amore di Guido Cavalcanti e i suoi antichi commenti*. Genoa: Il Melangolo, 1999.

Fink-Errera, Guy. "La produzione dei libri di testo nelle università medievali." In *Libri e lettori nel medioevo: Guida storia e critica*, edited by Guglielmo Cavallo, 131–164. Bari: Laterza, 1977.

Folena, Gianfranco. "Überlieferungsgeschichte der altitalienischen Literatur." In *Geschichte der Textüberlieferung der antiken und mittelalterlichen Literatur*, edited by Herbert Hunger, 2:319–537. Zürich: Atlantis Verlag, 1964.

Freccero, John. *Dante: The Poetics of Conversion.* Cambridge: Harvard University Press, 1996.

Giansante, Massimo, and Giorgio Marcon. "Frammenti di codici trecenteschi della *Divina Commedia* nell'Archivio di Stato di Bologna." *Rassegna degli archivi di stato* 50 (1990): 378–415.

———. *Giudici e poeti toscani a Bologna: Tracce archivistiche fra tardo stilnovismo e preumanesimo.* Bologna: Archivio di Stato, 1994.

Ginzburg, Carlo. *Clues, Myths, and the Historical Method.* Translated by John and Anne C. Tedeschi. Baltimore: The Johns Hopkins University Press, 1989.

Giunta, Claudio. *Due saggi sulla tenzone.* Rome: Antenore, 2002.

———. *Codici: Saggi sulla poesia del Medioevo.* Bologna: Il Mulino, 2005.

———. "Corrispondenze in canzoni (Per il restauro di Onesto da Bologna, 'Se co lo vostro val mio dir e solo.')" *Studi mediolatini e volgari* 41 (1995): 51–76.

———. "Un'ipotesi sulla morfologia del canzoniere Vaticano lat. 3793." *Studi di filologia italiana* 53 (1995): 23–54.

———. *La poesia italiana nell'età di Dante: La linea Bonagiunta-Guinizzelli.* Bologna: Il Mulino, 1998.

———. *Versi a un destinatario: Saggio sulla poesia italiana del Medioevo.* Bologna: Il Mulino, 2002.

Gorni, Guglielmo. *Il nodo della lingua e il verbo d'amore: Studi su Dante e altri duecentisti.* Florence: Olschki, 1981.

———. "Paralipomeni a Lippo." *Studi di filologia italiana* 47 (1989): 11–29.

Gozzadini, Giovanni. *Cronaca di Ronzano e Memorie di Loderingo d'Andalo Frate Gaudente.* Bologna: Società Tipografica Bolognese, 1851.

Grayson, Cecil. "'Nobilior est vulgaris': Latin and Vernacular in Dante's Thought." In *Centenary Essays on Dante by Members of the Oxford Dante Society,* 54–76. Oxford: Clarendon Press, 1965.

Guinizzelli, Guido. *Poesie.* Edited by Edoardo Sanguineti. Milan: Mondadori, 1986.

———. *Rime.* Edited by Luciano Rossi. Turin: Einaudi, 2002.

———. *Works.* Edited and translated by Robert Edwards. New York: Garland, 1987.

Guittone d'Arezzo. *Canzoniere: I sonetti d'amore del codice laurenziano.* Edited by Lino Leonardi. Turin: Einaudi, 1994.

———. *Lettere.* Edited by Claude Margueron. Collezione di opere inedite o rare 145. Bologna: Commissione per i Testi di Lingua, 1990.

———. *Le rime di Guittone d'Arezzo.* Edited by Francesco Egidi. Bari: Laterza, 1940.

Hanna, Ralph. *Pursuing History: Middle English Manuscripts and Their Texts.* Stanford: Stanford University Press, 1996.

Hartung, Stefan. "Guinizzelli e la teologia della grazia." In *Da Guido Guinizzelli a Dante: Nuove prospettive sulla lirica del Duecento,* edited by Furio Brugnolo and Gianfelice Peron, 147–170. Padua: Il Poligrafo, 2004.

Harvey, David. *The Condition of Postmodernity: An Enquiry into the Origins of Cultural Change.* Cambridge: Blackwell Publishers, 1990.

Havely, Nick. *Dante and the Franciscans: Poverty and the Papacy in the "Commedia."* Cambridge: Cambridge University Press, 2004.

Hawkins, Peter S. "Dido, Beatrice, and the Signs of Ancient Love." In *The Poetics of Allusion: Virgil and Ovid in Dante's Commedia,* edited by Rachel Jacoff and Jeffrey T. Schnapp, 113–130. Stanford: Stanford University Press, 1991.

———. "Watching Matelda." In *The Poetics of Allusion: Virgil and Ovid in Dante's Commedia,* edited by Rachel Jacoff and Jeffrey T. Schnapp, 181–201. Stanford: Stanford University Press, 1991.

Heilbronn, Denise. "Master Adam and the Fat-Bellied Lute (*Inf.* XXX)." *Dante Studies* 101 (1983): 51–65.

Hessel, Alfred. *Storia della città di Bologna dal 1116 al 1280.* Bologna: Alpha, 1975.

Hollander, Robert. "Dante's 'dolce stil novo' and the *Comedy.*" In *Dante: Mito e poesia; Atti del 2° Seminario Internazionale Dantesco,* edited by Michelangelo Picone and Tatiana Crivelli, 263–281. Florence: Franco Cesati Editore, 1998.

———. "Dante *Theologus-Poeta.*" *Dante Studies* 118 (2000): 261–302.

———. *Il Virgilio dantesco: Tragedia nella "Commedia."* Florence: Olschki, 1983.

Holmes, Olivia. *Assembling the Lyric Self: Authorship from the Troubadour Song to Italian Poetry Book.* Minneapolis: University of Minnesota Press, 2000.

Jacoff, Rachel. "Intertextualities in Arcadia: *Purgatorio* 30.49–51." In *The Poetics of Allusion: Virgil and Ovid in Dante's Commedia,* edited by Rachel Jacoff and Jeffrey T. Schnapp, 131–144. Stanford: Stanford University Press, 1991.

Jacopo della Lana. *Commento dantesco.* Edited by Luciano Scarabelli. Bologna: Tipografia Regia, 1886.

Kirkham, Victoria. *Fabulous Vernacular: Boccaccio's "Filocolo" and the Art of Medieval Fiction.* Ann Arbor: The University of Michigan Press, 2001.

Kleinhenz, Christopher. *The Early Italian Sonnet: The First Century (1220–1321).* Lecce: Milella, 1986.

———. "Pulzelle e maritate: Coming of Age, Rites of Passage, and the Question of Marriage in Some Early Italian Poems." In *Matrons and Marginal Women in Medieval Society,* edited by Robert R. Edwards and Vickie Ziegler, 89–110. Woodbridge: Boydell Press, 1995.

Koenig, John. *Il popolo dell'Italia del Nord nel XII secolo.* Bologna: Il Mulino, 1986.

Kripke, Saul A. *Naming and Necessity.* Oxford: Basil Blackwell, 1972.

Kullmann, Dorothea. "Osservazioni sui Memoriali bolognesi (con un frammento di lauda inedito)." *Zeitschrift für romanische Philologie* (2003): 256–280.

Lachin, Giosuè. "Partizioni e struttura di alcuni libri medievali di poesia provenzale." In *Strategie del testo: Preliminari Partizioni Pause: Atti del XVI e del XVII Convegno Interuniversitario (Bressanone, 1988 e 1989),* edited by Gianfelice Peron, 267–297. Padua: Esedra Editore, 1994.

Lane, F. C. "Double Entry Bookkeeping and Resident Merchants." *Journal of European Economic History* 6 (1977): 177–191.

Larson, Pär. "Appunti sulla lingua del canzoniere Vaticano." In *I canzonieri della lirica italiana delle origini,* edited by Lino Leonardi, 4:57–103. Florence: SISMEL-Edizioni del Galluzzo, 2001.

Le Goff, Jacques. *Time, Work, and Culture in the Middle Ages.* Translated by Arthur Goldhammer. Chicago: University of Chicago Press, 1980.

Lenzi, Domenico. *Il libro del Biadaiolo: Carestie e annona a Firenze dalla metà del '200 al 1348.* Edited by Giuliano Pinto. Florence: Olschki, 1978.

Leonardi, Lino. "Il canzoniere Laurenziano: Struttura, contenuti e fonti di una raccolta d'autore." In *I canzonieri della lirica italiana delle origini,* edited by Lino Leonardi, 4:153–214. Florence: SISMEL-Edizioni del Galluzzo, 2001.

———, ed. *I canzonieri della lirica italiana delle origini.* 4 vols. Florence: SISMEL-Edizioni del Galluzzo, 2001.

———. "Il *Fiore,* il *Roman de la Rose,* e la tradizione lirica italiana prima di Dante." In *The Fiore in Context: Dante, France, Tuscany,* edited by Zygmunt Barański and Patrick Boyde, 233–269. Notre Dame, IN: University of Notre Dame Press, 1997.

———. "Jacopone poeta francescano: Mistica e povertà contro Monte Andrea (e con Dante)." In *Francescanesimo in volgare: Secoli XIII–XIV; Atti del XXIV Convegno internazionale, Assisi, 17–19 ottobre 1996,* 97–141. Spoleto: Centro italiano di studi sull'alto Medioevo, 1997.

Letteratura italiana: Dizionario bio-bibliografico e indici. Edited by Giorgio Inglese, Luigi Trenti, and Paolo Procaccioli. 2 vols. Turin: Einaudi, 1990.

Levi, Ezio. "Cantilene e ballate dei sec. XIII e XIV dai Memoriali di Bologna." *Studi Medievali* 4 (1912–13): 279–334.

Levinas, Emmanuel. *Proper Names.* Translated by Michael B. Smith. Stanford: Stanford University Press, 1996.

Little, Lester K. *Religious Poverty and the Profit Economy in Medieval Europe.* Ithaca, NY: Cornell University Press, 1978.

Livi, Giovanni. *Dante e Bologna: nuovi studi e documenti.* Bologna: Zanichelli, 1921.

———. *Dante, suoi primi cultori, sua gente in Bologna.* Bologna: Cappelli, 1918.

Lusignan, Serge. *Parler vulgairement: Les intellectuels et la langue française aux XIIe et XIVe siècles.* Paris: J. Vrin, 1986.

Manselli, Raoul. "De Dante à Coluccio Salutati: Discussions sur la pauvreté à Florence au XIVe siècle." In *Etudes sur l'histoire de la pauvreté jusqu'au XVIe siècle,* edited by Michel Mollat, 637–659. Paris: Sorbonne, 1974.

Marchesi, Simone. "Dante's Vertical Utopia: *Aulicum* and *Curiale* in the *De Vulgari Eloquentia.*" In *Utopianism / Literary Utopias and National Cultural Identities: A Comparative Perspective,* edited by Paola Spinozzi, 311–316. Bologna: Cotepra, 2001.

Margueron, Claude. *Recherches sur Guittone d'Arezzo, sa vie, son époque, sa culture.* Paris: Presses universitaires de France, 1966.

Marti, Mario. *Cultura e stile nei poeti giocosi del tempo di Dante.* Pisa: Nistri-Lischi, 1953.

———. *Realismo dantesco e altri studi.* Milan-Naples: Ricciardi, 1961.

————. *Storia dello stil novo.* 2 vols. Lecce: Milella, 1973.

Martinez, Ronald L. "Cavalcanti's 'Man of Sorrows' and Dante." In *Guido Cavalcanti tra i suoi lettori,* edited by Maria Luisa Ardizzone, 187–212. Fiesole: Cadmo, 2003.

————. "Guido Cavalcanti's 'Una figura della donna mia' and the Spectre of Idolatry Haunting the *Stilnovo.*" *Exemplaria* 15.2 (2003): 297–324.

————. "Mourning Beatrice: The Rhetoric of Threnody in the *Vita Nuova.*" *Modern Language Notes,* 113:1 (1998): 1–29.

————. "Bolognese Smarts and Dubious Semblances: Guinizzelli's 'Al cor gentil.'" Paper presented at the Thirty-First International Congress on Medieval Studies, Kalamazoo, MI, May 12, 1996.

————. "The Pilgrim's Answer to Bonagiunta and the Poetics of the Spirit." *Stanford Italian Review* 3 (1983): 37–63.

Mazzotta, Giuseppe. *Dante, Poet of the Desert: History and Allegory in the "Divine Comedy."* Princeton: Princeton University Press, 1979.

McCash, J. H. *The Cultural Patronage of Medieval Women.* Athens: University of Georgia Press, 1996.

McGann, Jerome J. *The Textual Condition.* Princeton: Princeton University Press, 1991.

Meersseman, G. G. *Dossier de l'ordre de la pénitence au XIIIe siècle.* Fribourg: Editions Universitaires, 1961.

Melis, Federico. *Documenti per la storia economica dei secoli XIII–XVI.* Florence: Olschki, 1972.

————. *Storia della ragioneria.* Bologna: C. Zuffi, 1950.

Meneghetti, Maria Luisa. "Il corredo decorativo del canzoniere palatino." In *I canzonieri della lirica italiana delle origini,* edited by Lino Leonardi, 4:393–415. Florence: SISMEL-Edizioni del Galluzzo, 2001.

Mengaldo, Pier Vincenzo. "Dante come critico." *La parola del testo* 1 (1997): 36–54.

————. *Linguistica e retorica di Dante.* Pisa: Nistri-Lischi, 1978.

Migiel, Marilyn. *A Rhetoric of the "Decameron."* Toronto: University of Toronto Press, 2004.

Miglio, Luisa. "L'altra metà della scrittura: scrivere il volgare (all'origine delle corsive mercantili)." *Scrittura e civiltà* 10 (1986): 83–114.

————. "Considerazioni ed ipotesi sul libro 'borghese' italiano del Trecento." *Scrittura e civiltà* 3 (1979): 309–327.

————. "Criteri di datazione per le corsive librarie italiane dei secoli XIII–XIV. Ovvero riflessioni, osservazioni, suggerimenti sulla lettera mercantesca." *Scrittura e civiltà* 18 (1994): 143–157.

————. "Per una datazione del Biadaiolo fiorentino." *La bibliofilia* 77 (1975): 1–36.

Milner, Stephen J. "Exile, Rhetoric, and the Limits of Civic Republican Discourse." In *At the Margins: Minority Groups in Premodern Italy,* edited by Stephen J. Milner, 162–191. Minneapolis: University of Minnesota Press, 2005.

Moleta, Vincent. *Guinizzelli in Dante.* Rome: Edizioni di Storia e Letteratura, 1980.

Monte Andrea da Fiorenza. *Le rime.* Edited by Francesco Filippo Minetti. Florence: L'Accademia della Crusca, 1979.

Monteverdi, Angelo. "'Rosa fresca aulentissima . . . tragemi d'este focora.'" In *Studi e saggi sulla letteratura italiana dei primi secoli.* Milan-Naples: Ricciardi, 1954.

Mostra di codici romanzi delle biblioteche fiorentine. Florence: Sansoni, 1957.

Musseter, Sally. "*Inferno* XXX: Dante's Counterfeit Adam." *Traditio* 34 (1978): 427–435.

Najemy, John M. *Corporation and Consensus in Florentine Electoral Politics, 1280–1400.* Chapel Hill: University of North Carolina Press, 1982.

————. "Dante and Florence." In *The Cambridge Companion to Dante,* edited by Rachel Jacoff, 80–99. Cambridge: Cambridge University Press, 1993.

Nardi, Bruno. *Dante e la cultura medievale.* Bari: Laterza, 1942.

Nichols, Stephen G., ed. "The New Philology." Special issue, *Speculum: A Journal of Medieval Studies* 65.1 (1990).

Onesto da Bologna. *Le rime di Onesto da Bologna.* Edited by Sandro Orlando. Florence: Sansoni, 1974.

Ong, Walter J. *Orality and Literacy: The Technologizing of the Word.* London and New York: Routledge, 2002.

Orlandelli, Gianfranco. "Osservazioni sulla scrittura mercantesca nei secoli XIV e XV." In *Studi in onore di Riccardo Filangieri,* 445–460. Naples: L'Arte Tipografica, 1959.

Orlando, Sandro. "Best sellers e notai: La tradizione estravagante delle rime fra Due e Trecento in Italia." In *Da Guido Guinizzelli a Dante: Nuove prospettive sulla lirica del Duecento,* edited by Furio Brugnolo and Gianfelice Peron, 257–270. Padua: Il Poligrafo, 2004.

————. "Un piccolo canzoniere di rime italiane del secolo XIII (1288)." *Studi di filologia italiana* 36 (1978): 5–19.

————, ed. *Rime dei Memoriali bolognesi, 1279–1300.* Turin: Einaudi, 1981.

Paden, William D., ed. *The Future of the Middle Ages: Medieval Literature in the 1990s.* Gainesville: University Press of Florida, 1994.

Pagani, Ileana. *La teoria linguistica di Dante.* Naples: Liguori, 1982.

Pagliaro, Antonino. *Poesia giullaresca e poesia popolare.* Bari: Laterza, 1958.

Palma, Marco. "Osservazioni sull'aspetto materiale del canzoniere Vaticano." In *I canzonieri della lirica italiana delle origini,* edited by Lino Leonardi, 4:43–55. Florence: SISMEL-Edizioni del Galluzzo, 2001.

Panuccio del Bagno. *Le rime di Panuccio del Bagno.* Edited by Franca Bambilla Ageno. Florence: L'Accademia della Crusca, 1977.

Panvini, Bruno. "Studio sui manoscritti dell'antica lirica italiana." *Studi di filologia italiana* 11 (1953): 5–135.

Papahagi, Marian. "Guido Guinizzelli e Guittone d'Arezzo: Contributo a una ridefinizione dello spazio poetico predantesco." In *Guittone d'Arezzo nel settimo centenario della morte,* edited by Michelangelo Picone, 269–293. Florence: Franco Cesati, 1995.

Parkes, Malcolm Beckwith. "The Influence of the Concepts of *Ordinatio* and *Compilatio* on the Development of the Book." In *Medieval Literature and Learning: Essays Presented to Richard William Hunt,* edited by J. J. G. Alexander and M. T. Gibson, 115–141. Oxford: Clarendon, 1976.

Pertile, Lino. "Lettura dei sonetti CLXXI–CCX." In *Lettura del "Fiore,"* edited by Zygmunt Barański, Patrick Boyde, and Lino Pertile, 131–153. Letture Classensi 22. Ravenna: Longo, 1993.

Petrucci, Armando. "Fatti protomercanteschi." *Scrittura e civiltà* 25 (2001): 167–176.

————. "Le mani e le scritture del canzoniere Vaticano." In *I canzonieri della lirica italiana delle origini,* edited by Lino Leonardi, 4:25–41. Florence: SISMEL-Edizioni del Galluzzo, 2001.

————. "Modello notarile e testualità." In *Il Notariato nella civiltà toscana: Atti di un convegno (maggio 1981),* edited by Mario Montorzi, 123–146. Rome: Consiglio Nazionale del Notariato, 1985.

————. "Scrivere il testo." In *La critica del testo: Problemi di metodo ed esperienze di lavoro: Atti del Convegno di Lecce, 22–26 Ottobre 1984,* 209–227. Rome: Salerno Editrice, 1986.

————. "Storia e geografia delle culture scritte (dal secolo XI al secolo XVIII)." In *Letteratura italiana: Storia e geografia,* edited by Alberto Asor Rosa, 2:1193–1292. Turin: Einaudi, 1988.

————. *Writers and Readers in Medieval Italy: Studies in the History of Written Culture.* Edited and translated by C. M. Radding. New Haven, CT: Yale University Press, 1995.

Picone, Michelangelo. "Guinizzelli nel Paradiso." In *Da Guido Guinizzelli a Dante: Nuove prospettive sulla lirica del Duecento,* edited by Furio Brugnolo and Gianfelice Peron, 341–354. Padua: Il Poligrafo, 2004.

————. "Guittone e i due tempi del Canzoniere." In *Guittone d'Arezzo nel settimo centenario della morte: Atti del convegno internazionale di Arezzo,* edited by Michelangelo Picone, 73–88. Florence: Cesati Editore, 1995.

————. "Guittone, Guinizzelli e Dante." In *Intorno a Guido Guinizzelli,* edited by Luciano Rossi and Sara Alloatti Boller, 69–84. Alessandria: Edizioni dell'Orso, 2002.

Raimondi, Ezio. "I canti bolognesi dell'inferno dantesco." In *Dante e Bologna nei tempi di Dante,* 229–249. Bologna: Commissione per i Testi di Lingua, 1967.

Robinson, P. R. "The 'Booklet': A Self-Contained Unit in Composite Manuscripts." *Codicologica* 3 (1980): 46–69.

Rostagno, Enrico. "Frammenti di un codice di rime volgari affine al Vat. 3793." *Giornale storico della letteratura italiana* 26 (1895): 141–155.

Rubinstein, Nicolai. *La lotta contro i magnati a Firenze: le origini della legge sul "sodamento."* Florence: Olschki, 1939.

Russell, Betrand. *Logic and Knowledge: Essays.* Edited by R. C. March. London: George Allen and Unwin, 1956.

Salathiel Bononiensis. *Ars notarie.* Edited by Gianfranco Orlandelli. Milan: Giuffrè, 1961.

Salmi, Mario. *La miniatura fiorentina gotica.* Rome: Fratelli Palombi, 1954.

Sapori, Armando. *I libri degli Alberti del Giudice.* Milan: Garzanti, 1952.

———. *I libri di commercio dei Peruzzi.* Milan: S. A. Fratelli Treves, 1934.

Sarolli, Gian Roberto. *Prolegomena alla "Divina Commedia."* Florence: Olschki, 1971.

Scaglione, Aldo. D. "Dante and the Ars Grammatica." In *The "Divine Comedy" and the Encyclopedia of the Arts and Sciences,* edited by Giuseppe Di Scipio and Aldo Scaglione, 27–41. Acta of the International Dante Symposium, 13–16 Nov. 1983, Hunter College, New York. Amsterdam: John Benjamins, 1988.

Scariati, Irene Maffia, ed. *La corona di casistica amorosa e le canzoni del cosiddetto "Amico di Dante."* Rome-Padua: Antenore, 2002.

Schnapp, Jeffrey. *The Transfiguration of History at the Center of Dante's Paradise.* Princeton: Princeton University Press, 1986.

Searle, John. "Proper Names." *Mind* 67 (1958): 166–173.

Segre, Cesare. *Lingua, stile, e società. Studi sulla storia della prosa italiana.* Milan: Feltrinelli Editore, 1991.

———. "Review of *The Future of the Middle Ages.*" *Romance Philology* 51 (1998): 356–363.

Segre, Cesare, and Gian Battista Speroni. "Filologia testuale e letteratura italiana nel Medioevo." *Romance Philology* 45 (1991): 44–72.

Shoaf, R. A. *Dante, Chaucer, and the Currency of the Word: Money, Images, and Reference in Late Medieval Poetry.* Norman: Pilgrim Books, 1983.

Singleton, Charles S. *An Essay on the "Vita Nuova."* Cambridge: Harvard University Press, 1949.

Spitzer, Leo. "Note on the Poetic and Empirical 'I' in Medieval Authors." *Traditio* 4 (1946): 415–422.

Steinberg, Justin. "Bankers in Hell: The Poetry of Monte Andrea in Dante's *Inferno* between Historicism and Historicity." *Italian Studies* 58 (2003): 5–30.

———. "Merchant Bookkeeping and Lyric Anthologizing." *Scrittura e civiltà* 24 (2000): 251–269.

Storey, H. Wayne. "The Poetry and Literary Culture of Monte Andrea." Ph.D. dissertation, Columbia University, 1982.

———. "Lo 'stoscio' montiano-dantesco (*Inf.* XVII 118–123)." *Studi danteschi* 58 (1986): 385–389.

———. *Transcription and Visual Poetics in the Early Italian Lyric.* New York: Garland Publishing, 1993.

Strocchia, Sharon T. *Death and Ritual in Renaissance Florence.* Baltimore: Johns Hopkins University Press, 1992.

Stussi, Alfredo. *Tracce.* Rome: Bulzoni, 2001.

Suitner, Franco. *La poesia satirica e giocosa nell'età dei comuni.* Padua: Editrice Antenore, 1983.

Tabacco, Giovanni. *Egemonie sociali e strutture del potere nel Medioevo italiano.* Turin: Einaudi, 1979.

Tamba, Giorgio. "In margine all'edizione del XIV volume del Chartularium Studii Bononiensis." *Atti e memorie della Deputazione di storia patria per le province di Romagna,* n.s., 33 (1982): 151–168.

———. "I memoriali del Comune di Bologna nel secolo XIII: Note di diplomatica." *Rassegna degli archivi di stato* 47 (1987): 235–290.

———. *La Società dei Notai di Bologna.* Rome: Archivio di Stato, 1988.

Timpanaro, Sebastiano. *The Freudian Slip: Psychoanalysis and Textual Criticism.* Translated by Kate Soper. London: NLB, 1976.

Toesca, Pietro. *Il Trecento.* Turin: UTET, 1951.

Vinay, Gustavo. "Ricerche sul *De vulgari eloquentia. Giornale storico della letteratura italiana* 136 (1959): 236–74, 367–88.

———. "La teoria linguistica del *De vulgari eloquentia*" *Cultura e scuola* 5 (1962): 30–42.

Vitale, Vito. *Il dominio della parte guelfa in Bologna (1280–1327).* Bologna: A. Forni, 1978.

Vittorio, Franchini. "L'instituto dei 'Memoriali' in Bologna nel secolo XIII." *L'Archiginnasio* 9 (1914): 95–106.

Wallace, David. *Chaucerian Polity: Absolutist Lineages and Associational Forms in England and Italy.* Stanford: Stanford University Press, 1997.

Ward, John O. "Rhetorical Theory and the Rise and Decline of Dictamen in the Middle Ages and Early Renaissance." *Rhetorica* 19 (2001): 175–223.

Wilkins, E. H. *The Invention of the Sonnet, and Other Studies in Italian Literature.* Rome: Edizioni di Storia e Letteratura, 1959.

Yamey, B. S. "Scientific Bookkeeping and the Rise of Capitalism." *Economic History Review* 2 (1948): 99–113.

Zaccagnini, Guido. *Cino da Pistoia: Studio biografico.* Pistoia: D. Pagnini, 1918.

———. "Gherardo da Castelfiorentino: Notizie intorno alla sua vita e ad una sua ballata." *Giornale storico della letteratura italiana* 73 (1919): 208–209.

Index of Names and Notable Matters

Index of Passages from Dante's Works

JUSTIN STEINBERG

is assistant professor of Italian at the University of Chicago.